Shinra Myōjin and Buddhist Networks of the East Asian "Mediterranean"

Shinra Myōjin and Buddhist Networks of the East Asian "Mediterranean"

Sujung Kim

HAWAI

University of Hawaiʻi Press
Honolulu, Hawaiʻi

Printed in the United States of America

25 24 23 22 21 20 6 5 4 3 2 1

Library of Congress Cataloging-in-Publication Data

Names: Kim, Sujung, author.
Title: Shinra Myōjin and Buddhist networks of the East Asian "Mediterranean" / Sujung Kim.
Description: Honolulu, Hawaiʻi : University of Hawaiʻi Press, [2020] | Includes bibliographical references and index.
Identifiers: LCCN 2019010538 | ISBN 9780824877996 (cloth ; alk. paper)
Subjects: LCSH: Shinra Myōjin (Buddhist deity) | Buddhism—Japan—History—1185–1600. | Buddhism—Korea—History.
Classification: LCC BQ4890.S55 K56 2020 | DDC 294.3/42113—dc23
LC record available at https://lccn.loc.gov/2019010538

ISBN 978-0-8248-8844-2 (pbk.)

University of Hawaiʻi Press books are printed on acid-free paper and meet the guidelines for permanence and durability of the Council on Library Resources.

Cover art: Shinra Myōjin, thirteenth c., colors on silk. Onjōji, Shiga Prefecture.

To my parents,
Bokim Kim and Dongsu Kim

Contents

Acknowledgments

My first encounter with Shinra Myōjin was in a graduate seminar course I took in the spring of 2009 in which we explored the wondrous world of medieval Japanese gods through reading the *Keiran shūyōshū*. I still vividly remember how excited I was about Shinra Myōjin, and this book is the outcome of a long labor.

So many people have helped the book come into being. Intellectually, it owes its greatest debt to my teachers at Columbia University, first and foremost, Bernard Faure, as well as Chün-fang Yü, Max Moerman, Michael Como, and David Lurie. My profound gratitude goes to Jacqueline Stone, Paul Groner, Saitō Hideki, Dongwu Kwon, Iyanaga Nobumi, Abe Yasurō, Mizukami Fumiyoshi, Lucia Dolce, Siñead Vilbar, Lan Wu, Michaela Mross, Seung Hae Yu, Michael Pye, Jin Y. Park, Youngjin Kim, Wendi Adamek, Mark Blum, Steve Covell, Fabio Rambelli, Paul Swanson, and Marcus Bingenheimer, all of whom taught me what the bodhisattva truly means.

I also owe profound debts to my friends and colleagues who offered me their kindest help along the way. Above all, I would like to thank Luke Thompson, who has read several versions of my manuscript and significantly improved it. Bryan Lowe, too, kindly read the entire manuscript and provided insightful and invaluable suggestions. I am also grateful to Kevin Buckelew and Heather Blair for sharing their generous feedback with me.

Two anonymous readers prompted crucial rewrites that have made the book immeasurably stronger, and I believe that their suggestions are largely responsible for what I consider some of the best parts of my book. Nonetheless, I must take responsibility for any flaws and errors that remain. I also want to express my sincere gratitude to my editors at University of Hawai'i Press—Stephanie Chun, Cheryl Loe, and Barbara Folsom—who have not only been passionate but immensely patient supporters of my project.

At DePauw, I must thank all my colleagues in the Religious Studies and Asian Studies departments for their support. My special thanks go to my writing partners Pauline Ota, Danielle Kane, and Tineke D'Haeseleer, who spent numerous early morning hours with me in the library. Beth Wilkerson helped with two maps, and I thank her very much. The office of Academic Affairs at DePauw provided generous support for the final process of publication.

This book was made possible thanks to library travel grants from the Center for East Asian Studies at the University of Chicago in 2016, and the Center for East Asian Studies, Stanford University, in 2017. Furthermore, I was very fortunate to find myself in a supportive community and with access to extensive library materials at Kyushu University during my visiting professorship there in the spring of 2018. Cynthea Bogel made my stay in Fukuoka most enjoyable, and I am extremely grateful for her friendship. Special thanks go to Mr. Fuke Toshihiko, the chief administrative official of Onjōji, who generously provided me with Onjōji documents and Shinra Myōjin images.

My heartfelt gratitude goes to my family, both the Kims in South Korea and the Johnsons in Indiana, USA. I owe this humble achievement to them and their love. My fondest thanks also to my cousin Jiyoon Kim in Osaka for her selfless care whenever I needed it.

Last, this book would simply have been impossible without the never-ending support of my coach, colleague, and companion Paul M. Johnson. My deepest affection and gratitude go to my husband Paul and our newborn daughter, Reina.

Abbreviations

DNBZ	*Dai Nihon Bukkyō zensho*
KT	*Kokushi taikei*
NBT	*Nihon bungaku taikei*
NKBT	*Nihon koten bungaku taikei*
SNKBT	*Shin Nihon koten bungaku taikei*
ST	*Shintō taikei*
T	*Taishō shinshū daizokyō*
T zuzō	*Taishō shinshū daizōkyō zuzō*
ZGR	*Zoku gunsho ruijū*

Introduction

Shinra Myōjin in the East Asian "Mediterranean" Network

One day in 858 CE, a boat traveling the maritime expanse that stretched from China to Japan found itself battered by angry waves and on the verge of capsizing. Enchin 円珍 (814–891), a Japanese Tendai Buddhist monk aboard the ship, sensed that his life was in great danger. He was returning to Japan after having completed five years of study of Buddhism in China. In desperation, he prayed to the gods for protection. As Enchin began to pray, an old man suddenly appeared above the boat and declared: "I am a deity of the Silla Kingdom (Shinra Myōjin 新羅明神). I will protect your practice of Buddhism until the Buddha Maitreya comes into this world." Having said this, the old man vanished.[1]

This legend illustrates the connection between Shinra Myōjin and Enchin. Enchin is best known for reviving Onjōji 園城寺 temple in Ōmi 近江, which eventually became the headquarters of the Tendai 天台 Jimon 寺門 tradition. The Tendai Jimon, along with the Sanmon 山門 tradition, which is headquartered in the temple Enryakuji 延暦寺 on Mt. Hiei, are the two major branches of Japanese Tendai Buddhism.[2] The split between the Sanmon and the Jimon was one of the most important events in the history of the Tendai tradition (and of Japanese Buddhism more broadly), and Shinra Myōjin was at the heart of the Jimon's institutional development following this split. While Shinra Myōjin's name immediately alerts us to possible connections to the Korean kingdom of Silla 新羅 (57 BCE–935 CE), it also served as a collective name for a network of Silla deities.[3]

This book is about Shinra Myōjin. However, its focus is not limited to this single figure, but addresses the sociocultural and mythological networks within which this deity was embedded. My overarching question is this: Why did a deity whose name clearly refers to the Korean kingdom of Silla become the protector deity of a Japanese Buddhist sect? The answer to this question, laid out in the pages that follow, challenges the delimitation of research topics according to modern-day national borders and identities. Rather than treating Shinra Myōjin as a Korean deity, a Japanese deity, or something in between, this study locates Shinra Myōjin within a network that includes and also transcends those borders and identities.

I call this network the East Asian "Mediterranean." Within it we find Sillan immigrant communities in Japan and China, communities that were able to retain their cultural identity and religious practices for at least a few generations post-emigration. Official mercantile ties between Silla and Japan were terminated in the late ninth century, but through memories, imagination, and reinterpretation, this network of people, cultic practices, and ideas continued into Japan's medieval period. In this book, I argue that we cannot fully understand the development of Shinra Myōjin in medieval Japan unless we look beyond the Japanese archipelago and consider the networks that linked Japan, the Korean Peninsula, and other parts of mainland East Asia.

The concept of the East Asian "Mediterranean," first coined by Angela Schottenhammer, provides a fruitful framework for understanding the diffusion, interaction, and density within the networks that linked China, Korea, Japan, and other locations.[4] While this term can refer to the actual bodies of water we now call the East China Sea, the Yellow Sea, and the East Sea/Sea of Japan, instead I use the word "Mediterranean" to draw the reader's attention to the way in which these waters did not separate China, Korea, and Japan but rather served as the primary conduit for cross-cultural influence and exchange. The idea of the "Mediterranean"—*la Méditerranée*—as a conceptual category derives from the theories of the *Annales* historian Fernand Braudel.[5] In his magisterial book, *The Mediterranean and the Mediterranean World in the Age of Philip II* (first published in French in 1949), Braudel plumbed both spatiality and temporality in pursuit of new methods of historical enquiry. In his broader vision of space, Braudel uses the term "Mediterranean" to refer to a large geographic region that is connected by sea; he emphasizes the role that seas play in connecting far-flung lands rather than their potential to separate such lands.[6] He makes it clear that the Mediterranean Sea—literally, a sea amid lands—has been the major channel for economic and cultural communication between the countries that border it. With this shift in thinking, the sea becomes the spatial center as well as the channel through which connections are made and maintained. When we closely examine the East China Sea and surrounding waters in a similar manner, we begin to see connections between Buddhists and Buddhist institutions in China, Korea, and Japan in a completely new light.

Braudel's concept of temporality provides another crucial methodological framework in my study of Shinra Myōjin. Throughout his work, Braudel differentiates between three scales of temporality: the long duration of change (*longue durée*) over several centuries or even a millennium; the middle span of trends (*conjonctures*) of a generation or more; and last, the short timescale of events (*l'histoire des événements*)—all of which are interrelated.[7] These three scales of analysis can help us come to a more holistic understanding of Shinra Myōjin and his place in the networks of Silla deities. While the institutional growth of Shinra Myōjin in Japan and the historical development of the Jimon tradition can be understood within the medium and short-term time frames, the larger narrative arc of Shinra Myōijn can only be fully appreciated if we look at the long duration.

The *longue durée* trajectory of the worship of Shinra Myōjin can be divided into three stages, and this book is accordingly organized into three sections. The first stage was the pre–Shinra Myōjin period, being the time of loose networks of Silla deities that was characterized by fluidity between immigrant groups and ideas within the East Asian Mediterranean. This was also a period during which there was little in the way of an established institution of Shinra Myōjin worship. The second stage consisted of the Jimon's efforts to sedentarize Shinra Myōjin.[8] The successful localization and institutionalization of this deity ended up transforming Shinra Myōjin into the protector deity of the mountain behind Onjōji, Mt. Nagara 長等. By being tied closely to a particular location, Shinra Myōjin came to be recognized as an individual divinity of Silla origin, and this individuation in turn led to the deity playing a central role in the creation of a flourishing Jimon network during the medieval period. The third stage was a reversal of the second stage. Ironically, once fully sedentarized and domesticated, the deity recovered its fluidity again, taking on a number of functions and symbolic identities. His coming full circle was made possible by two developments: (1) the emergence of a new mythic consciousness known as new medievalism (explained later); and (2) the reemergence and reinterpretation of mythic symbols shared by the deities within the network of Silla gods. To better understand how a cult of Shinra Myōjin specific to a particular location was transformed through structural time I draw on Braudel's reconfiguration of space and time.

While I use Braudel's epistemological position in my analysis of Shinra Myōjin, I recognize that the phrase "East Asian 'Mediterranean'" can be problematic, not only because of its political overtones, but also because of its reliance on artificial, binary relations centered in, and on, the West.[9] In this book, reference to an East Asian Mediterranean is not intended to create another geopolitical model or to claim that Braudel's Mediterranean and the world of maritime East Asia were identical, for I use "Mediterranean" to denote a quality rather than an object. Having said that, the reader should keep in mind that here I am concerned with the Yellow Sea, the Sea of Japan/East Sea, the East China Sea, and the coastal regions that border these bodies of water, as seen in Map 1.[10] The contested nature of this nomenclature is another reason why "Mediterranean" functions as a viable terminological alternative.

Although the sea is featured as a perilous space in Shinra Myōjin's *engi* (origin) story, the same sea served as a conduit that connected Buddhist monks, teachings,

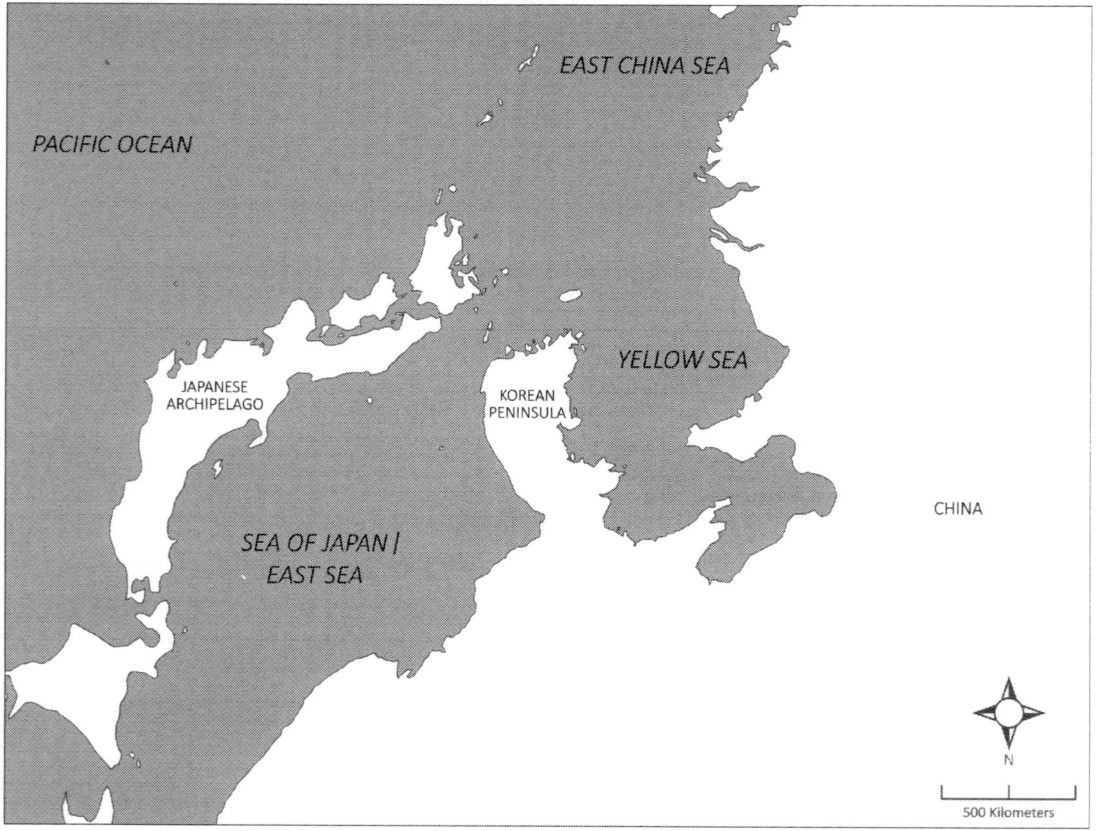

MAP 1. East Asian "Mediterranean."

and gods. In the history of Buddhism, the sea was indeed not a barrier but a contact zone.[11] When we examine the history of Japanese Buddhism with this insight in mind, it becomes clear that the sea did as much to connect the Japanese archipelago to mainland Asia as it did to isolate it, serving as a transportation route that linked people by creating various contact points.[12] When we move beyond the premise that culture only migrates over land, we arrive at a more nuanced view of the migration and circulation of Buddhist culture in the main coastal areas and among the islands dotting the sea around China, Korea, and Japan. The East Asian Mediterranean functioned as a medium and as a hybrid space populated by humans, buddhas, and gods, all of whom coexisted in this shared territory.[13] When it comes to the world of gods, which is the focus of this book, we still have a very limited understanding of how gods traveled via maritime networks and how they interacted with humans therein. By looking at East Asian sea networks, this book hopes to portray a broader perspective that is both relational and transnational.

For the study of Shinra Myōjin, interactions between the Korean Peninsula and the Japanese islands are particularly important. Whereas many scholars have drawn our attention to the Chinese cultural influence on all things Japanese, little attention has been paid to the Korean transmission of Buddhist culture to Japan.[14] The contribution of Korean immigrants to Japanese Buddhism and religion has similarly been ignored; scholars tend to characterize these phenomena collectively as "bridges," assigning importance to Korea only insofar as it served as a link between China and Japan. In recent years, however, some Anglophone scholarship has begun to recognize the significance of the religious interactions that took place between Korea and Japan during the premodern era.[15] As can be seen from these works, Korea was a "bastion of Buddhist culture in East Asia" in its own right.[16] Following Robert Buswell's challenge to the view of Korea as "a bridge for the transmission of Buddhist and Sinitic culture from the Chinese mainland to the islands of Japan,"[17] in this book I highlight the Korean impact on Japanese religions by showing that in the figure and worship of Shinra Myōjin we see the lingering influence of Korean culture on medieval Japanese religion. Looking at the worship of Shinra Myōjin in the East Asian Mediterranean network also allows us to observe other exchanges between the major players in East Asian Buddhism. In this way, the book attempts to move away from the constraints imposed by the boundaries and identities of modern nation-states.

I focus on Shinra Myōjin as this deity was understood and worshipped during the medieval period (ca. twelfth to seventeenth centuries). It has been generally assumed that the influx of Korean elements—technological, material, and ritual—into Japanese religion largely stopped sometime during the ninth century. To date, even studies illuminating religious connections between Korea and Japan have focused predominantly on the late ancient and early classical periods (ca. fourth to twelfth centuries), whereas the medieval connections between the archipelago and peninsula remain unexplored. While the medieval period may have witnessed a certain decrease in interactions and exchanges between Korea and Japan, Korean religious elements did not just disappear. Rather, they were appropriated in more creative ways—through myths, imagination, and symbolism. This is particularly true of Shinra Myōjin.

Primarily, though, my approach prioritizes the Japanese medieval imagination/*imaginaire* of Silla, as well as its concomitant religious symbolism and significance. While I do detect and identify Korean influences, I am more interested in explaining how the medieval Japanese conception of Silla was translated into the cult of Shinra Myōjin, and how the cult further reinforced the image of Korea as it existed in the Japanese imagination. What I mean by *imaginaire* is the imagined worlds created and shared by members of a society or social group and that had an enduring ideological impact.[18] In this conceptual framework, I attempt to discuss the Japanese *imaginaire* of Korea/Silla to see how specific ways of perceiving the world were collected and coded in Japanese culture.

Throughout the book, I use the term "medieval" in two different yet interrelated ways: it denotes both a historical period *and* a conceptual framework.[19] As a conceptual framework "medieval" refers to the process by which Japanese religion was transformed by the infusion of continental civilization and by the Japanese internalization and altering of that civilization. This idea of "medieval" is closely related to the so-called new medievalism, the scholarly attempt to explain religious history from socioeconomic and political perspectives, an attempt exemplified by the work of Kuroda Toshio and Amino Yoshihiko.[20] Kuroda's work focused primarily on rulership, and he dealt extensively with what he identified as the three major "power blocs" (J. *kenmon* 権門): the court nobles, the warrior aristocracy, and shrines and temples. However, when we shift our attention from power blocs to the realm of gods, mythology, and imagination, we are better able to explain how the unseen world was constantly connected to the seen world during the medieval period.

Although Shinra Myōjin's name means "the deity of Silla," there is no historical connection between Shinra Myōjin and Silla. The name "Shinra Myōjin" does not appear in any Korean sources. The earliest appearance of the name comes from the *Onjōji ryūge-e engi* 園城寺龍華会縁起 (1062), in which the deity introduces himself as Shinra Myōjin to Enchin while Enchin's ship is in the waters off the coast of Silla. Shinra Myōjin is not a classical Japanese deity either; the name shows up in neither the *Kojiki* 古事記 nor the *Nihon shoki* 日本書紀, which contain most of the deities important in early Japanese religion. Nor does Shinra Myōjin appear in canonical Buddhist literature. It is fair to say that he is neither a Korean nor a Japanese deity; neither a Buddhist deity nor a Shinto *kami*. As Fabio Rambelli and Mark Teeuwen put it, Shinra Myōjin is a "moot" divinity—that is, a deity that cannot be fit into a traditional category of deities and that falls outside of the broader medieval religious paradigm of "original forms and local traces" (J. *honji suijaku* 本地垂迹), a combinatory system in which local gods were identified as transmuted manifestations of buddhas and bodhisattvas.[21]

While Shinra Myōjin himself does not fit into this paradigm, he nevertheless developed close associations with other divinities worshipped in the Buddhist and Shinto pantheon. Not only was he associated with major Buddhist deities such as Mañjuśrī and Vimalakīrti, but he was also said to have numerous original forms (J. *honji*):[22] he was identified as Susanoo no Mikoto 素戔嗚尊 (the brother of royal ancestor Amaterasu 天照); other medieval gods such as Sonjōō 尊星王 (a star deity in the esoteric ritual of the Tendai Jimon); Matarajin 摩多羅神 (the guardian of the Jōgyō zanmai-dō 常行三昧堂 at Enryakuji); and the divine old man (J. *okina* 翁), a mysterious elderly male figure who famously appears in Noh plays.[23] These various identifications are an indication of Shinra Myōjin's hybrid nature, and I address these in the chapters that follow. Recognizing his complexity, I take this deity as a lens through which to explore two dimensions of medieval religiosity: first, the way in which the Japanese understood and incorporated Sillan religious elements into their myths and rituals; and, second, the way in which Japanese religious institutions used individual deities and the larger networks of symbols in which those deities participated in creating their own institutional identities and historical narratives.

I want now to turn to the place of Shinra Myōjin within the study of Japanese religion. In recent decades, Japanese scholars have rediscovered a large body of medieval religious literature produced in the context of medieval Shinto-Buddhist syncretism. These texts—origin stories, *kami* (deity) tales, and treatises—focus on the deities and myths found in the *Kojiki* and *Nihon shoki* (the so-called *kiki shinwa* 記紀神話). However, whereas the myths of the *Kojiki* and the *Nihon shoki* are primarily concerned with tales of *kami* that promoted the political interests of the court and ruling elite, these medieval texts contain the voices and concerns of a far greater diversity of social groups and religious institutions. These groups and institutions hoped to promote worship of *kami* associated with themselves, and they did so by producing new types of mythic concerns and accompanying rituals, mostly based on a reinterpretation of the *kiki shinwa* and the incorporation of Buddhist doctrines.

Several scholars have recognized these narratives and rituals as unique medieval phenomena in need of attention, and methodological approaches were devised for such study.[24] For instance, Yamamoto Hiroko uses the term *chūsei shinwa* 中世神話 (medieval mythology) to refer to the medieval religious literature based on mythological ideas, on the one hand, and to a methodological concern for studying this corpus, on the other.[25] However, it is also crucial to understand Yamamoto's scholarly positioning. From the beginning the field of medieval mythology was driven by a certain ideological bent. Yamamoto's *chūsei shinwa* was devised as a response to previous scholarship's tendency to ignore or devalue mythological literature produced at shrine-temple complexes during the medieval period. The previous attitude had been that such literature degraded the myth of the *Kojiki* and *Nihon shoki*, the study of which was highly valued.[26] In contrast, a new group of scholars, including Yamamoto, thought it imperative to rectify previous generations' dismissal of medieval religiosity as being marred by apocryphal texts deemed impure.[27] This corrective was welcome and necessary, and yet it inevitably led to a fetishization of the medieval world by focusing on the uniqueness of medieval mythology vis-à-vis ancient mythology. The result was an overemphasis on a distinctive Japanese medieval episteme.

My approach to the study of Shinra Myōjin builds on and further develops the established approach to medieval mythology.[28] Yamamoto rightly points out the degree to which gods permeated all levels of medieval religiosity—from mythological thought to ritual activity—and how central these "eccentric gods" (J. *ishin* 異神) were to the esoteric Buddhist pantheon during the medieval period.[29] Furthermore, she shows the degree to which Shinra Myōjin and deities such as Sekizan Myōjin 赤山明神, Matarajin 摩多羅神, Ugajin 宇賀神, and Gozu Tennō 午頭天王 were intimately linked to each other as members of a medieval pantheon.

And yet Yamamoto fails to explain the emergence of Shinra Myōjin or to address the deity's broader cultural and geographical connections. These gaps result in a view of Shinra Myōjin worship as being merely an isolated, medieval cult located at one particular Buddhist institution. In order to arrive at a fuller understanding of Shinra Myōjin, therefore, we need to examine how he and other "eccentric gods" all possessed certain "foreign" traits developed in specific locales and how they were tied to broader cultural issues over a much longer period of time. Furthermore, in order to explain the ways in which Shinra Myōjin was inscribed into the Japanese religious landscape and how this deity operated within the East Asian Buddhist context, it is necessary to widen a narrow institutional focus, to look beyond the specific institutions with which Shinra Myōjin was associated during the medieval period.[30]

One way to move away from the Japan-centric tendency is to turn to the idea of Buddhist mythology (J. *bukkyō shinwa* 仏教神話), a notion used to great effect by Iyanaga Nobumi. Buddhist mythology refers to the study of deities that appear in Buddhist texts and are incorporated into Buddhist cosmology and ideology.[31] While medieval mythology is most interested in myth-as-ideology, and only within Japan, Buddhist mythology is concerned with myth as it appears in religious practice more broadly and throughout Buddhism. As a methodology, Buddhist mythology is inspired in large part by structuralism, with an emphasis on the historical and ideological significance of the myths being studied. I follow the Buddhist mythology approach insofar as I emphasize the structures of the expansive networks of which Shinra Myōjin was a part, which allows me to expand the study of Shinra Myōjin beyond Japan.

I also bring network theory to bear on my understanding of Shinra Myōjin worship in the East Asian Mediterranean. More specifically, actor-network theory helps us think about deities as in some sense having agency.[32] In this theory, "actants" (meaning human and nonhuman actors) are shaped through relationships with other actors and transformed through these relationships within networks. This idea of "actants" helps to offset our conventional bias of agency. As William Sax has pointed out, the bias is the effect of "Euro-American ways of perceiving and interpreting the world," but nonhuman agency "can be compared with Foucault's notion of intentionality without a subject, and is thoroughly consistent with realist, individualist theories of social action."[33] Expanding this idea to my study of Shinra Myōjin, I think it is essential to treat both humans and nonhumans—including deities, institutions, and other complex entities—as actors and participants in their own right.

In this book I deal with two different but related networks: the network of Korean/Silla immigrants, and that of Silla gods within the East Asian Mediterranean. The two do not necessarily overlap in terms of their respective historical periods, but they do share a great number of cultural symbols and mythic signs. The two are "parallel *and yet* overlapping networks."[34] To understand religious networks one must take into account different types of religious movements, interactions, and permutations. In order to explain Shinra Myōjin's position within a complex web of actants, I trace the movement, settlement, and connections between people and gods. By focusing on actants' mobility, fluidity, and hybridity, I show that human actors and gods operate alike. In this way, instead of making Shinra Myōjin an immobile, dead god locked in the ritual altar and in texts, I aim to reveal the historical, cultural, social, and mythological webs surrounding him.

However, there are necessary caveats concerning the use of network theory. Manuel Vásquez warns of foreseeable problems when social network analysis is directly applied to humanistic subjects, particularly to religion, the primary problem being the theory's tendency to reduce networks and actants to functions. Vásquez further notes that network theory never resolves the issue of intentionality.[35] As a potential remedy, he suggests viewing networks not as closed and linear systems but rather as "flexible, highly dynamic, non-totalizing, and multi-directional structures of relationality."[36] My treatment of Shinra Myōjin takes this critique into account; I do not intend to argue that gods act on their intentions, although gods do make human beings act.

A similar concern is expressed by Bernard Faure, whose analysis of the medieval Japanese pantheon complicates our view of the religious network even further.[37] In his recent works Faure describes the entire network of Japanese gods as a rhizome-like, fluid network of mythic symbols.[38] In his kaleidoscopic treatment of the pantheon, he underlines both the insights and the limitations of structuralism and draws his theoretical position from actor-network theory. Acknowledging the methodological efficacy of Faure's scholarship, I hope my study of Shinra Myōjin will serve as a complementary work that illustrates the same kind of complexity but approaches it through focusing on a single god. Ultimately, the book aims at revealing the flexibility and fluidity that characterized the networks in which Shinra Myōjin existed and is intended to capture the ways in which different actants exchanged and expressed their ideas and practices in the East Asian Mediterranean.

The seven chapters of this book are organized both chronologically and thematically. Part 1—chapters 1 and 2—focuses on Shinra Myōjin prior to his medieval domestication and traces the connections between immigrant cultures within the East Asian Mediterranean. Chapter 1 introduces the origin story of Shinra Myōjin, which tells us that Enchin's decision to build Onjōji and to build it where he did was guided by Shinra Myōjin, whom he had encountered during his return voyage from China. This origin story hints at the transcultural nature of the emergence of Shinra Myōjin worship, and I argue that the network of the Silla immigrants crisscrossing the East Asian Mediterranean was largely responsible for this emergence.

Chapter 2 explains that the emergence of Shinra Myōjin at Onjōji must be understood in light of the presence of Korean immigrant communities settled around Lake Biwa 琵琶 in Ōmi Province, the ancient imperial palace of Japan between the years 667 and 672 and the location of Onjōji. These Korean immigrants supported and sustained the network of Silla-related gods at the shrines and temples in the region. The presence and activity of these Silla immigrant communities must, in turn, be perceived within the larger context of the East Asian Mediterranean and its multicentered network of Silla merchants, Silla immigrants, and Tendai Buddhist monks.

With part 2—chapters 3 and 4—we move on to the process by which Shinra Myōjin acquired a new role as a localized mountain deity during the medieval period, a process that eventually resulted in Shinra Myōjin becoming the principal deity of the entire Jimon tradition. On the one hand, this transformation of Shinra Myōjin allowed him to become a local god and shed his foreign identity. On the other hand, although he acquired new characteristics and roles, through this process he also lost his fluidity and vitality as he was made to fit the rigid political reality and ideological struggle of which the Jimon was a part.

Chapter 3 examines the ideological nature of Shinra Myōjin's transformation within the Jimon's medieval institutional history. The chapter focuses on the spread of Shinra Myōjin through the Minamoto 源 clan, one of the two major clans vying for control of Japan during the medieval period, and through networks that later developed into what we now call Shugendō 修験道 (the way of cultivating special powers). One of the pivotal moments in the transformation of Shinra Myōjin was the fixing of his location, a process by which this deity of the sea turned into a mountain deity residing next to Lake Biwa. This process was necessary if Shinra Myōjin was to become the main protector deity of the Jimon. The Jimon's attempt to establish its own ordination platform played a pivotal role in duplicating this deity of Silla into two distinct gods: Sekizan Myōjin 赤山明神, who protected the Sanmon, and

Shinra Myōjin, who guarded the Jimon. The mutual borrowings and appropriations between the Sanmon and the Jimon were responsible for the duplication of this deity, and these two deities subsequently grew in importance and popularity.

In chapter 4 I explore the Jimon's projection of its stories of legitimation onto the deity through literature, legends, performing arts, and rituals. Through these media, in which the deity revealed his many roles at the temple, this noncanonical deity established his importance and became the divine representative of the entire Jimon tradition. Shinra Myōjin's multifaceted nature and many roles further allow us to understand that this deity was an integral part of the Jimon's everyday ritual space. The constant interplay between the Onjōji clerics and Shinra Myōjin was crucial to constructing the Jimon's collective identity. The deity's permeation of every corner of temple life suggests that he was both a source and a concrete expression of the temple's political and institutional legitimation.

In part 3—chapters 5, 6, and 7—I turn to the broader mythological network of Silla gods in which Shinra Myōjin participated to illustrate how the deity regained fluidity by being linked to other Korean/Silla deities. Chapter 5 describes Shinra Myōjin's association with Sonjōō 尊星王 (literally the monarch of the revered star), focusing on Sonjōō's historical background, ritual, and iconography. At Onjōji, the worship of Shinra Myōjin reached its zenith with the use of Sonjōō as the main focus of worship (J. *honzon* 本尊) of the esoteric star ritual during the Insei 院政 period (1086–1185). With its creation of Sonjōō and linking of Shinra Myōjin with Sonjōō, the Jimon created one of its most important deities, and the Sonjōō star ritual contributed to an increase in the Jimon's political power.

Chapter 6 examines the way in which Silla's position within the Japanese *imaginaire* led to Shinra Myōjin's transformation into a god of pestilence. This chapter explains how the Japanese came to associate the Korean kingdom of Silla with pestilence, and how Japanese views of Silla facilitated the identification of Shinra Myōjin with Susanoo, a paradigmatic Japanese god who supposedly traveled to Silla. Here I argue that the mythological development of Shinra Myōjin was largely a response to the medieval Japanese Buddhist imagination's understanding of the ancient Korean kingdom of Silla. I further show that this mythic confusion helped Shinra Myōjin transform from a god of Silla into a god who conquered Silla.

Chapter 7 addresses the significance of visual representations that portray Shinra Myōjin as a divine old man, showing that the iconography of Shinra Myōjin was influenced by images of the divine old man that appear in Mañjuśrī paintings known as *Mañjuśrī Crossing the Sea from Mt. Wutai* 五台 (Tokai Monju 渡海文殊) or as Mañjuśrī Pentad (Monju Gosonzō 文殊五尊像). This chapter further explores the network of old-man deities, almost all of whom were connected to Korean immigrants. I thus argue that Shinra Myōjin's iconography was part of a larger network of the old-man deity, a complex and broad cultural phenomenon found in a number of East Asian religious traditions. This chapter's analysis of Shinra Myōjin iconography helps us see that this deity came to be visualized through an accommodation of the existing iconographical traditions and reveals the ways in which his visual appearance reflected cultural symbolism held in common by multiple East Asian religious networks.

Part I

Maritime East Asia

Networks of Immigrants and Silla Shrines/Temples

Chapter 1

Between History and Story

In this chapter I outline the history of Onjōji, which is inseparable from the history of Shinra Myōjin. I also introduce the *engi* of Shinra Myōjin, which served as the scriptural basis for Shinra Myōjin worship. This background information will help the reader to understand the place of this deity within the broader religio-political milieu of medieval Japan. Despite Onjōji's importance as one of the four most powerful esoteric Buddhist institutions of the medieval period (alongside Tōji 東寺, Kōfukuji 興福寺, and Enryakuji 延暦寺), there has been very little research on its history.[1] This is in part due to the fact that many medieval sources that might tell us about Onjōji were destroyed during the many years of fighting between the Sanmon and Jimon.

Onjōji was first founded in 668 as Sūfukuji 崇福寺 (also known as Shigaji 志賀寺 and Shigazanji 志賀山寺) and has remained at its current site ever since. Sūfukuji was built by Emperor Tenji 天智 (r. 661–672) after he moved his palace to nearby Ōtsu 大津 in 667 in response to the threat of an invasion by the Tang-Silla alliance. Ōtsu was the largest settlement on Lake Biwa, and the considerable presence of continental immigrants in the area was one of the main reasons why Ōtsu was chosen as the new imperial capital. Sūfukuji was among several temples built to protect the new palace, and it was established with the sponsorship of the Ōtomo 大友 clan,[2] one of the largest immigrant groups in the Ōmi area.[3] The Ōtomo may very well have originally come from Silla, and thus their presence in Ōmi may in part account for the later prominence of the worship of Silla deities, and specifically Shinra Myōjin, in this area. However, the textual record suggests a number of different geographical origins for this clan, and there is no scholarly consensus as to whether the Ōmoto were indeed from Silla, so the Silla-Ōtomo connection must for the time being be treated as speculative. Some clan members claimed that the Ōtomo were descendants of the Chinese emperor Xian 献 (r. 189–220) of the Later Han, while others claimed descent from Paekche. Whatever the clan's origins may have been, what is clear is that it established close ties with Emperor Tenji. When Emperor Tenji moved the palace to Ōmi, the Ōtomo clan provided invaluable political and technological support. In return, the emperor had his son change his name from Prince Iga 伊賀 to Prince Ōtomo 大友 shortly after the move to Ōtsu.[4] However, during the Jinshin war (J. *jinshin no ran* 壬申の乱), a succession dispute occurred between Prince Ōtomo and Emperor Tenmu 天武 (r. 673–686) and the prince was killed; shortly thereafter, in 687, Emperor Tenmu rebuilt the main hall of Sūfukuji with the help of the Ōtomo clan as a way of pacifying the spirit of Prince Ōtomo.[5]

Sūfukuji secured its official association with Tendai Buddhism through the appointment of Enchin as its chief monk in 866.[6] A *daijōkanchō* 大政官牒 (an official document from the Daijōkan, or Ministry of State) issued the same year documents the court's approval of Enchin's request to affiliate Sūfukuji with the Tendai school.[7] After Enchin took charge of the temple, its name changed to Onjōji.[8] This new name, however, still exhibits the lingering presence of the Ōtomo: the name of the temple originated from a manor named "Onjō" 薗城, which the Ōtomo clan owned.[9] Even after the Ōtomo ceased to be the temple's primary patron in the late Heian period the Ōtomo continued to support Onjōji.[10]

Onjōji is also known as Miidera 三井寺 (Temple of Three Wells, also written 御井寺, or Temple of the Imperial Well). The name Miidera exemplifies Onjōji's strategic use of Sūfukuji's legacy. Through the Sūfukuji connection, Onjōji linked itself to imperial support and claimed that the name Miidera resulted from the temple's association with three emperors—Tenji, Tenmu, and Jitō 持統 (r. 690–697). Onjōji developed a legend stating that when these emperors were born, water from the well of Onjōji was used for their bathing rituals, and that it was because of this that the temple was called Miidera.[11] In this way, although Onjōji was in no way related to these three emperors, it was able to fabricate an imperial connection.

The Jimon's appropriation of the legacy of Sūfukuji can also be seen in the temple's principal object of worship (J. *honzon*). When Onjōji was established on the previous site of Sūfukuji, it inherited many of Sūfukuji's traditions, including Sūfukuji's central icon. The *honzon* of Sūfukuji was Maitreya (J. Miroku 弥勒), the Future Buddha.[12] Sūfukuji's association with the Maitreya cult reflects the earlier significance of Maitreya in the Ōmi area, and Onjōji's continued interest in Maitreya worship can be explained in this context.[13] What is interesting, however, is the way in which Onjōji used this particular Maitreya statue to claim historical superiority, a move that entailed the conflation of an ideological claim and a historical truth. In the *Onjōji denki*, we read:

> Onjōji is the first Buddhist monastery in Japan. Forty-four years after the establishment of Onjōji, Kōfukuji was established. Fifteen years after that temple [was built], Tōdaiji

> was then established. About one hundred years after the establishment of Miidera [Onjōji], Enryakuji was built. Our temple is the first temple in the history of Buddhism [in Japan]. Emperor Tenji strove to build that temple during his reign and enshrined Maitreya as its *honzon*. This is the very Maitreya enshrined there today. Both the *honzon* and the temple are the oldest in Japan.[14]

Here Onjōji claims that Sūfukuji's *honzon* is Japan's oldest Maitreya image, and that since Onjōji succeeded this image of Maitreya, Onjōji is the oldest Buddhist temple in Japan. The earliest Buddhist image in Japan was in fact a statue of Maitreya, but this does not mean that the Maitreya found in Sūfukuji was that same early statue. The *Nihon shoki* states: "In 584 during the reign of Emperor Bidatsu 敏達 (r. 572–586), a stone statue of Maitreya was transmitted from Paekche."[15] This event marks for Japanese Buddhists the official transmission of the Maitreya cult to Japan.[16] Although the above passage does not explicitly make the link between Onjōji's *honzon* and the Maitreya image mentioned in the *Nihon shoki*, the text is speaking to an audience who will understand that the text is making this link. In this passage, we see Onjōji's attempt to establish religious authority and antiquity by linking itself to the first Maitreya statue (and first Buddhist statue) to come to Japan. By making such a bold, polemical statement, Onjōji was attempting to show itself to be, not only the most ancient site of Maitreya worship, but also the most authentic and authoritative temple in Japan.

The worship of Shinra Myōjin was indeed developed as part of a broader revival of the Maitreya cult during the tenth and eleventh centuries in the Jimon. In the Maitreya image (figure 1), which was produced at Onjōji, Maitreya is the centerpiece of the Jimon's ritual altar and of its iconographic tradition along with Enchin and Shinra Myōjin.[17] It has been assumed that the Maitreya cult was most active in Nara Buddhism and in temples affiliated with the Hossō 法相 school. However, the Maitreya cult in the Jimon suggests that Maitreya played an important role in early Tendai history as well.[18]

Shinra Myōjin became a leverage point when Onjōji began trying to establish a new Tendai esoteric Buddhist center. After Enchin returned from China, bringing with him new esoteric Buddhist images as well as his own experience of studying esoteric Buddhism there, his disciples could claim to possess superior esoteric Buddhist knowledge vis-à-vis the monks at Enryakuji. This eventually led to the Jimon's Tendai teaching being more esoteric than those of the Sanmon.[19] Although there is no concrete evidence that Enchin actually worshipped Shinra Myōjin, this deity became a central institutional feature of the Jimon from the tenth century onward.[20] Though the Sanmon-Jimon split that characterized much of early Tendai rivalry did not occur until the end of the tenth century, the seeds of discontent were already being sown during the early ninth century.[21] The eighteenth Tendai *zasu* 座主 (the chief abbot of Tendai) Ryōgen 良源 (912–985) was in part responsible for the Tendai

FIGURE 1. Maitreya accompanied by Enchin and Shinra Myōjin, Miroku bosatsu zō, thirteenth c., ink and colors on silk. Kyoto National Museum, Kyoto.

schism.[22] When Ryōgen became *zasu*, he attempted to eradicate a factional division on Mt. Hiei.[23] However, his reform failed and instead contributed to the permanent division. The schism was caused by many factors, but the two primary ones were (1) disagreement over control of the Tendai *zasu* and, later, (2) concerns about the creation of an independent ordination platform at Onjōji.

By the time of Ryōgen's death in 985, the Tendai community on Mt. Hiei had completely separated into two opposing groups: the Saichō-Ennin line and the Gishin-Enchin line. This split was related to a succession problem originating in the fact that Saichō had named two different monks—Enchō 円澄 (771–836) and Gishin 義真 (781–833)—as successors at different times.[24] Ryōgen was succeeded by his disciple Jinzen 尋禅 (943–990), son of the powerful Fujiwara no Morosuke 藤原師輔 (909–960). Four years later, Jinzen became Tendai *zasu*. When he resigned from the office in 989, the court appointed the Onjōji monk Yokei 余慶 (919–991), Ryōgen's rival, to be Jinzen's successor as Tendai *zasu*. The monks of the Saichō-Ennin line vehemently protested the appointment of Yokei and refused to cooperate with him. Within three months, Yokei had to resign and return to Onjōji, where he died in 991. Yokei was the last Tendai *zasu* from the Gishin-Enchin line to live on Mt. Hiei.

During the severe factionalism between the two Tendai branches in the late tenth century, monastic military forces became involved, and each side's protector deity took on a new importance. A major military clash between the Sanmon and the Jimon branches occurred during the eighth month of 993; some Jimon followers of Jōsan 成纂 (925–998), a disciple of Shōsan 勝算 (939–1011), destroyed a number of religious icons at the Sekizan Zen'in 赤山禅院, a shrine dedicated to Sekizan Myōjin and located at the western foot of Mt. Hiei. By this time Sekizan Myōjin, the purported protective deity brought back from China by Ennin, had already become a powerful symbol of the Sanmon, whereas there was no mention of the Shinra Myōjin Shrine during this initial conflict. Two days later, armed monks of the Saichō-Ennin line attacked a number of the Gishin-Enchin line monks who were still living on Mt. Hiei and drove them out.[25] In the end, over one thousand monks from Enchin's lineage fled to Onjōji never to return, thereby cementing the split between the two Tendai traditions.

Kanshū 勧修 (945–1008) and Shōsan, both of whom left Mt. Hiei in 981, were leading figures in the split, and they eventually became leaders of the new group, namely the Jimon. After the split, the Sanmon and Jimon factions never reconciled their differences.[26] Whereas Jimon monks fought to establish their independence, arguing for the superiority of their practices, Sanmon monks maintained that the Jimon was part of the overall Tendai denomination. The new tradition sought political support, and soon they found powerful patrons among courtiers, chief among them Fujiwara no Michinaga 藤原道長 (966–1028). In their efforts to strengthen their political power, the Jimon provided shelter for dharma princes (J. *hōshinnō* 法親王) by appointing them to the abbotship of Onjōji.[27] Dharma princes were sons within the royal family who received the status of imperial prince after entering the monkhood. Having a prince as *chōri* 長吏 (Onjōji's designation for abbot) became an effective strategy for controlling not only the temple's estates but also important religious ceremonies and armed followers.[28]

Onjōji never subdivided into denominations, although it did create its own network of temples and collective identity, differentiating itself from the Sanmon. During the eleventh century, however, several imperial princes took up residence at Onjōji sub-temples, and three imperial temples (J. *monzeki* 門跡): Enmanin 円満院, Shōgoin 聖護院, and Jissōin 実相院 came to be affiliated with the Jimon.[29] These temples were institutions that were operated by an aristocratic or imperial lineage, and this setup had a significant role in the growth of the Jimon network. In addition, these institutions increased the artistic and cultural production within the Jimon tradition.[30] Throughout the medieval period, Onjōji owned a large area of territory around Mt. Nagara 長等 and had five sub-temples (J. *bessho* 別所): Bizōji 尾蔵寺, Gonshōji 近松寺, Bimyōji 微妙寺, Jōzaiji 常在寺, and Suiganji 水観寺. Devotion to Shinra Myōjin spread throughout this network, and Jimon temples such as Nyoiji 如意寺 and Mimurotoji 三室戸寺 became homes for the worship of Shinra Myōjin.[31]

Throughout the medieval period the Jimon remained deeply involved with court politics and the Kamakura shogunate. When the Minamoto family was in power between 1180 and 1219, the Jimon enjoyed the Minamoto shogun's favor. However, at the end of the twelfth century, Onjōji became involved in the Genpei 源平 War (1180–1185), and parts of the temple turned into a battleground.[32] Onjōji maintained close ties with the Minamoto clan, and when the Fujiwara clan took over the shogun's post, the temple also managed to gain the Kujō family's patronage (the Kujō being a branch of the Fujiwara family). Kujō Yoritsune 九条頼経 (r. 1226–1244), the fourth shogun of the Kamakura shogunate, was a major patron of Onjōji and invited Onjōji monks to Kamakura to perform esoteric rituals for him.[33] When Hōjō Sudatoki 北条貞時 (r. 1284–1301) and Hōjō Takatoki 北条高時 (r. 1316–1326) were regents, esoteric rituals generated more interest, in part due to the attempted Mongol invasions (1274–1281), and Onjōji's esoteric rituals acquired strong support from the shogun.

The Muromachi period (1136–1573) was also a generally fortunate one for Onjōji. The temple and the first Ashikaga shogun, Ashikaga Takauji 足利尊氏 (r. 1338–1358), maintained a close relationship from the very beginning of the period. But in 1336, the temple was destroyed again by the joined forces of the imperial troops and the Sanmon's armed monks. After the war, the temple recovered with the support of the shogun. Ashikaga Takauji helped revive the dharma lecture series for Shinra Myōjin (J. *Shinrakō* 新羅講) in 1340 and sponsored the rebuilding of the Shinra Myōjin Shrine in 1347.[34] It was around this time that Onjōji monks such as Zōki 増基 (1282–1352) and Bōsen 房仙 (fl. fourteenth c.) performed rituals for the Muromachi shogunate.[35] Despite the vicissitudes of the shogun government's fortunes during this period, Onjōji maintained its position as a powerful institution through highly politicized religious rituals.

During the peacetime, Onjōji was able to reclaim previously held temple estates and compiled several temple chronicles, including the *Record of Onjōji* (*Onjōji denki* 園城寺伝記, fourteenth c., ten fascicles), the *Complementary Record of the Jimon* (*Jimon denki horoku* 寺門伝記補録, ca. 1394–1427, twenty fascicles), and the *Continued Record of the Transmission of Miidera* (*Mii zokutōki* 三井続燈記, 1483, ten fascicles).[36] This last compilation reflects Onjōji's self-awareness as an independent institution, which was reinforced by the continuous string of crises that plagued it throughout the medieval period. Peace continued until 1595, when Oda Nobunaga 織田信長 (1534–1582) decided to destroy the Tendai institutions on Mt. Hiei. Since its warrior monks were no match for Nobunaga's large, well-trained army, much of Onjōji was razed at this time. Although it suffered from the incident, the temple was restored during the Keichō 慶長 era (1596–1615) with the support of Toyotomi Hideyoshi 豊臣秀吉 (1536–1598). The Onjōji monk Dōchō 道澄 (1544–1608), who won Toyotomi's favor, undertook the reconstruction of the temple.[37]

Worship of Shinra Myōjin continued during the Edo period, although the scale was smaller when compared to the medieval period. The *Old Record of Onjōji* (*Onjōji koki* 園城寺古記, 1739), a document that records the daily rituals conducted at the temple, begins with a description of a ceremony at the Shinra Myōjin Shrine in the ninth month of 1583.[38] The ritual for Shinra Myōjin was also revitalized. As a way to realign ritual manuals, the Onjōji monk Enshin 圓親 retranscribed a ritual text titled the *Instructions for the Buddhist Ritual of the Three Shrines* (*Sansha hōe hōsoku* 三社法会法則, 1367) in 1615.[39] Here "three shrines" refers to shrines for Mio Myōjin 三尾明神, various dharma protecting deities, and Shinra Myōjin. The Shinra Myōjin section of this work is a liturgy for the Shinra Myōjin ritual, and is still used even today.[40]

Onjōji's association with military power continued into the modern period. During the Meiji government's forced separation of Shinto from Buddhism, the temple suffered from massive alteration and destruction. In 1875, when the Ninth Infantry's Japanese Imperial barracks were moved from Osaka to Ōtsu, the temple complex was devastated yet again. Various military facilities, such as a hospital and juvenile air force academy were installed in the northern part of the temple complex during the Showa period (1926–1989).[41] After the Pacific War, the ground was occupied by the US army in 1945, known as "Camp Ōtsu Area-A."[42] The area was returned to Ōtsu city in 1958, but public office buildings and a memorial park for Emperor Kōbun 弘文 (r. 671–672) were built on the Onjōji grounds. This postwar rearrangement resulted in a total separation of the Shinra Myōjin Shrine from the rest of the temple complex. Although worship of Shinra Myōjin continues today, its history after the sixteenth century will not concern us. I want to now turn to the textual tradition of the Jimon in order to shed light on the formation and development of Shinra Myōjin worship in the Jimon.

MAJOR ONJŌJI TEXTS RELATED TO SHINRA MYŌJIN

The Jimon produced temple chronicles throughout the medieval period. These texts recorded both its history and accounts of eminent monks. However, due to the frequency with which Onjōji was attacked, few records from the medieval period have survived to the present day. Extant Jimon sources date mostly to the Muromachi and Edo periods, making reconstruction of earlier periods somewhat difficult.[43] Because of this, it is fairly challenging to reconstruct the history of Shinra Myōjin worship in great detail.

However, there are two extremely valuable Jimon textual sources on which this study heavily relies: the *Onjōji denki* and the *Jimon denki horoku*. The *Onjōji denki*'s final entry records events from the year 1343, meaning the work was compiled sometime after this date. The text lacks coherent organization, and entries concerning Shinra Myōjin mostly appear in fascicles one, three, and four. In these sections, the text explains numerous aspects of the deity: its origin, ritual protocols, poems and eulogies for the deity, local legends, miracle stories, and iconographical details. The latter text, the *Jimon denki horoku*, serves as a supplement to the *Onjōji denki* and contains more detail and annotations. The Jimon monk Shikō 志晃 (fl. early fifteenth c.) compiled the *Jimon denki horoku* during the Ōei 応永 era (1394–1424). Being more chronologically organized than the *Onjōji denki*, it spans a period of several centuries; the entries begin with the first year of the female ruler Jitō and end in 1397. Entries on Shinra Myōjin are concentrated in the first three fascicles.

The portrayal of Shinra Myōjin in these texts was determined in large part by the ideological landscapes of their respective times. By the time that these Jimon chronicles were compiled, the worship of *kami* by Buddhist monks had grown in importance.[44] Due to this new relationship between monks and the *kami*, Jimon scholar-monks became actively involved in the production of new knowledge related to shrine cults, and, in turn, Shintō rituals were incorporated into Buddhist ceremonies.[45] In the *Onjōji denki* and the *Jimon denki horoku* we see the simultaneous influence of the dominant ideology of "original substance, manifest traces" (J. *honji suijaku*) and that of its reverse (J. *han honji suijaku* 反本地垂迹), a theory that was developed by Tendai monks around the fourteenth century.[46] While the term "*honji suijaku*" was derived from the Buddhist doctrine of multiple manifestations of the Buddha, in medieval Japan the doctrine provided a conceptual tool for incorporating local *kami* into Buddhism. Other than these two texts, there are several others that help us to develop a fuller picture of Shinra Myōjin worship (see table).[47]

Jimon Textual Sources That Discuss Shinra Myōjin

Text Title	Date	Compiler
Onjōji ryūge-e engi 園城寺龍華会縁起	1062	Fujiwara no Sanenori 藤原実範
Shinra Myōjin ki 新羅明神記	Early 13th c.	Unknown
Jitokushū 寺徳集	1344	Suishin 水心
Keiran shūyōshū 渓嵐拾葉集	1347	Koshū 光宗
Onjōji denki 園城寺伝記	After 1379	Unknown
Jimon denki horoku 寺門伝記補録	1394–1427	Shikō 志晃
Shinra ryakki 新羅略記	Early 15th c.	Unknown
Onjōji engi 園城寺縁起	920?	Unknown
Shinra no kiroku 新羅之記録	1646	Unknown

The *Onjōji ryūge-e engi* (1062) is thought to be the oldest *engi* to reference Shinra Myōjin. Before I introduce the *Onjōji ryūge-e engi*, I want to briefly discuss another text that the Jimon claimed to be the earliest record of Shinra Myōjin. The text in question is titled the *Onjōji engi* 薗城寺縁起, and in it we find the claim that this text is based on a secret oral transmission that can be traced back to Enchin. Currently only one copy of the text survives: a handwritten manuscript copied during the Kamakura period.[48] The *Onjōji engi* consists of three parts: a declaration about Onjōji's territory, the *engi* story of Onjōji as provided by Enchin, and two official documents.[49] The story of Shinra Myōjin appears in the second part of the *engi*, and the story found here is almost identical to that found in the *Onjōji ryūge-e engi*.

The authenticity of the *Onjōji engi*, however, has been challenged: in premodern times by the Sanmon, and more recently by modern scholars.[50] A Sanmon text entitled *Sanmon sōjō* 山門奏状 (1215), for example, accused the *Onjōji engi* of being apocryphal. Despite these critiques, in the Jimon tradition the text's authority was never questioned, and it continued to be read and cited, as can be seen in works such as the *Asabashō* 阿娑縛抄 (1275) and the *Tengu zōshi* 天狗草紙 (thirteenth c.).[51] According to the colophon, the *Onjōji engi* was compiled in 920, which would make it a least a century older than the *Onjōji ryūge-e engi*. Akamatsu Toshihide and Oyamada Kazuo have both expressed doubts about this date and argue that it is a forgery.[52] Setting aside the dating of the text, what is intriguing is the text's attempt to create a substantial link between Enchin and Shinra Myōjin. Shinra Myōjin does not appear in any official documents related to Enchin that were produced during his lifetime. It is possible that as Jimon monks began to promote the cult of Shinra Myōjin, they became aware that this absence of a link in older sources would be a problem, and they may have therefore created the *Onjōji engi* to address this absence.

As can be seen in the table above, there are several other texts related to Shinra Myōjin that have been preserved in the Jimon tradition, including the *Shinra Myōjin ki* 新羅明神記, *Shinra ryakki* 新羅略記, and *Shinra no kiroku* 新羅之記録. The *Shinra Myōjin ki*, compiled during the early thirteenth century, is one of the main sources for our understanding of Shinra Myōjin; the only extant manuscript of this work is currently housed in the archives of Tokyo University.[53] The text contains one section about Enchin and another that relates various miracle tales about Shinra Myōjin. The *Shinra ryakki* is an abridgement of another text, the *Shinra ki* 新羅記, which is no longer extant.[54]

The third of these three texts—the *Shinra no kiroku*—was compiled in 1646 by Matsumae Kagehiro 松前景広 (1600–1658), the sixth (or seventh) son of Matsumae Yoshihiro 松前慶広 (1548–1616), the first feudal lord (J. *hanshu* 藩主) of the Matsumae 松前 domain in present-day Hokkaido.[55] This text contains the oldest extant local history of Matsumae. It is comprised of three parts,[56] the first of which focuses on the origin of Shinra Myōjin, whose *engi* story was told to Matsumae Kagehiro during a trip he made to Onjōji. Several sentences from the text are identical to sentences found in the major Onjōji chronicles, and it is highly possible that Matsumae actually read those Onjōji documents. The Matsumae clan considers Minamoto no Yoshimitsu 源義光 (1045–1127)—popularly known as Shinra Saburō 新羅三郎—to be its clan ancestor. After Kagehiro's visit to Onjōji in 1646, he was even more convinced that the people of Matsumae were the descendants of Minamoto no Yoshimitsu and that Shinra Myōjin was the protector god of the Matsumae clan.[57]

Before I get into the details of the story of Shinra Myōjin, it is useful to think about the nature of the *engi* literature that we are going to look at.[58] The *Onjōji denki* and the *Jimon denki horoku* belong to a genre of temple and shrine origin legends known as *jisha engi* 寺社縁起, a type of literature usually associated with Japan's medieval period.[59] Earlier scholars neglected *jisha engi* literature because they regarded such works as forgeries or fictions, and thus as unreliable sources for historical scholarship.[60] The *jisha engi* were said to have been created by temples and shrines that wished to assert their spiritual authority, institutional legitimacy, political autonomy, economic power, and ritual continuity. In this way, *engi* writing, compilation, and promotion have been understood either as a means of gaining political favor (and thus support) or economic power (usually in the form of donations). In addition, unlike work with traditional historical sources, dealing with the *jisha engi* can be extremely challenging, for their content and structure is complex; this fact has further dissuaded scholars from using these works as sources for the study of medieval Japanese religions.[61] But these records should not be regarded simply as self-serving, self-promoting narratives. Rather, this literature offers tremendous insights into and information about medieval religion, history, and art (both material and performed).[62]

As works of the *jisha engi* genre, the *Onjōji denki* and the *Jimon denki horoku* focus on the origins and benefits of particular *kami* or buddhas related to Onjōji in an attempt to promote the temple's uniqueness and importance. The rise in the popularity of *engi* and the increase in their production by individual temples was in part a result of the collapse of the *ritsuryō* 律令 system, a centralized government structure used between the seventh and tenth centuries.[63] During the late Heian period, the court's control of individual temples and shrines weakened, and in response temples and shrines sought new ways of managing their local economies. One way they did this was by operating their own manors, independently fund-raising for religious rituals, and securing wealthy patrons to finance the production of art. It was in this context that they began to create their own histories and disseminate miracle tales; such stories helped them establish economic stability, promote their own political independence, and continue ritual practices for a variety of patrons. While there are a few *jisha engi* produced by aristocratic patrons or worshippers in order to record their own individual memories or religious inspirations, *jisha engi* were for the most part produced by elite Buddhist priests who were concerned first and foremost with re-creating the history of their temple and with advertising the powers of the *kami* or buddhas enshrined therein.

In trying to understand how *engi* literature functioned, the concept of "mythistory" proves useful. Introduced by William H. McNeil and developed by Joseph Mali, mythistory defies easy categorization and challenges us to think more carefully about embellishment and redaction in premodern texts.[64] Just as in many ancient texts and worldviews, in Japanese temple chronicles' sacred narratives the distinction between history and myth is not clear, or sometimes even irrelevant. Endowed with truth-bearing power, *jisha engi* are neither myth nor history, even as they contain elements of both. On the one hand they are concerned with specific historical events, while on the other they are also permeated by a collective consciousness teeming with spirits, gods, and demons. While we can understand in retrospect the specific religious and historical contexts in which these texts were produced, we should keep in mind that for the producers of these narratives, the mythical-religious world of these stories was intimately related to their perception of reality, and the narratives in the *jisha engi* literature were seen as the most powerful medium for conveying human experiences and human imagination. By reading *jisha engi* as mythistory, we can better understand how the symbolic schemes and the temple's worldview operated within this specific genre. It is for this reason that I view the temple chronicles of Onjōji as a type of "mythistorical literature" and use these narratives to understand how specific religious experiences were collectively created and transformed into stories without abandoning the distinction between myth and history.

To acknowledge mythistory's dual potential is not simply to recognize its paradoxical nature but also to provide a method for more nuanced readings of those written sources. Being aware of the nature of the *jisha engi* genre, we should be more careful and critical in examining the ways in which the Jimon used the past and in which Jimon monks transmitted their experiences in narrative form. These chronicles do not relate "history" in our sense of the word; they are ideological documents that contain mythic elements and that seek to re-create a certain past rather than to produce a neutral and accurate account of previous events. However, they are still historical insofar as they explicitly describe and implicitly allude to a number of factual events that led to the authorship or compiling of the text. To read between the lines of the *jisha engi* is to understand how these stories linked history to a timeless origin and to a particular temple's sanctity. It further helps us see that there is no clear separation between history and myth, because the power of belief, on the one hand, and the will to believe, on the other, each functions as a point of convergence where myth reveals history while history becomes myth. With this in mind, I now turn to Shinra Myōjin's origin story as found in the *Onjōji ryūge-e engi*.

SHINRA MYŌJIN'S *ENGI* STORY

The *engi* story of Shinra Myōjin reveals two apparently contradictory features. On the one hand, it shows the worship of this deity to be a local phenomenon; this *engi*, as a narrative about a specific religious space and time, becomes a source of authority and legitimating power of a particular site. At the same time, however, it demonstrates the translocal character of this deity. This *engi* contains a tension between local and translocal concerns. While one could read it as a story about the localization of a foreign origin deity, the translocal nature of the deity remains at the core of his character, allowing him to be associated with other Korean/Silla deities through their respective *engi*. In addition to the translocal character of the deity, the physical mobility of the *engi* contributed to the translocality of the deity. Through associated networks of temples, shrines, and people, *engi* stories circulated and were read widely. The *engi* of Shinra Myōjin was part of the same movement that created and sustained the network of the Silla deities.

The *Onjōji ryūge-e engi* is one of the earliest *engi* to highlight an eminent Japanese monk's bond with a foreign deity.[65] The author of the text, Fujiwara no Sanenori 藤原実範 (fl. 1023–1062), had a connection to Onjōji in part through his wife's family, the Ono 小野 clan, which was based in Ōmi. In addition, he was connected to the temple through the Onjōji *chōri* Myōson 明尊 (971–1063), a member of the Ono family. Myōson played a key role in formulating the worship of Shinra Myōjn in the Jimon. In 1039, during his *chōri* tenure, Myōson was also appointed as the twenty-ninth Tendai *zasu*. The Enryakuji monks opposed him, though, so much so that his abbacy lasted only three days. As the schism between the two Tendai factions—the Sanmon (being the Saichō-Ennin lineage) and the Jimon (being the Gishin-Enchin lineage)—developed, Myōson was forced to devise ways to secure the Jimon's –religious and political independence, and it was in this context that the *Onjōji ryūge-e engi* was compiled.

More specifically, the *Onjōji ryūge-e engi* did two things. First, it helped establish the Dharma assemblies (J. *hōe* 法会) of Maitreya, which Onjōji used to compete with the *hōe* performed at other major temples. Second, it reconfirmed Enchin's tie with the Jimon, even though in actual fact Enchin himself did not have an exclusive tie with Onjōji during his lifetime.[66] The text begins with Enchin's encounter with Shinra Myōjin on his return trip from China, while sailing across what we now call the East China Sea. In the story, an elderly man suddenly appears in front of Enchin and introduces himself as Shinra Myōjin.

> During the Jōwa 承和 era (834–848), Master Chishō 智證 [Enchin] crossed the sea and entered Tang China in search of the Dharma. He waited for wind for safe sailing, but in a seaway the boat reached the outskirts of Wanliu 万柳 in China. With the divine protection of the Three Treasures from his home temple, the master was at last able to reach Qinglongsi 青龍寺 in Chang'an 長安. At the temple, he learned all the Dharma from his master (Skt. *ācārya*). One by one, he received all the teachings of the exoteric and esoteric traditions, and finally received transmission. After the master completed his mission, he decided to come back to Japan. On his boat, an old man suddenly appeared and declared: "I am a deity (J. *myōjin* 明神) of the Silla Kingdom. I will protect your practice of Buddhism until the Buddha Maitreya comes to this world." Having said this, the old man disappeared.[67]

This is one of the oldest stories in which a Japanese monk encounters a foreign deity and receives the deity's protection, but the narrative is not unique to Shinra Myōjin. Thus, before I analyze the *engi* story, I want first to describe the complex web of narrative traditions of which the Shinra Myōjin *engi* story is a part. This narrative structure has since been copied and modified, sometimes with a twist for some ideological purpose. For instance, a similar narrative appears in popular tale collections, such as the *Konjaku monogatari shū* 今昔物語集 (early twelfth c.) and the *Kokon chōmonjū* 古今著聞集 (1254), and the historical epic *Taiheiki* 太平記 (fourteenth c.). While the general plot in which an eminent monk receives protection from a deity on his way back to Japan from China is maintained, the deity differs in each story. In the *Konjaku monogatari shū*, the god who appears to Enchin is not Shinra Myōjin but the Yellow Fudō Myōō (Ki Fudō Myōō 黄不動明王).[68] In the *Taiheiki*, Shinra Myōjin and Fudō both appear in front of Enchin instead of Shinra Myōjin alone.[69]

Among this same group of *engi* stories, the most noteworthy is the story of Ennin and how he invoked Sekizan Myōjin. The narrative exhibits the same storyline, except that Ennin takes the place of Enchin, and Sekizan Myōjin replaces Shinra Myōjin. A similar story is found in the *Keiran shūyōshū* 渓嵐拾葉集 (ca. 1311–1347). Here we read that Ennin encountered not Sekizan Myōjin but Matarajin, another complex deity later worshipped on Mt. Hiei and at Tōji. This story also provides the origin story of Matarajin, although the narrative structure is exactly the same as that of Shinra Myōjin, which became the prototype. These stories are not just analogous ones; they reveal a deeper layer of mythological logic. In the subsequent self-duplicating narrative structure, not only deities in the story, but the narrative structure itself operates as a collective agency to create its own mythological reality while fulfilling its primary operation of making new connections between foreign deities and eminent monks from Japan.

Although the *engi* story of Shinra Myōjin serves as the archetype of a certain "medieval myth," the mythic elements found in these narratives are also part of a long tradition of sea narratives dating back to premedieval times. For example, it reflects a widespread recurring motif in tale literature (J. *setsuwa* 説話), which we see in the story of Shiotsuchi no oji 塩土老翁 (Old Man Tide Spirit). This story, which appears in the *Kojiki* and *Nihon shoki*,[70] concerns two brothers: Umi no sachi (Sea Luck) and his younger brother, Yama no sachi (Mountain Luck). When Yama no sachi took the elder brother's fishhook and went to the sea to fish, he lost the fishhook. While Yama no sachi tried to find the fishhook on the seashore, Shiotsuchi no oji appeared in front of him. Thereupon, Shiotsuchi no oji made a skiff and invited Yama no sachi to the palace of the sea god. What is relevant to our discussion at this point is Shiotsuchi no oji's identity. He is a deity who appears as an old man and a god of fishing, of navigation, and, subsuming all these, of the sea. This makes him very similar to Shinra Myōjin, who is a god of seafaring and is also regarded as the son of the Sagara Dragon King.[71]

Another story that reveals parallels with the Shinra Myōjin *engi* is the account of the monk Gyōzen 行善, which appears in the *Nihon ryōiki* 日本霊異記 (ca. 822). According to this tale, Gyōzen was sent to Koguryŏ for his studies. After Koguryŏ was defeated by a Silla-Tang alliance, he had to leave there and head to Tang China. Arriving at a river and lacking a means to cross it, he began to meditate upon Avalokiteśvara (J. Kannon 観音). Suddenly, an old man in a boat appeared and ferried him to the other shore. Gyōzen realized that the old man was an incarnation of Kannon. Upon reaching China, he made an image of the bodhisattva and worshipped it. Even after his return to Japan, Gyōzen venerated the bodhisattva until he died.[72]

The stories of Gyōzen and Enchin reveal several intriguing similarities. First, both monks are faced with some water-related danger or trouble, and both are saved by a deity who appears as an old man. Second, both encountered the water-related danger or trouble somewhere between China and Japan: Gyōzen on the Korean Peninsula, and Enchin out at sea. Third, although one story appears to be about the worship of Kannon and the other about Shinra Myōjin, at Onjōji these two were regarded as being the same, perhaps due to the fact that both were connected with water.[73] So what do these similarities tell us? Could it be that the story of Shinra

Myōjin is a conflation of these two well-known stories, that of Shiotsuchi no oji and that of Gyōzen? It is highly possible that the compiler of the Shinra Myōjin *engi* was well versed in *setsuwa* literature and might have been inspired or even influenced by them. Currently it is impossible to say with any certainty. But this examination of possible sources for the Shinra Myōjin origin story suggests that it arises from a much broader folkloric tradition, and not simply from Buddhist or elite sources, as has sometimes been assumed.

Returning to the *Onjōji ryūge-e engi*, the central aim of the first part of the story is to explain Shinra Myōjin's connection to Enchin. This part of the story also suggests that Shinra Myōjin's primary role is to protect those at sea. With this protection Enchin arrives safely back in Japan. In the second part of the story, set back in Japan, the deity reappears to the master. In contrast to Shinra Myōjin's role as a sea deity, in this section of the story the deity takes on the role of a mountain deity and introduces Enchin to the future site of Onjōji. After this he disappears. As the story unfolds, the focus shifts from Enchin's relationship with Shinra Myōjin to his interactions with Kyōtai, an old man who had been living at the site where Onjōji would later be built. After the mysterious Kyōtai explains the history of the temple to Enchin, he vanishes, echoing Shinra Myōjin's earlier disappearance. This part of the *engi* reads:

> After the master returned to Japan, the court asked him to present what he had learned and collected in China to the Daijōkan 太政官 (the statutory Council of State). At that very time, the same old man from the previous day reappeared and stated: "In Japan there is an auspicious place. You should build a Buddhist temple on that land, and enshrine the teachings that you received."
>
> Thereupon, the master arrived at Onjōji in Shiga district 滋賀郡 in Ōmi Province 近江國. He asked monks at the temple about [the temple's] origins. However, no one knew about them except an old monk named Kyōtai 教待. He approached the master and told him: "I am a hundred and sixty-two years old. This temple was established one hundred and eighty years ago. There is a descendant of our patron clan."
>
> Kyōtai called to the person, and the person came and introduced himself: "My ancestor is Ōtomo no Yotaō 大友与多王. He established the temple for Emperor Tenmu. Originally the territory was part of the family land of Prince Ōtomo, the prime minister of the Daijōkan 大友太政大臣. Following Emperor Tenji's imperial decree, the minister built Sūfukuji at this very site. A sixty-foot-tall Maitreya statue was enshrined at the temple."[74]

According to the following section of the *engi* story, Enchin was intrigued, explored the area, and learned more about Kyōtai by visiting Kyōtai's hut. There, Enchin was told that as a monk Kyōtai always caught fish and tortoises, but when Enchin saw these they suddenly transformed into lotus flowers. Enchin then realized that Kyōtai was not just a mysterious informant but a manifestation of Maitreya.[75] This revelation of Kyōtai's true nature highlights the connections between Maitreya worship and the Sūfukuji, as well as the temple's and Enchin's devotion to Maitreya.[76] What is interesting in this part of the *engi* story is the fluid identity of Kyōtai. There have been a number of theories about the identity of Kyōtai.[77] Some suggest that his name indicates a connection with Maitreya: awaiting (*tai*) the teaching (*kyō*), that is, awaiting the time when he, as Maitreya, will give the teachings. On the other hand, Kyōtai should be understood more generally as a particular archetype. On this issue, Edward Drott suggests that he is "a composite figure—the product of multiple layers of legend," and he bears a remarkable resemblance to the aged fisherman, a common literary motif in Japanese religious narratives during the medieval period.[78] The *engi* story also leaves open the possibility that Kyōtai is an avatar of Shinra Myōjin: in the guise of an old fisherman, Kyōtai is connected to Shinra Myōjin through their common associations with the sea and fishing.

To sum up, the first part of the Shinra Myōjin story highlights Enchin's miraculous encounter with the deity on his way back from China to Japan, while the second half explains how the deity led Enchin to the site of the future Onjōji and how Enchin learned about the history of this site. The text is very likely a synthesis of two different stories, and they point to two different functions of Shinra Myōjin: in the first half of the *engi*, Shinra Myōjin is presented as a god who guarantees safe passage across the sea, whereas in the latter half, he is a mountain god, who guides Enchin to the site where Onjōji will be built. In this way, the deity acquires the legitimate role of a *genius loci*, or landlord deity (J. *jinushi* 地主), who will protect the mountain of the Jimon forever after. Here we have a Shinra Myōjin who has become domesticated (in the sense of being tied to a single location) and institutionalized. The story portrays him as a divine old man who can sacralize and secure the Jimon's position as a new headquarters for Tendai activity. This is a new identity, yet one that draws on much older sources.

This chapter outlined the establishment of Onjōji, clarified the context in which textual sources related to Shinra Myōjin were produced, and introduced the origin story of Shinra Myōjin. A careful analysis of the Jimon's temple chronicles suggests that Onjōji built on Sūfukuji's traditions. In their attempt to establish a new powerful Tendai center, Enchin's followers strategically appropriated the history of Sūfukuji. By doing so Onjōji was able to inherit Sūfukuji's religious legacy and political ties with the imperial court. Sūfukuji's connections with imperial power and the Ōtomo, one of the most powerful immigrant clans in the region, were immensely desirable for Enchin and his followers as they sought to establish a new center for Tendai independent of Mt. Hiei.

Turning to the main textual sources for understanding the early history of Onjōji and Shinra Myōjin, I noted that, while the temple chronicles contain much that we might think of as myth, they are also valuable sources for historical inquiry. The *engi* of Shinra Myōjin, which appears to be part of a broader mythic and secular narrative tradition stretching back to the ancient period, set a precedent for the Buddhist adaptation of those mythic elements and that narrative structure, and it helped to create a subgenre of *engi* narratives. The analysis of the *engi* story of Shinra Myōjin allows us to see the recurring themes and patterns in the story as well as the main functions of the story. While decoding the origin story of Shinra Myōjin, several key features of the earlier development of the worship of Shinra Myōjin were revealed, such as the deity's many roles: that of a seafaring deity, a landlord deity, and a mountain deity, all of which grant Shinra Myōjin an exalted status in the later history of the Jimon tradition.

To understand the way in which these mythic stories were perceived is crucial when we begin to ask what historical facts we can glean from a literature that is a product of the intersection between mythological consciousness and historical imagination. As seen in the case of Shinra Myōjin, myths bear witness to the process by which shared knowledge was internalized, altered, and preserved. But myth was also the location at which historical consciousness and mythic imagination converged and were contested. In this way, the *engi* of Shinra Myōjin reveals the importance placed on history, but also the prominence of myth and imagination, within East Asian Buddhist networks. These networks in turn created channels of communication, allowing the deity to become an integral part of the larger network in the East Asian Mediterranean, a topic to which I now turn my attention.

Chapter 2

The Network of Silla Immigrants and the Emergence of Shinra Myōjin

I shall now turn my attention to Silla immigrants, their networks (which crisscrossed the East Asian Mediterranean), and the connection between these immigrant networks and the emergence of Shinra Myōjin worship. The Silla networks provided conduits for the movement and circulation of people, ideas, and gods. The result was a number of Silla enclaves beyond the Korean Peninsula, most of them along the coasts of China and Japan. In this chapter I focus on major Silla-immigrant strongholds—the Ōmi 近江 region (modern-day Shiga Prefecture) in Japan and the Shandong 山東 Peninsula in China—and argue that the interplay between the two played a key role in the transformation of Shinra Myōjin into an individualized and prominent god in the Tendai tradition.

The network of humans and their gods is something of an anchor for my investigation from this chapter onward. In the East Asian Mediterranean, these immigrants and their gods functioned as what Bruno Latour has termed "mediators."[1] According to Latour, a mediator is not just an intermediary being or meaning. Rather, it is an agent of transformation and makes other mediators or agents do unexpected things.[2] Silla immigrants who settled in Ōmi in Japan and, in later periods, on the Shandong Peninsula in China actively transformed the local culture in which they lived in part by introducing new ideas and practices. One result of all this was the worship of Shinra Myōjin.

The term "immigrant" plays a key role in this study and thus needs to be addressed here. Although scholars often maintain that some common identity and some notion of "Japanese" was formed around 700 CE, it is not entirely clear what "Japanese" meant during this period, between the seventh and ninth centuries.[3] When it comes to ancient history, and particularly when the focus is on interactions between the Korean Peninsula and the Japanese archipelago, nationalist tendencies in modern Korean and Japanese scholarship further complicate the matter. In thinking about this, I have benefited from the work of Michael Como, who contends that "'immigrant' kinship groups came to be defined as such not simply in terms of customs followed but rather in terms of their claims to lineal descent from ancestors from across the sea."[4] Following Como's lead, I take an immigrant group to be a self-identified group that traces its ancestry to the continent and maintains a distinguishable cultural identity. In Japanese scholarship both *kikajin* 帰化人 and *toraijin* 渡来人 are used to refer to immigrants from the continent. In this study, however, rather than using *kikajin* ("naturalized" citizen), which is a somewhat derogatory term in modern Japanese, I use the word "immigrant" as an English equivalent of the Japanese word *toraijin*, which refers to those people from overseas who settled in ancient Japan and became integral members of Japanese culture.[5]

One wonders how long *toraijin* retained their cultural identity and at what point they stopped self-identifying as *toraijin*. To state it differently, it is usually not clear when a *toraijin* group becomes fully "native," and thus it can be difficult to distinguish between the two. Some *toraijin* retained their foreign identity over several centuries while others did not. During the sixth and seventh centuries a massive number of immigrants from the Korean kingdoms arrived in Japan and established the settlements of Koma-gun 高麗郡 and Shiragi-gun 新羅郡.[6] The *New Selection and Record of Hereditary Titles and Family Names* (*Shinsen shōjiroku* 新撰姓氏録, 815) lists over a hundred clans who traced their genealogy to Korean kingdoms such as Koguryŏ 高句麗, Paekche 百濟, Silla, and Gaya 加倻 (42–532 CE).[7] This evidently suggests that, even after the edict of 757 that instructed all immigrants to be naturalized by changing their family names and eliminating all indications of their continental origin,[8] some groups continued to identify as descendants of various Korean kingdoms.[9] This also means not only that the process was a long and complicated one but also that different kinship groups went about identifying their respective ethnic communities in very different ways.[10]

Further complicating the matter is the diverse and ambiguous status of immigrants in ancient Japan, a status that changed according to historical circumstances and political contingencies. Depending on the time period, an "immigrant" might have been perceived as a visitor, a merchant, a refugee, or a pirate. There were three main waves of Korean emigration to Japan: one from the late fourth to early fifth century, another during the last half of the fifth century, and finally one in the late seventh century, when the three kingdoms were unified into a single realm.[11] Each period resulted in the emigration of a different group of people to Japan, and how those people were perceived once in Japan depended in large part on the current political relationship between Japan and the kingdom from which the group came. For instance, between the 780s and Silla's demise in 935 there was another massive migration from Silla to Japan, and during this time the Japanese were not always sure whether those people were pirates or simply immigrants.[12] What becomes clear when one examines this fluid human migration and integration process is that these immigrants played a pivotal role in creating larger networks of hybrid culture in which old and new ideas were sustained and transformed. In what follows I present an outline of these immigrant networks by revealing the connections between a number of Silla immigrant hubs, beginning with Ōmi Province in Japan.

SILLA IMMIGRANTS IN ŌMI

Ōmi, the birthplace of Shinra Myōjin, was one of Japan's Korean-immigrant strongholds.[13] Archeological findings around Lake Biwa suggest that a large number of Korean immigrants settled in this area.[14] From the late fourth to the late seventh century, a large influx of immigrants settled in various areas of Japan.[15] It was also during this period that Ōmi was chosen to be the location of the new imperial palace. From 667 to 672, Emperor Tenji's palace was in Ōtsu 大津 in Ōmi. According to Mizuno Masayoshi—who conducted archeological surveys of the Sūfukuji site in Ōmi—immigrants were the primary force behind the decision to construct the palace in this region.[16] The Shiga and Ōtomo clans were the two major groups involved in building the Ōtsu palace. Evidence of a Korean-style fortress around the Ōtsu palace further supports Mizuno's claim that the area was heavily populated by Korean immigrants and that their fortress-building technology may have been used in the construction of the new imperial space at Ōmi.[17]

Ōtsu, the hometown of Onjōji, was the biggest port on Lake Biwa and was also located about thirteen kilometers to the east of Kyoto. Its proximity to the capital meant that Ōtsu could connect all the major transport routes, including those coming in from the Tōgoku 東国 and Hokkoku 北国 areas, to the capital. And yet, being on the water and at a slight remove from the capital, it was connected to many water-transport routes and through these to the sea.[18] As a major transportation hub located not far from the Yamato region, it drew immigrants who brought with them advanced continental culture and technologies and who established villages along the shores of the lake. Ōtsu was not only an important trading post, but was also the administrative and mercantile nexus for major Buddhist complexes. This led to the spread of continental Buddhist culture throughout the Lake Biwa region, and merchants, monks, traders, and artisans found themselves living side by side.[19] It was in this context that many immigrant shrines and temples were built around the lake, some of which were reminiscent of ancient Korean kingdoms. There once stood a temple called Kōraiji 高麗寺.[20] Another example is Hyakusaiji 百済寺 (or Kudaraji), built by the Hata 秦 clan, which was of Silla origin.

Lake Biwa effectively functioned as an inland sea, facilitating the spread of immigrant culture in the area. Beginning in the fifth century, shrines and temples whose

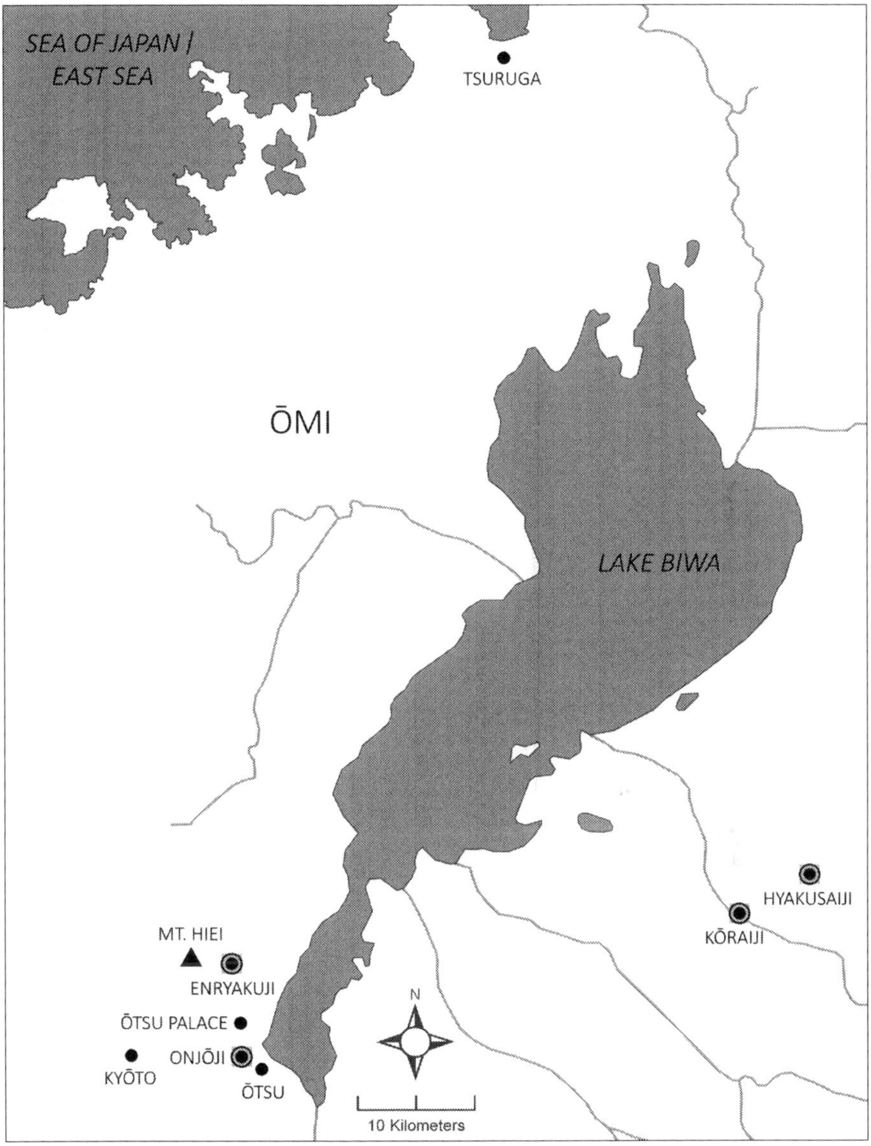

MAP 2. Temples and Major Places around Lake Biwa.

names contain "Silla" began to appear all over Japan, although such Silla shrines and temples tended to be concentrated around the lake. According to Dewa Hiroaki's field research, the numerous Silla shrines and temples found in Japan can be divided into two types: (1) Silla immigrant clan shrines that are not directly related to the Jimon's Shinra Myōjin Shrine; and (2) shrines associated with the Jimon's Shinra

Myōjin Shrine.[21] In the case of the former, the name Silla is used due to the clan's connection with Silla; these shrines constitute an older layer of the network. The latter type of shrine, on the other hand, represents a more organized form of Silla-deity worship and one that is more characteristically and institutionally Buddhist. While these two networks initially may have developed separately, the Shinra Myōjin Shrine at Onjōji became a point of convergence for the two, and an important nodal point in the "Silla" network.

SILLA IMMIGRANTS IN CHINA AND ENNIN'S SEKIZAN MYŌJIN

So far I have examined the evidence for the presence and influence of Korean immigrants in Ōmi and around Lake Biwa, including the network of Silla-named shrines and temples in the region. I want to now shift my geographic focus to the other side of the East Asian Mediterranean and look at Silla immigrants on China's Shandong 山東 Peninsula. I shall look in particular at information about these immigrants found in the *Record of a Pilgrimage to Tang in Search of the Dharma* (*Nittō guhō junrei kōki* 入唐求法巡礼行記), a travel diary written by the Japanese Tendai master Ennin 圓仁 (794–864) during his sojourn in China (838–847).[22]

By the early ninth century there were sizable Korean diasporic communities spread out over the Shandong Peninsula and Jiangsu 江蘇, the eastern-central coastal area of China. Although these communities included people from Koguryŏ and Paekche, Silla immigrants were the most prominent Korean group at this time, and there is evidence that they were largely responsible for the establishment and maintenance of Korean communities in these areas. These Silla immigrants enjoyed relative judicial autonomy due to the Tang dynasty's (618–907) liberal policies toward non-Han ethnic groups. With their cultural and linguistic advantages, these immigrants settled permanently or semipermanently in China and established mercantile networks.

Using Philip Curtin's terminology, these communities functioned as "nodes of trade diasporas" and achieved a certain degree of social cohesion.[23] Numerous local institutions in the area used the term "Silla" in their names, signifying the strong presence of a Silla immigrant culture. For instance, Silla communities were called Silla villages (Kor. Silla-bang 新羅坊). The administrative institutions of the Silla villages were called Silla offices (Kor. Silla-so 新羅所).[24] There was also a local institution called the Silla lodging (Kor. Silla-gwan 新羅館), located in Penglai 蓬萊 village in Shandong. The Silla lodging was established by Silla immigrants as a space for official envoys and other visitors from Silla. Many Silla envoys stayed here before continuing on to Chang'an 長安 (modern-day Xi'an 西安), the capital of Tang China.

As attested to in Ennin's records, Silla immigrants were actively involved in trade that connected China, Japan, and the Korean Peninsula.[25] After Silla's unification of the Korean Peninsula in 668 CE, political and economic instability led a large number of people to emigrate to China, where they established colonies on or near the coast. The cessation of diplomatic relations between Silla and Japan in 779 offered a unique opportunity to these Silla merchants, who were engaged in the triangular trade among China, Japan, and Silla.[26] The termination of official diplomatic relations unexpectedly promoted trade within the private sector, and suddenly individual merchants were able to thrive by stepping into the vacuum and supplying trade services that were previously available via official, diplomatic trade and tributary missions.[27] China-based Silla merchants engaged in a great deal of trade with Japan. Records indicate a continuous stream of Silla merchants arriving in Dazaifu during the ninth century. Japanese monks from major Buddhist monasteries were some of the primary consumers of imported goods from China and the Korean Peninsula.[28] According to the *Anshōji garan engi shizaichō* 安祥寺伽藍縁起資財帳 (867), a record kept by the Japanese Buddhist monk Eun 恵運 (768–869) of Kannonji 観音寺 in Dazaifu, Silla goods such as copper bowls and lacquered wooden dishes were popular items.[29]

Buddhist monks were particularly active consumers within the mercantile world of the East Asian Mediterranean, as seen in the case of Ennin. Ennin traveled to China with one of Japan's *kentōshi* 遣唐使 (Japan's official missions to China), although the practice of sending *kentōshi* was beginning to wane by this period.[30] Most Japanese student-monks, Ennin included, who traveled to China with *kentōshi* during the eighth and ninth centuries had to rely on commercial ships owned by Silla merchants and often formed close relations with Silla people during their journeys.[31] The *kentōshi* also commonly hired interpreters from Silla, who proved to be indispensable to the missions. As mentioned in Ennin's diary, several Silla interpreters accompanied the *kentōshi* fleet heading to Tang. Interpreters such as Kim, Chŏngnam 金正南 (fl. ninth c.), and Tohyŏn 道玄 (fl. ninth c.) guided Ennin and introduced him to various people in China, which allowed him to travel and study with relative ease.[32] Ennin also developed close relationships with Silla merchants in China, and in particular with the renowned merchant Chang Pogo 張保皐 (?–841?).[33] Ennin had heard of Chang Pogo even before his arrival in China; the head official of Chikuzen Province (J. *Chikuzen daishu* 筑前大守) knew Chang Pogo and wrote a letter of introduction for Ennin, though Ennin lost the letter en route and thus never actually presented it to Chang Pogo.[34] Chang Pogo possessed exceptional maritime knowledge and navigational skills, and his trade between China, Korea, and Japan was so successful that he achieved a near trade monopoly in large parts of the East Asian Mediterranean.[35] By the ninth century, he was widely known as one of the most successful merchants in China, Korea, and Japan.

Prior to Chang Pogo, commercial trade between Silla and Japan had not been officially recognized. Moreover, piracy was rampant in the waters separating the two countries, due in part to a lack of maritime rules or any party powerful enough to control the marauding. It was Chang Pogo who organized individual merchants from both China and Silla and started a triangular international trade, connecting Chishan 赤山 port in China, Ch'ŏnghaejin 清海鎮 in Silla, and Dazaifu in Japan. Chang Pogo's rise also motivated the Japanese court to organize its first commercial legislation in Dazaifu in 831.[36] However, after Chang Pogo's sudden death in 846, that legislation was abolished, and trade between Silla and Japan was reduced again to exchange between private parties.[37] Ch'ŏnghaejin, which was Silla's trade hub, was destroyed in 851 and never recovered.[38]

Chang Pogo and other Silla people helped Ennin in many ways during his stay in China.[39] Ennin stayed at a Silla temple called the Lotus Flower Monastery of Mt. Chi (Kor. Chŏksan Pŏbhwa-wŏn 赤山法華院, also known as Silla-wŏn 新羅院), which was a temple established by Chang Pogo and maintained by his community.[40] Upon his arrival in China, Ennin faced a serious problem: he had failed to receive official permission from the Tang government to stay in China, and at one point even considered returning prematurely to Japan. Chang Yŏng 張詠 (fl. ninth century), one of the merchants who worked closely with Chang Pogo, resolved the issue, and Ennin was able to secure official permission to stay in China as a student-monk.[41] He received his travel permission from the Chinese authorities in 840, his second year of residence at the Lotus Flower Monastery of Mt. Chi. During his stay at the temple, Ennin also revised his travel plans. He had originally intended to travel to Mt. Tiantai 天台. However, he was advised by the Silla monk Sŏngrim 聖林 (who resided at the Lotus Flower Monastery) to go to Mt. Wutai 五台 instead.[42] In his diary, Ennin further records that it was due to the help of Silla people that he was able to eventually return to Japan, which he did upon a Silla trade boat; he departed from the port in Mt. Chi at the very eastern tip of the Shandong Peninsula, which was under the political control of Chang Pogo. His close relationship with Silla people is made clear in a letter he wrote to Chang Pogo in 840:

> I, Ennin, have stayed in the mountain cloister, passing the year with much good luck. I have received the warm kindness of the monks, which has greatly consoled my worries as a traveler. This is all the Guard Officer's kind doing. Your protection has been extensive. How can I, insignificant man that I am, repay you? . . . Our return home depends solely on your great assistance, and we shall be overwhelmed with gratitude to you.[43]

Ennin's ties with Silla merchants, monks, and immigrants in China were the primary reason for his worship of a Mt. Chi 赤 god, later known as Sekizan Myōjin. After presenting this letter of gratitude to Chang Pogo, Ennin boarded a Japan-bound vessel, and, according to the *Sekizan Daimyōjin engi* 赤山大明神縁起 (948), when that ship encountered a storm during the voyage, Sekizan Myōjin appeared to Ennin in the form of an old man. With Sekizan Myōjin's protection, the ship was able to weather the storm and Ennin returned safely to Japan.[44]

Ennin's official biography (*Jikaku daishi den* 慈覚大師伝, 939) presents a slightly different picture of Ennin's relationship with Sekizan Myōjin. The biography does not mention Sekizan Myōjin by name, though it does tell us that Ennin prayed to a mountain deity of the Mt. Chi region.[45] It also states that when Ennin was staying at the temple of Mt. Chi, a deity appeared to him in a dream in the guise of an elderly merchant, an appearance that suggests an affinity between Sekizan Myōjin and Chang Pogo.[46] In this dream, Ennin bought a scale from the old man, which enabled him to acquire a great deal of new knowledge.[47] Afterwards, Ennin purportedly made a vow that upon his return to Japan he would establish a temple and would worship the deity of Mt. Chi.

The construction of the Sekizan Zen'in 赤山禅院 at the western foot of Mt. Hiei in Japan cemented the tie between Ennin and Sekizan Myōjin. This does little, however, to clarify with much certainty the actual origins of Sekizan Myōjin or of this deity's name. While the *Jikaku daishi den* informs us that Ennin prayed for the deity of Mt. Chi before his return trip, the name "Sekizan Myōjin" appears in neither the *Jikaku daishi den* nor Ennin's diary.[48] These two stories, both of which explain the genesis of the relationship between Ennin and Sekizan Myōjin, portray Sekizan Myōjin as a seafaring deity with close ties to the Silla immigrants in China. The relationship between Sekizan Myōjin and the Silla community is further reinforced by the fact that the deity appeared as a merchant, reminding us of Chang Pogo and pointing to the Silla-immigrant community's primary economic activity.

After his return to Japan, Ennin wanted to build a shrine for the god of Mt. Chi but was not able to accomplish this during his lifetime. According to the *Sekizan Daimyōjin engi*, he did, however, instruct his disciples to build a shrine for the deity.[49] Accordingly, Ennin's disciples obtained some land on the western slope of Mt. Hiei (Nishi no Sakamoto 西坂本) and built a shrine on this land.[50] Significantly, the land on which the shrine was built had originally belonged to Minabuchi no Toshina 南淵年名 (808–877), an administrator of Dazaifu. Minabuchi and his son were also involved in international trade with Chang and other Silla merchants based in China.[51] In 888, the construction of Sekizan Zen'in was completed.[52] Ennin's disciples chose the Nishi Sakamoto area for Sekizan Zen'in because it was on the side of Mt. Hiei opposite from the side on which the shrine to Sannō 山王 was located, Sannō being the principal autochthonous deity of the entire Tendai tradition on Mt. Hiei.[53] In other words, with the invitation of Sekizan Myōjin, the eastern side of Mt. Hiei (represented as Higashi hongū 東本宮) and the western side of the mountain (Nishi hongū 西本宮) were both protected by divine powers.[54]

Ennin and his followers' worship of Sekizan Myōjin demonstrates a process by which one idea or practice becomes a nodal point of adaptation and permutation. Ennin's personal interactions with and memories of the Silla people in China during his trip were directly responsible for the formation of Sekizan Myōjin worship on Mt.

Hiei. But this is not the end of the story. As I shall explain in the following chapter, Ennin's Sekizan Myōjin worship triggered the creation of the *engi* of Shinra Myōijn in the Jimon, whose story and function within the Jimon is identical to the story and function of Sekizan Myōjin within the Sanmon. The two deities are essentially the same deity but with different names. Although the Jimon claims that Shinra Myōjin was brought to Japan by its founder, Enchin, in fact Shinra Myōjin was not Enchin's but rather Ennin's deity, which was then appropriated by Enchin's followers.

This chapter has examined the network of Silla immigrants in Japan and China in order to provide the background necessary for understanding Shinra Myōjin's emergence in the Jimon tradition. The appearance of Shinra Myōjin at Onjōji can best be understood against the larger backdrop of Silla-immigrant networks, which comprised a large number of Silla communities located in coastal areas around the Yellow Sea, East China Sea, and Sea of Japan/East Sea. Onjōji's location was crucial to the transformation of a generic "deity of Silla" into the individualized deity of the Jimon. All of this demonstrates that East Asian maritime connections extended far beyond the well-known ports in Kyushu, stretching far inland all the way to Ōmi. Being connected to the East Asian maritime through Lake Biwa, Ōmi experienced a constant circulation of ideas and cultural influences that flowed between the capital and the Lake Biwa communities. While the lake functioned as an inland sea and was a part of the broader East Asian Mediterranean network, the local environment also contributed to the later emergence of Shinra Myōjin's cult in this particular region.

However, the travel of particular individuals also contributed to the formation of this new cultic practice. In the case at hand we saw from Ennin's diary that his voyage to China and the relationships he formed there with Silla immigrants on the Shandong Peninsula were also crucial elements, and that this in turn was related to the birth of Sekizan Myōjin worship in Japan. Understanding Sekizan Myōjin is key to understanding the emergence of Shinra Myōjin. If one confines oneself to a sectarian reading of the Onjōji chronicles, one comes away convinced that it was Enchin who initiated worship of Shinra Myōjin, and that he did this because the deity asked him to do so. But Shinra Myōjin is none other than Sekizan Myōjin, a point I shall expand upon in the next chapter. Moreover, it was Enchin's followers who formulated and appropriated Silla immigrants' worship of a Silla deity under a new, individualized name—Shinra Myōjin.

In short, the emergence of Shinra Myōjin's cult can be fully understood when viewed within the context of the East Asian Mediterranean Buddhist network, in which merchants, immigrants, and Buddhist monks all played a prominent role in the exchange of cultic practices. Within this network the mediating role of immigrants was of central importance. Whether they intended it or not, their new religious culture created something that had not existed previously, exemplified by

Shinra Myōjin and other immigrant deities. In this way, immigrants and immigrant communities were not just transmitters but also transformers. Further, analyzing this transcultural network allows us to explore the diversity and density of a cultic network that included a large number of nodal points in China, Korea, and Japan. These East Asian Mediterranean networks help us to understand the circulation of goods and gods, Shinra Myōjin being a prime example.

Part II

Sedentarization

Networks of Silla Deities and Shinra Myōjin

Chapter 3

The Medieval Transformations of Shinra Myōjin

The previous chapter presented the network of Silla immigrants as the sociohistorical context responsible for the emergence of Shinra Myōjin worship in the pre-Nara, Nara, and early Heian periods. The following two chapters will examine the institutional development of Shinra Myōjin in the Jimon tradition from the late Heian period through the early Muromachi period, a time during which both the cult of Shinra Myōjin and the power of the Jimon were at their zenith. By the time the power struggle between the Jimon and the Sanmon reached its crescendo in the mid-eleventh century, Shinra Myōjin had become the chief deity of the Jimon and was the central symbol of the entire Jimon tradition.

While Shinra Myōjin was previously perceived as the protector god of the Jimon,[1] his role was not limited to that of dharma protector (J. *gohōjin*) or protective *kami* of the shrine and temple (J. *garanjin* 伽藍神). The deity had other functions as well, and in this chapter I focus on the process by which Shinra Myōjin was "sedentarized," that is, by which he came to be thoroughly intertwined with Japanese Buddhism, politics, and culture. Continuing with the previous chapter's discussion, I examine how Shinra Myōjin was cloned from Sekizan Myōjin. Central to this process was Shinra Myōjin's transformation from a generic deity of the sea into an individualized mountain deity. While the individualization of Shinra Myōjin was in part a result of Japanese Tendai's internal schism, the worship of Shinra Myōjin spread far beyond Tendai. We shall examine that spread, looking at two key networks around the deity: one associated with the Minamoto clan, and the other with a nascent network of mountain religious practitioners that would later develop into what we now call Shugendō.

Before further exploration of the association between Shinra Myōjin and Enchin, the founder of the Tendai Jimon, I want first to provide a brief outline of his life. Enchin was born in Sanuki 讃岐 Province in 814.[2] Through his mother he was related to Kūkai 空海 (774–835). At the age of fifteen he went to Mt. Hiei and became a student of Gishin. At the age of twenty he received the Bodhisattva precepts and began a twelve-year period of study and practice at Enryakuji. In 853 he traveled to China, where he learned Tiantai doctrines on Mt. Tiantai and also studied esoteric rituals with Faquan 法全 (fl. ninth c.) at Qinglongsi 青龍寺, the same master who had transmitted esoteric Buddhist teachings to Ennin. Enchin also collected and brought back to Japan seminal esoteric Buddhist texts and iconographic drawings, all of which provide visual and ritual knowledge that was newer and different from what Kūkai had introduced.[3] Similarly to Ennin, Enchin was helped and supported by Silla people during his sojourn. For example, Enchin developed a friendship with Tohyŏn, a Silla Buddhist monk who had previously served as Ennin's interpreter.[4] Enchin returned to Japan in 858 and stayed briefly at Kōrokan 鴻臚館 in Dazaifu. A letter written by Tohyŏn at Kōrokan suggests that he and Enchin maintained a close relationship during the latter's stay in China.[5] In 859, the year after he returned from China, Enchin was sent to Onjōji and began to revitalize the temple. While the Jimon tradition asserts that Enchin built Onjōji's Shinra Myōjin Shrine in 860, the evidence that he personally worshipped Shinra Myōjin in any way during his life is shaky at best.[6] From 868 until his death in 891 he served as Tendai *zasu* on Mt. Hiei. During his lifetime Enchin had more institutional ties with Enryakuji than Onjōji.

BETWEEN THE SEA AND THE MOUNTAIN

While Enchin may not have perceived Shinra Myōjin as the god who protected him during his return voyage and guided him to Onjōji, later Jimon monks certainly believed this to be the case. As the *engi* story suggests, one of Shinra Myōjin's primary functions is to ensure the safety of those traveling by sea. While this function is not limited to Shinra Myōjin, most of the major sea-related deities in the Japanese pantheon are connected to Korea in some way. Well-known examples include Myōken 妙見, Sumiyoshi 住吉, Hachiman 八幡, Kawara 香春, and Munakata 宗像, all of whose cults emerged in Kyushu, where contact between Japan and the Korean Peninsula was frequent from the ancient period onward.[7] The worship of these gods was always associated with seafaring, and all of the myths about these deities contain elements from Korean culture.

As in any culture in constant contact with the ocean, the anxiety about the dangers of the perilous sea often found expression in the worship of sea deities. Prior to a sea voyage, one would typically pray to a sea god in order to secure safe passage. However, mountain gods were also often invoked together with sea gods on such occasions. As scholars of Japanese folklore have noted, sea gods and mountain gods are functionally related and at times were but two sides of the same coin.[8] We observe this mutual permeability in the rituals performed to appease the gods of both realms. For example, sea gods were thought to favor mountain animals as offerings, whereas mountain gods preferred sea creatures.[9] The sea and the mountain each represents a polarized territory, and through exchange they complement one another. In this duality, the sea is not separate from the land but rather is a link between this and the other world. To set sail was therefore to enter a liminal stage, and praying to both sea and mountain gods prior to the voyage was a powerful means of securing bidirectional protection.

Praying to a mountain god for safe sea passage was common among the early Japanese Tendai Buddhist masters who traveled to Tang China; Saichō, Ennin, and Enchin all made such prayers.[10] Securing the divine protection of a mountain god for the duration of the trip was a central duty of Buddhist monks on board. The *Shoku Nihon kōki* 続日本後紀 (869) and other Tendai documents state that while Saichō was waiting to depart from Buzen 豊前 in the years 803 and 804, he visited the mountains of northern Kyushu to pray to several gods, including the god of Mt. Kawara, who was associated with Silla.[11] In so doing, he may have been attempting to please the sea deity on the Silla side of the maritime expanse that he was to cross, or the deity that would be encountered en route.

Following Saichō, Ennin and Enchin are said to have prayed to the deity at the Kawara Shrine before embarking for China.[12] According to his diary, prior to his return trip from Tang China to Japan, Ennin sought to secure safe passage by invoking a number of gods during his sutra chanting and prayers; Kawara was one of them.[13] An official letter written by Enchin in the year of 852 also mentions that Enchin prayed to the Kawara deity.[14] All of this suggests that early Tendai masters who went to China were familiar with the practice of praying to a mountain god prior to sea travel, and that Kawara deity, a god associated with Silla, was included in their prayers. Worship of the Kawara deity may not be directly related to the later worship of Sekizan Myōjin and Shinra Myōjin within Tendai, but it helps us to understand the larger context of a practice of invoking Silla deities for safe sea travel.

As noted in the previous chapter, Shinra Myōjin's dual role as a god of both sea and mountain finds expression in his *engi* story, which concludes with the deity guiding Enchin to the future site of Onjōji. The story presents Shinra Myōjin as having been the landlord deity (J. *jinushigami*) of Mt. Nagara for a period of eons, disguised as an elderly man.[15] By definition, the *jinushigami* is a god who asserts his authority over a specific tract of land.[16] Claiming that a foreign deity is a *junishigami* seems paradoxical, as the claim to territorial antiquity and supremacy should belong to an indigenous deity. This claim is key, then, for once Shinra Myōjin was perceived as *jinushigami*, he was no longer a foreign deity: the deity was perceived not as being *from* Silla but rather as having *returned* from Silla. This inverted logic is also found in Shinra Myōjin's mythological association with Susanoo, which I address in chapter 6. By turning Shinra Myōjin into a *jinushigami*, this story conveniently avoids the dichotomy between foreign and native gods.

The transformation of Shinra Myōjin into the *jinushigami* of the Jimon was in part an ideological response to the Tendai cult of Sannō 山王 (Mountain King). Sannō, whose cult began at Hie (or Hiyoshi 日吉) Shrine at the eastern foot of Mt. Hiei, is the most prominent deity within the Tendai tradition.[17] Because Sannō was the *sine qua non* deity for Tendai monks from early on, he remained significant to the Onjōji monks even after the full-scale schism during the eleventh century. Because of this, Sannō was venerated within the Jimon, even though the highest position was reserved for Shinra Myōjin. The Sanmon tradition, however, never recognized the status of Shinra Myōjin or Enchin's association with him. For example, the fragmented diary of Enchin that he wrote during his trip to Tang, the *Commentaries on [Enchin's] life* (*Gyōrekishō* 行歷抄, 859) is silent on this matter, though it highlights the importance of Sannō for Enchin.

Enchin was closely associated with the Sannō cult. During his tenure as *zasu* on Mt. Hiei, Enchin was called Sannōin 山王院, the name of his residential hall. Sannō's association with Enchin is also confirmed by Enchin's biography, the *Tendaishū Enryakuji zasu Enchin kashō den* 天台宗延曆寺座主円珍和尚伝 (also called the *Chishō daishiden* 智証大師伝), a text compiled in 902 by Miyoshi Kiyoyuki 三善清行 (847–918), a literatus of the Heian period. According to the text, the master's decision to go to China was due to an oracle that he received from Sannō in a dream he had in 850.[18] Though it was Shinra Myōjin who appeared to Enchin, telling him where to build Onjōji and how to worship him, the text still gives partial credit to Sannō, stating that both Shinra Myōjin and Sannō guided Enchin to the future site of Onjōji. After this, Sannō returned to Enryakuji alone, whereas Shinra Myōjin remained at this site. The tie between Sannō and Enchin continued even after the latter's death. Enchin's relics were enshrined not only in Onjōji's Tōin 唐院 but also in Enryakuji's Sannōin.[19] With the spiritual growth of Shinra Myōjin and, in parallel, the growth of Onjōji's institutional power, Shinra Myōjin's prestige came to exceed that of Sannō at Onjōji.

DOUBLING IDENTITY: SEKIZAN MYŌJIN AND SHINRA MYŌJIN

In this section, I show that the Sanmon-Jimon sectarian rivalry led to the duplication of a Silla deity: Shinra Myōjin and his cult were a deliberate appropriation of Sekizan Myōjin and that deity's cult. With the competition between the followers of Ennin and those of Enchin, in the tenth century we see the emergence of polemical attacks between the two groups and the groups' production of similar myths and iconography. Ennin's followers invoked Sekizan Myōjin, while Enchin's followers called on Shinra Myōjin. Contrary to what the traditions themselves say, neither Ennin nor Enchin was directly involved in this process. In fact, while alive both Ennin and Enchin attempted to resolve partisanship among Tendai monks, and at times Enchin even expressed deep admiration for Ennin.[20] It was the later followers of these two monks who created the association between Ennin and Sekizan Myōjin, and between Enchin and Shinra Myōjin.

Although both of these deities are often described as assuming the appearance of an old man, and despite the fact that the two are in some sense the same deity, their iconography is not entirely identical. While it became standard to represent Shinra Myōjin as an elderly man in the attire of a Tang official, there was much greater diversity in visual representations of Sekizan Myōjin. One typical image has him as an official in a red robe and headgear (similar to that of the Ten Kings or *jūo* 十王, the rulers of the underworld from the *Sutra of the Ten Kings*) and a bow. Sekizan Myōjin also appears in the clothes of a Tang official, with a wooden wand (J. *gohei* 御幣) in his hand (e.g., as in the Hie Sannō Mandala). Sometimes Sekizan Myōjin is described as a general in full armor.[21]

Although a somewhat distinctive iconography of each deity contributed to the construction of individuality in the later periods, as the analysis of the *engi* story and institutional history suggests, Sekizan Myōjin is in many ways identical to Shinra Myōjin. The worship of Sekizan Myōjin was very likely established earlier than that of Shinra Myōjin. However, it was Enchin's followers who appropriated and further popularized the cult of the Silla deity through the creation of various Shinra Myōjin legends, rituals, and iconography. They strategically adopted the name "Silla" for the deity, very possibly because the name echoes the temple's ancient past—its strong connection with immigrant groups in Ōmi, which resembles Ennin's connection with Silla immigrants in China. As the Jimon's institutional power increased, Enchin's followers further adapted the story of their master's encounter with the Silla god to make it their own. By building up Shinra Myōjin in this way, the Jimon was able to gain legitimacy as a new center of Tendai learning and power, completely independent of Enryakuji; the deity was the unifying force that allowed this to happen. Through the Jimon's history Shinra Myōjin has even been thought of as Onjōji monks' alter ego.

The rise of Shinra Myōjin as a powerful foreign god is intimately related to the Jimon's relationship with the Sanmon, as well as to a peculiar form of political structure after which the Insei 院政 period (1086–1192) is named.[22] The term "Insei" refers to a system of government in which decisions of state were made by the retired sovereign. In this system, a retired emperor, rather than the reigning emperor, exercised political power from his cloister (J. *in* 院) or monastery. Emperor Gosanjō 後三条 (r. 1068–1073) initiated the Insei system by stepping down from the throne prior to his death; he did this in an attempt to curtail the influence of the Fujiwara regents and reassert the power of the imperial house. But Gosanjō died before fully realizing his plan, and it was his son, Emperor Shirakawa 白河 (r. 1073–1087), who established the system upon his father's abdication.

This period also witnessed the emergence of a new ideological configuration, which resulted in both conflict and collaboration between imperial law (J. *ōbō* 王法) and Buddhist law (J. *buppō* 仏法), and between the retired emperor and powerful Buddhist temples.[23] By this time, the mutual dependence between major temples and the court was not simply a relationship between two major power blocs, sacred and secular, but was based on a broader interpretation of Buddhism as the central element upon which political and social order was founded and upon which it relied. For a time, Enryakuji was the only relevant Tendai institution within this system, but from the tenth century on, Onjōji tried to gain recognition as a new power bloc. One of its immediate concerns was thus to establish full autonomy.

There were two important issues for Enchin's followers at Onjōji: (1) making sure that Onjōji monks could be appointed Tendai *zasu*; and (2) the establishment of its own ordination platform (J. *kaidan* 戒壇). The ordination platform would allow Onjōji to ordain monks independently from Enryakuji.[24] The confrontation over the issue of the Tendai *zasu* appointments intensified with the intervention of aristocratic political power. In 1038 Fujiwara no Yorimichi 藤原頼通 (992–1074), the eldest son of Fujiwara no Michinaga, supported the promotion of the Onjōji monk Myōson to the rank of Tendai *zasu*. However, Myōson's abbacy lasted only three days on account of Enryakuji's resistance. After the Myōson incident, only monks from the Sanmon held the post. On the few occasions when Onjōji monks were appointed, their efforts were sabotaged by the Sanmon and their tenure never lasted long.

This growing antagonism led to a new urgency around the need to establish an independent ordination platform at Onjōji, and Onjōji's attempt to acquire its independence can be seen in a series of petitions to the court. However, the court could not satisfy Onjōji without incurring Enryakuji's wrath. Enryakuji monks claimed that a single school—Tendai—could not have two ordination platforms. Onjōji monks responded by arguing that, since the temples were already separate, they should have distinct ordination platforms. Caught between these warring factions, the court continually postponed its decision, thus leading to increased discord and bouts of violence between the Sanmon and Jimon. Between 1081 and 1121, for instance, Onjōji was burnt down by the Sanmon a number of times.[25]

This led to a situation in which, during the eleventh century, Onjōji monks received full precepts, not at Enryakuji, but rather at Tōdaiji 東大寺 in Nara.[26] This use of Tōdaiji's ordination platform allowed Onjōji both to protest Enryakuji's recalcitrance and to avoid dependence upon Enryakuji for new monks. As it turned out, Enryakuji could not accept this practice. In 1162, for example, when the Jimon monk Kakuchū 覚忠 was appointed Tendai *zasu*, Enryakuji monks denounced him, noting that he had been ordained at Tōdaiji. They dismissed Nara ordinations as being based on Hīnayāna teachings and thus insufficient.[27] In 1163, Enryakuji monks petitioned the court to prohibit Onjōji monks from being ordained at temples in

Nara.[28] Although Goshirakawa personally favored Onjōji, the court proclaimed that only a monk ordained on Enryakuji's platform could be appointed *zasu* of Tendai.[29] Onjōji monks were deeply dissatisfied with the court's decision and ignored this stipulation by secretly continuing the practice of going to Nara for ordination.

It was against this backdrop that Onjōji began to use the *sanmaya* precepts (J. *sanmaya kai* 三昧耶戒) as a way of ordaining monks independently from Enryakuji and without official approval.[30] Shinra Myōjin was key in this process, for through this deity the Jimon could link their new ordination practice to continental Buddhist traditions, thereby allowing it to be portrayed as ancient and authentic. According to the *Onjōji denki*:

> Shinra Myōjin received the precepts from [the Vinaya master] Daoxuan on Mt. Zhongnan 終南. The *sanmaya* 三昧耶 precepts that Enchin brought back to Japan are fundamentally based on Daoxuan's *vinaya* teachings. As an opening, the *sanmaya* precepts are performed and the *abhiṣeka sanmaya* (J. *kanjō sanmaya kai* 灌頂三昧耶戒) precepts follow. Shinra Myōjin manifests himself to protect the precepts. When Shinra Myōjin resided in the kingdom of Silla, he received the methods of the three attainments (J. *sanshu shichi hō* 三種悉地法)[31] from the Silla preceptor (Skt. *ācārya*) Hyŏnch'o 玄招. The teaching was transmitted exclusively to our Jimon lineage. Thus, the master Enchin said in his commentary that "I transmit the *sanshu shichi hō* and protect the whole world." In order to protect the teaching, [Shinra Myōjin] resides [in the ritual]. Because of this karmic connection, the mantra of the *sanshu shichi* is recited [in front of the deity]."[32]

In this passage, Shinra Myōjin plays a central role in justifying the legitimacy of the *sanmaya* precepts by linking the practice with the Chinese *vinaya* master Daoxuan 道宣 (596–667), the founder of the Nanshan *vinaya* school (Ch. Nanshan lü zong 南山律宗).[33] It is also intriguing to note the way in which the Silla monk Hyŏnch'o's story is interwoven with the myth. During his stay in China, Hyŏnch'o was a disciple of Śubhakarasiṃha (Ch. Shanwuwei 善無畏, 637–735), the eminent Indian monk of esoteric Buddhism. Hyŏnch'o was later a teacher of Huiguo 惠果 (746–806), and Kūkai in turn studied under Huiguo. In this lineage, Hyŏnch'o was thus only one generation removed from Kūkai, the founder of Shingon Buddhism in Japan. Hyŏnch'o was active primarily in China, but evidently his Silla connections led to the invention of a mythological genealogy chart wherein Shinra Myōjin became an orthodox Buddhist deity.

The Jimon monks grew increasingly resentful of the court due to its indecision about the ordination issue, and they expressed their frustration in the form of popular tales, many of which included or echoed Shinra Myōjin–related imagery. One relevant narrative here is the story of the Onjōji priest Raigō 頼豪 (1004–1084). According to the *Heike monogatari* 平家物語, the story begins in 1074 when Emperor Shirakawa 白河 (r. 1072–1086) declined Onjōji's request yet again.[34] In the meantime,

Shirakawa had been praying that his Fujiwara consort would produce a male heir. Upon the emperor's request, Raigō, who was Shirakawa's spiritual adviser, prayed for a son. Soon afterward, Prince Atsufumi (敦文, 1075–1077) was born. As a reward, Raigō asked the emperor to grant Onjōji an ordination platform.[35] However, foreseeing the Enryakuji monks' opposition, the emperor declined the request. Dispirited by Shirakawa's refusal, Raigō starved himself to death and returned as a vengeful spirit (J. *onryō* 怨霊). Shortly thereafter Prince Atsufumi unexpectedly died, and it was believed that Raigō's curse had caused his death. Raigō's (or, more accurately, the Jimon's) attack on imperial power did not cease, however. According to the *Heike monogatari*, Raigō's vengeful spirit even transformed into a thousand rats that infested Enryakuji and caused great damage, including destroying the emperor's sacred texts.[36]

The legend of Raigō's vengeful spirit was repeated, and many versions circulated widely within literary circles throughout the medieval period.[37] In the *Hie Sannō rishōki* 日吉山王利生記 (ca. thirteenth c.) and the *Genpei jōsuiki* 源平盛衰記 (or *Genpei seisuiki*, ca. late Kamakura or early Nanbokuchō), Sekizan Myōjin makes an appearance in order to defend the Sanmon; he threatens Emperor Shirakawa in an attempt to dissuade him from granting Onjōji a separate ordination platform.[38] While in the *Hie Sannō rishōki* Sekizan Myōjin's presence is limited to the sound of his arrow, the *Genpei jōsuiki* provides a more detailed image of him. According to this version, sometime after he promised Onjōji that he would allow the independent ordination platform, Shirakawa had a dream in which a divine old man in a red dress, holding a bow and arrows, appeared to him. The old man introduced himself as Sekizan Myōjin and warned Shirakawa not to grant Onjōji's wish.[39] After waking, Shirakawa decided not to authorize Raigō's request. His decision caused Raigō to withdraw to Onjōji and fast to death, resulting in Raigō's transformation into an angry spirit.[40]

What is noteworthy in these stories is that Raigō is identified as Shinra Myōjin. It is not coincidental that Raigō's vengeful spirit appears in the form of a divine old man carrying a staff—precisely the form that Shinra Myōjin usually assumes.[41] Indeed, Shinra Myōjin retained the character of a typical vengeful spirit (J. *tatarigami* 祟り神), a deity who can bestow blessings, but who can also curse those who have offended him.[42] The curse of a *tatarigami* was a source of great fear, and the portrayal of Shinra Myōjin as one helped the Jimon depict this deity as a powerful spirit able to curse anyone who opposes him. Indeed, the *Jimon denki horoku* tells us that Shinra Myōjin's resentment was the cause of another emperor's death. Like the previous story, this emperor incurred the deity's wrath by his refusal to support Onjōji's bid for an independent ordination platform.[43] The more wrathful the deity in these stories, the merrier the Jimon was in real-world politics.

Shinra Myōjin's curses continued alongside the Jimon's desire to build its own ordination platform, and similar tales appeared, all emphasizing the deity's asperity. According to another legend in the *Jimon denki horoku*, Shinra Myōjin cursed

Emperor Nijō 二条 (r. 1158–1165) when the emperor sided with the Sanmon.[44] In this account, Nijō fell ill and was possessed by Hannya 般若, one of Shinra Myōjin's acolytes, and by Kuro'o Myōjin 黒尾明神, one of the acolytes of Mio Myōjin 三尾明神, an ancient local deity worshipped at Onjōji. Shinra Myōjin then expressed his anger through the mouth of the emperor, saying, "I cannot forgive you for smiling in the direction of Mt. Nyoi 如意 (meaning Onjōji) when the temple was burnt down."[45] The acolytes then struck Nijō with a staff (J. *shakujō* 錫杖), and the emperor died several months later.[46] These stories suggest that the threat of *tatari* was very real for emperors who ran afoul of the Jimon. These tales functioned not only as a mimesis of the Jimon's politics, but also as a way of pushing the Jimon's agenda forward. Significantly, Shinra Myōjin represented Onjōji's aspiration to establish an independent ordination platform.

While Shinra Myōjin continued to advocate for the interests of Onjōji in the world of myth, the Jimon's petition for installing its own independent ordination continued in the real world. Beginning in the third month of 1257, several Onjōji monks solicited support from the Kamakura shogunate, as well as from the court. With the support of the shogunate, the Onjōji monk Ryūben 隆弁 (1208–1283), a descendant of the powerful Hōjō 北条 family, took a leading role and, having raised an army of hundreds of soldiers, he protested in Kyoto. Pressured by the military presence, in 1260 the court finally accepted Onjōji's request for an official ordination platform.[47] However, Enryakuji protested, backed by its superior military might, and in 1264 Onjōji had to agree with the court's reversal of this decision. Despite this setback, Onjōji monks did not give up. In the early fourteenth century, they again presented the court with a petition for official recognition of their independent ordination platform, though this effort also proved to be in vain.

Although its attempt to establish a separate ordination platform ultimately did not succeed, the Jimon nevertheless established itself as a powerful Tendai institution equipped with its own set of rituals, divinities, legends, and history. The Jimon's endeavor to distinguish itself from the Sanmon can therefore be seen as a partial success, despite the many scars the Jimon incurred in the process. Despite the internecine destruction that characterized this period of Japanese Tendai history, the emergence of Shinra Myōjin was a constructive trend within this turmoil. In the following section, I turn to the spread of Shinra Myōjin worship outside of Onjōji.

THE SPREAD OF SHINRA MYŌJIN BEYOND ONJŌJI

As seen in the *engi* story of Shinra Myōjin, the Ōtomo clan was one of Onjōji's main sponsors during the temple's formative years. The Ōtomo clan was closely related to the cult of Shinra Myōjin at Onjōji. For instance, the first priest of the shrine was a man from the Ōtomo family named Kiyomura 清村 (fl. tenth c.).[48] From that time until the fifteenth century, the priestly lineage of the Shinra Myōjin

Shrine was limited to members of the Ōtomo clan.[49] The colophon of the *Shinra Myōjin ki* 新羅明神記 informs us that it was the Ōtomo family who guarded and passed on the secret transmission of the deity.[50] With the wane of the Ōtomo clan, however, beginning in the eleventh century another powerful warrior clan, the Seiwa 清和 branch of the Minamoto, became one of the Jimon's major patrons.[51]

The Seiwa Genji 清和源氏 was one of the most successful subclans of the Ōmi-based Minamoto, and the clan was a major patron of Onjōji from the eleventh to the early fourteenth century.[52] The Minamoto's patronage of Onjōji began with Minamoto no Yoriyoshi 源頼義 (988–1075), the head of the Minamoto. During the Former Nine Years' War (J. *zenkunen no eki* 前九年の役, 1051–1062) in northern Mutsu 陸奥, Yoriyoshi vowed at the shrine of Shinra Myōjin that if his military campaign was successful he would dedicate one of his sons to Onjōji. He won the battle and, in accord with his promise, celebrated the coming-of-age rites (J. *genpuku* 元服) of his third son, Minamoto no Yoshimitsu 源義光 (1045–1127), at the Shinra Myōjin Shrine. After that, Minamoto no Yoshimitsu became a devotee of Shinra Myōjin and came to be known as Shinra Saburō. Following the establishment of this relationship, Yoshimitsu and his descendants continued to maintain close ties with Onjōji. For example, Yoshimitsu provided the funds for the construction of Konkōin 金光院, a sub-temple in the Onjōji temple complex near the Shinra Myōjin Shrine, and had his son Kakugi 覚義 appointed as the first abbot of Konkōin.[53]

The Minamoto clan was instrumental in spreading the worship of Shinra Myōjin outside the Ōmi region, largely through the Minamoto clan's military campaigns and subsequent influence throughout the country.[54] Elements of the Shinra Myōjin cult spread as far as Hokkaido. The *Records of Shinra* (*Shinra no kiroku* 新羅之記録, 1646), a seventeenth-century document of the Matsumae 松前 clan, for instance, demonstrates that Shinra Saburō's association with Shinra Myōjin helped the deity travel far beyond the Ōmi region.[55] The *Shinra no kiroku* is the earliest record from Hokkaido's Matsumae domain (J. Matsumae-han 松前藩).[56] In this text, the Matsumae clan claims that Shinra Saburō is their ancestor. Because of this, when Matsumae Kagehiro 松前景広 (fl. seventeenth c.), who compiled the *Shinra no kiroku*, finished the work, he paid a visit to Onjōji in 1643 to dedicate the text to Shinra Myōjin at Onjōji. During his visit, he learned more about Shinra Myōjin and the deity's legends, and he inserted this information into the text in 1646.[57] Because Shinra Myōjin was perceived as the protector of Shinra Saburō, Matsumae regarded Shinra Myōjin as a prominent deity of the Matsumae clan as well.

While the Minamoto family was closely involved in the promotion of the worship of Shinra Myōjin, it had also developed a strong spiritual tie with another Silla-related deity, Hachiman 八幡. According to his origin story, Hachiman ordered the female ruler Jingū to destroy the Silla kingdom.[58] Hachiman was popularly worshipped among the warrior clans, as he was thought to ensure military success. Ironically, Hachiman is a Silla-related deity whose cult was closely associated with Shinra

Myōjin—Shinra Myōjin being the god of Silla, and Hachiman being the archenemy of Silla. But for the Minamoto clan, the antagonistic relationship between the two deities appears not to have posed a problem.

The formal connection between Hachiman and the clan goes back to Minamoto no Yorinobu 源頼信 (968–1048). Yorinobu started worshipping Hachiman as an ancestral deity and attributed his father's military success to Hachiman's powers. In the eleventh century, Minamoto Yoriyoshi's first son Minamoto no Yoshiie 源義家 (1041–1108) formed a more direct association with Hachiman. In 1048 Yoshiie had his coming-of-age ceremony at Iwashimizu Hachiman 石清水八幡 Shrine, which had begun to develop official ties with Onjōji. After this he became known as Hachiman Tarō 八幡太郎.[59] In order to commemorate the successful military campaign of the Former Nine Year's War, in 1063 Yoriyoshi, Yorinobu's son, established a shrine-temple complex dedicated to Hachiman in Yuigahama 由比ヶ浜, near present-day Kamakura. This marked the first of its vast network of Hachiman shrines, and the Minamoto, bit by bit, built a vast network of shrines and temples dedicated to Hachiman on their estates and battlefields.[60]

The founder of the Kamakura shogunate, Minamoto no Yoritomo 源頼朝 (1147–1199), was responsible for an additional link between the Minamoto clan and Onjōji. Yoritomo became a lay disciple of the Onjōji *chōri* Kōken 公顕 (1110–1193) and maintained a close relationship with both Kōken and Kōken's disciple Kōin 公胤 (1145–1216). Yoritomo was also responsible for strengthening the clan's association with Hachiman, who was a much needed deity for a warrior clan.[61] In his attempt to revitalize the Hachiman cult, Yoritomo moved the Hachiman Shrine from Yuigahama to Tsurugaoka 鶴岡, closer to the headquarters of his military government. In 1180, he established the Tsurugaoka Hachiman 鶴岡八幡 Shrine, thereby shifting the cultic center closer to the headquarters of his military government.[62]

The Tsurugaoka Hachiman Shrine became the central ritual space for the Minamoto family, and Jimon monks played a significant role in this, conducting esoteric Buddhist rituals at the shrine. Many of the monks at the Tsurugaoka Hachiman Shrine came from Onjōji, and it was common for Onjōji monks to simultaneously hold posts at both the Tsurugaoka Hachiman Shrine and Onjōji.[63] In 1182 Yoritomo invested the Onjōji monk Engyō 円暁 as the first chief administrator (J. *bettō* 別当) of the shrine, further cementing the tie between Onjōji and the shrine.[64] For the next three generations the post was held by disciples of Engyō: Songyō 尊暁, Jōgyō 定暁, and Kōgyō 公暁.[65] The Onjōji monk Ryūben, previously mentioned, performed the role of a protector monk (J. *gojisō* 護持僧 or 御持僧), and was tasked with praying and performing rituals for the protection of the Minamoto clan, as well as for the health of the shōgun.[66] Ryūben became the *bettō* of the shrine in 1247, and during his twenty-seven-year tenure, the Jimon's political influence increased due to its ties with the Minamoto. Dōkyō 道慶 (?–1285) was another monk from Onjōji who helped reify the Jimon-Minamoto relationship. However, after Ryūben and Dōkyō,

Onjōji monks were ousted from power and Sanmon monks took key posts at the Tsurugaoka Shrine.[67]

Beginning in the early twelfth century, through the Minamoto association, both the Tsurugaoka and Iwashimizu Hachiman Shrines developed close institutional ties to the Jimon.[68] The Minamoto patronage of Onjōji led to the dissemination of the Shinra Myōjin and Hachiman cults as they existed at Onjōji beyond the so-called *miyako* Tendai (Tendai limited to the capital area), which was centered in Ōmi Province, the birthplace of both Shinra Myōjin and the Minamoto clan. The two overlapping networks—that of the Minamoto and that of the Jimon—served as the "concatenations of mediators,"[69] or as the nexus of symbols, ideas, and practices around the cult of Shinra Myōjin.

SHINRA MYŌJIN AND THE JIMON'S KUMANO PILGRIMAGE NETWORKS

The Jimon's association with the tradition of ascetic practice in the mountains that later came to be called Shugendō played a significant role in spreading Shinra Myōjin worship beyond the Jimon.[70] This network also helped to extend the Jimon's religious authority and cultural capital to Kumano 熊野, one of the most significant imperial pilgrimage sites in medieval Japan.[71] In essence, the Jimon's interests in the Kumano pilgrimage was part of its attempt to strengthen its ties with court elites.[72] This association can be traced back to the eleventh century, when Onjōji monks were associated with imperial pilgrimages to the Kumano region. The monastic and administrative network linking the retired emperors, Onjōji, and Kumano was formed in 1090 when retired emperor Shirakawa established the new office of "overseer of the three Kumano shrines" (J. *Kumano sanzan kengyō* 熊野三山検校) by appointing the Onjōji *chōri* Zōyo 増誉 (1032–1116) to the position.[73] As the first overseer, Zōyo became a protector monk who offered prayers for the health and the well-being of the retired emperor during the period of pilgrimage, and Shirakawa finished his first pilgrimage to Kumano with Zōyo's assistance. In the same year, Shirakawa elevated Zōyo to the abbacy of Onjōji, and from that time onward, the majority of Onjōji's *chōri* also served as overseers of the three Kumano shrines.[74]

During the Insei period, pilgrimage to the Kumano area became popular among emperors and aristocratic families, and the Jimon served to connect the central authorities in Kyoto to the religious practices in Kumano. Retired emperors Toba (r. 1108–1123), Goshirakawa (r. 1156–1158), and Gotoba (r. 1184–1198) all made pilgrimages to Kumano, and all were led by *gojisō* monks associated with the Jimon.[75] Within a century, the Jimon had created a monopoly on the Kumano overseership. While the Jimon increased its presence in Kumano, Kumano's religious culture also infiltrated Kyoto. In 1160, for instance, the devout Kumano pilgrim and retired emperor Go Shirakawa enshrined the Kumano Gongen on the imperial palace grounds in Kyoto and sponsored the building of a new Kumano shrine (J. Shin Kumanosha 新熊野社) on the spot.[76] By periodically serving as Kumano overseers, Onjōji monks fortified their relationships with retired emperors and exercised their institutional power over popular imperial pilgrimage sites. A legend found in the *Kōfukuji sōjō* 興福寺奏状 (1205), for instance, tells us that "Enchin prayed to Shinra Myōjin at Kumano for the prosperity of his lineage."[77] This passage suggests that during this formative period, the Jimon strategically established connections with Kumano, resulting in new legends that connected the Jimon to Kumano.

One of the *monzeki* cloisters of the Jimon, Shōgoin 聖護院 in Kyoto, was more involved with the Kumano *sanzan* pilgrimage during the Ōei 応永 era (1394–1428).[78] Shōgoin slowly acquired management rights at local shrines in Kumano and financial and institutional control of regional pilgrimage networks.[79] During the fifteenth century, Shōgoin eventually established itself as the headquarters of the Honzan 本山 branch of Shugendō, and Shōgoin came to control a number of mountain sites (e.g., Kumano, Ōmine 大峰, and Yoshino 吉野) and extended its devotional community even further with the support of the Ashikaga shoguns.

This is also the time when Shōgoin became an integral part of the dissemination of Shinra Myōjin worship through the Kumano Shugendō network. Shōgoin sponsored numerous images of Shinra Myōjin, among them a mandara.[80] Known as the Kumano honji suijaku mandara 熊野本地垂迹曼荼羅 (hereafter Kumano mandara),[81] it depicts Shinra Myōjin appearing alongside other deities and Enchin, thereby symbolizing a synthesis of Buddhism and Kumano religious practices and ideas.

A closer examination of the Kumano mandara gives us a better idea of how Shinra Myōjin was perceived by Shugendō groups, or at least of the way in which the Jimon wished to portray Shinra Myōjin to a new audience. Figure 2 is a mandara from the Kamakura period and is currently stored at Tōsen 湯泉 Shrine. The mandara can be divided into two parts. The upper half depicts the *honji suijaku* relationship of various Kumano deities. The lower half illustrates the twelve manifestations (J. *gongen* 権現) of Kumano. Below Zaō Gongen 蔵王権現[82] Shinra Myōjin appears as an old man seated on a high chair, wearing a hat and holding a staff. Surrounded by popular deities of Kumano, such as Aizen Myōō 愛染明王, Bishamonten 毘沙門天, Inari Myōjin 稲荷明神, Fudō Myōō 不動明王, and Kangiten 歓喜天, Shinra Myōjin appears in the center of the mountains. This central position of Shinra Myōjin in the mandara mirrors Onjōji's influence in the Kumano region.

It is noteworthy that this particular image of Shinra Myōjin echoes that of Shugendō's purported founder, En no Gyōja 役行者 (ca. seventh c.), who is also depicted as an old man wearing a hat and holding a staff. Concerning the relationship between En no Gyōja and Shinra Myōjin, Miyake Hitoshi argues that the visual overlap between the two figures speaks to Onjōji's interests in controlling the Kumano region. According to Miyake, the iconography of En no Gyōja appeared only after the Kamakura period, and judging from the earlier dates of the Shinra

FIGURE 2.
Shinra Myōjin in the Kumano honji mandara, Late Kamakura period, ink and colors on silk. Tōsen Shrine, Hyōgo.

Myōjin iconography, it is highly likely that these visual portrayals of Shinra Myōjin influenced later visual representations of En no Gyōja.[83] Furthermore, some Kumano mandaras have En no Gyōja while others show Shinra Myōjin where En no Gyōja should be, indicating that these two figures were perceived as interchangeable.[84] This also suggests that the promotion of En no Gyōja's iconography coincided with the institutionalization and legitimization of Shugendō, and that Shinra Myōjin played a role in this process.

As the image of Shinra Myōjin from the Kumano honji suijaku mandara shows, the cult of Shinra Myōjin continued to circulate during the medieval period, and this circulation was made possible by imperial pilgrimages to Kumano and the activities and movements of Shugendō practitioners, through whom the imperial family, Onjōji, and Kumano were linked. While he continued his sedentarization process even in mountainous Kumano, Shinra Myōjin became mobile again through the networks of Shugendō practitioners and pilgrims. The Kumano mandara, then, reveals the Jimon's larger goals: political patronage from the court, economic power beyond the capital, and cultural impact as an independent religious institution.

Furthermore, the Kumano mandara points to several facets of the spread of Shinra Myōjin worship. First, Shōgoin was an active participant in the promotion of the Shinra Myōjin cult. Second, through the Kumano pilgrimage, divinities of the Jimon came to be worshipped by a large range of social and religious groups, including imperial pilgrims, aristocrats, Shugendō practitioners, and numerous other people on the Kii Peninsula who were in contact with these groups. Third, the travel route to Kumano was the primary channel through which stories and images of Shinra Myōjin were transmitted. In this way, the Kumano pilgrimage was one of the key channels for disseminating the cult of Shinra Myōjin to a wide audience, and Shōgoin's role was key in this.

This chapter focused on Shinra Myōjin's role in the Jimon's institutional growth during the medieval period. Here, we see the transformation of Shinra Myōjin in one of the most inland parts of the East Asian Mediterranean. Shinra Myōjin began as a sea deity, but acquired new functions and characteristics as his importance within the Jimon grew. Chief among these was his role as a mountain deity, a role that was distinct yet intimately related to his association with the sea. This deity's sedentarization was a never-ending process, however, and developed in multiple directions. In this sense, his sedentarization was not simply a linear progression, but entailed a constant negotiation of boundaries of influence in a circular manner.

Within the history of Japanese Tendai, nothing was more destructive than the feud between the Sanmon and the Jimon. The growth of Shinra Myōjin emerged out of this feud, and specifically as part of the Jimon's efforts to secure the right to perform its own monastic ordinations, independently of Mt. Hiei. The Jimon's frustration led to great creativity, as can be seen in the stories about Raigō, who is a doppelgänger of sorts of Shinra Myōjin. Through such stories, and by turning Shinra Myōjin into a deity able to curse his opponents, the Jimon gained a symbolic victory over the Sanmon and its supporters. Later, due to the relationship between Onjōji and the Minamoto clan, the cult of Shinra Myōjin spread far beyond the Ōmi area as the Minamoto racked up military victories as far north as Hokkaido. The spread of the Shinra Myōjin cult was also facilitated through the Jimon's relationship with Shugendō and with the Kumano area.

Sectarian conflict was central to the growth of Shinra Myōjin. And yet the spread of Shinra Myōjin worship was also a product of carefully crafted institutional efforts and the networks in which the Jimon participated. All of this suggests that Shinra Myōjin was not simply the paramount deity of that tradition, but also the symbol for that institution's history, and for the very institution itself. With the spread of Shinra Myōjin worship, the Jimon could establish itself as an influential center of esoteric Buddhist doctrine and practice.

Chapter 4

Shinra Myōjin, the Multifaceted Deity

This chapter continues to explore the Jimon's efforts to sendentarize Shinra Myōjin by examining the deity's many roles at Onjōji. It focuses on how the deity was portrayed in narratives, poems, Buddhist rituals, and performing arts that were produced in the Jimon network. Beginning with two literary works—*A Long Tale for an Autumn Night* (*Aki no yo no nagamonogatari* 秋夜長物語, ca. 1300s) and *A Collection of Sand and Pebbles* (*Shasekishū* 沙石集, 1279–1283)—I explain how Shinra Myōjin was perceived in the popular imagination as the patron deity of the Jimon, as well as the deity of Japanese poetry (J. *waka* 和歌). I then turn to the crucial role this deity played in rituals at Onjōji, from small-scale rituals to large, annual festivals. By revealing Shinra Myōjin's multidimensional character and many roles, I show that his growth went hand in hand with the institutional development of the Jimon tradition, and that Shinra Myōjin was at the core of Jimon's evolution as a new esoteric Tendai Buddhist center.

Although the centuries-long clash between the Tendai branches caused incredible damage to Onjōji, there was a silver lining: the destruction served as artistic inspiration and fueled the literary imagination. *A Long Tale for an Autumn Night* is the oldest known *chigo monogatari* 稚児物語, a genre of love stories that focuses on young boys.[1] The work is of unknown authorship, but given the historical details found in the story, the author must have either witnessed or heard about the last burning of Onjōji in 1319.[2] The text is an invaluable source, not only because it includes a detailed story of the Sanmon-Jimon battle and a faithful description of historical events and figures, but also because it provides a glimpse of how Shinra Myōjin was portrayed in popular literature of the period.[3]

The narrative revolves around the love between Keikai 桂海, a Tendai priest of the Eastern Pagoda of Mt. Hiei, and Umewaka 梅若, a youth (J. *chigo* 稚児) at Onjōji.[4] When Keikai was passing by Onjōji, he encountered the youth, realized that he had already met Umewaka in a dream, and fell in love with the boy. This story was later produced as an illustrated handscroll (J. *emaki* 絵巻), and the oldest copy dates to 1377.[5] The handscroll comprises three sections, and figure 3 is from the first of these. Here, we see Keikai lost in a daydream, thinking of his young lover. Umewaka (literally "young plum blossom"), in accord with his name, is symbolically represented as a blossoming plum tree in this picturesque scene.

The love story, however, turns into a disaster when an aged mountain ascetic (J. *yamabushi* 山伏) absconds with the temple acolyte to the goblin nest on Mt. Ōmine. The Onjōji priests blamed Keikai, who was an Enryakuji monk, for Umewaka's disappearance. Tensions between Onjōji and Enryakuji were already tense over the issue of the ordination platform, and the two had already engaged in several martial conflicts. In the story, the Onjōji monks launched an attack on Enryakuji in response to Umewaka's disappearance, and a massive number of Enryakuji monks, including Keikai, then counterattacked. Afterwards, when Umewaka was released from captivity, he and his attendant visited Onjōji only to find that everything had been burnt to ashes. Only the shrine for Shinra Myōjin had survived, and Umewaka sought shelter therein. The enmity between the two Tendai branches ended with the young boy's unexpected suicide, which then served as a catalyst for Keikai's awakening (figure 4).

Although this didactic tale is in large part a story about the salvation of a Buddhist monk, Shinra Myōjin's role as Onjōji's religious anchor is given a prominent place in the narrative.[6] He appears throughout the story, but it is really at the end of the tale that his importance becomes clear. After Onjōji has been completely destroyed by the Sanmon monks, thirty dispirited Onjōji monks experience a collective dream in

FIGURE 3. Umewaka's death, a scene from the *Aki no yo no nagamonogatari*, late fourteenth c., ink, color, and gold on paper. The Metropolitan Museum of Art, New York.

FIGURE 4. Keikai's daydreaming, a scene from the *Aki no yo no nagamonogatari*, late fourteenth c., ink, color, and gold on paper. The Metropolitan Museum of Art, New York.

which they see Shinra Myōjin and Sannō joyfully banqueting together.[7] After Sannō returns to Mt. Hiei, one of the Onjōji monks asks Shinra Myōjin why he was so welcoming toward Sannō, the deity of the temple responsible for Onjōji's destruction. Shinra Myōjin replies that humans cannot understand the divine will, but that with the collaboration of Sannō the whole affair was designed to guide all the involved people to supreme enlightenment. Shinra Myōjin further reveals that Umewaka was not an ordinary boy but a manifestation of Kannon of Ishiyamadera 石山寺 in Ōtsu. After the revelation of the divine scheme, the deity encourages Onjōji monks to reconstruct the lost buildings and recopy Buddhist texts for attaining merits and enlightenment. The story ends with the listener's admiration of an old man who has apparently narrated the entire tale. The old man echoes the appearance of Shinra Myōjin, creating something of a metanarrative structure in which Shinra Myōjin is both in the story and the narrator of the story.

This portrayal of Shinra Myōjin as the source of the Onjōji monks' religious inspiration was taken up by other writers during the thirteenth century.[8] For instance, in a collection of Buddhist didactic literature entitled *A Collection of Sand and Pebbles*, compiled by the monk Mujū Ichien 無住一円 (1227–1312), we find a similar story that emphasizes the benevolent nature of Shinra Myōjin.[9]

> Long ago, Miidera was burned down by monks from Enryakuji, and nothing remained of the halls and pagodas, monks' quarters, Buddhist images, or sutras. The monks were

> dispersed throughout the fields and mountains, and Miidera became a completely uninhabited temple. One of the monks made a pilgrimage to the Shinra Myōjin Shrine and there spent the night. In his dream, the monk saw the deity push open the doors of the shrine. Because the deity appeared to be in a very good mood, the monk was emboldened and addressed him. "When I consider your august vow to protect the Buddhist teachings of this temple and think how profound your sorrow at what has been completely lost must be, why is this not reflected on your countenance?" "How could I not feel grieved?" replied the god. Shinra Myōjin continued, saying: "But even so, it pleases me that this incident should give rise to a genuine desire for enlightenment in a single monk. One can always restore the halls, pagodas, images and sutras if one has the money. But it is the man aspiring to Buddhahood, though one in ten million, who is to be valued highly." After hearing this, the monk awoke from his dream and realized how wondrous the divine will was, and made a sincere vow for enlightenment.[10]

In this story, Shinra Myōjin is presented as being unconcerned with worldly matters, almost like a Daoist sage. He urges Onjōji monks to turn the destruction of the temple into an opportunity to reach enlightenment. To the monk who complains about Shinra Myōjin's inability to protect Onjōji from destruction, the god replies that he does not protect every monk at the temple but only those who are determined to reach enlightenment.[11] This image of Shinra Myōjin is drastically different from the fearful image of the deity in the story of Raigō discussed in chapter 3. To his enemies, Shinra Myōjin could be a threatening, cursing deity who pursued the institution's political independence with militant zeal. But to the Jimon followers, he was a compassionate, protective deity who encouraged the monks to transcend mundane matters and take Buddhist ideals seriously. In both cases, he served as a mouthpiece for the Jimon, constantly promoting the political and religious interests of the Jimon monks.

SHINRA MYŌJIN: THE *WAKA* DEITY OF ONJŌJI

As literary accomplishment increasingly became the basis for recognition and advancement at court during the Heian period, composing poems became an important skill among the literati. With the growing popularity of *waka* composition, Buddhist ideas came to be an accepted theme within official court poetry. By the late Heian period, aristocrats had taken over a majority of the important ecclesiastical positions in Buddhist institutions. High-ranking monks were often members of the imperial family or aristocracy. With this development, aristocratic culture permeated Buddhist monastic culture, and *waka* competitions involving both monks and aristocrats became a familiar scene at Buddhist temples.

Beginning in the early eleventh century, Shinra Myōjin became a *waka* deity in the Jimon tradition. The deity's newly acquired role was part of a broader reinterpretation of *waka* within esoteric Buddhist circles that began in the late Heian period with the *waka-dhāraṇī* theory.[12] Interpreting *waka* poetry through an esoteric Buddhist lens, Buddhist elites theorized that among the various art forms, *waka* poetry was the ultimate expression of sacred words in the regulated exchange between the visible and invisible worlds. As shown in the preface of the *Collection of Waka, Old and New* (*Kokin wakashū* 古今和歌集, ca. 905–914), the first anthology of Japanese poetry to be compiled by imperial commission, *waka* poetics already contained a nativist discourse that stressed the inherent value of things that were uniquely Japanese and put forward the idea that *waka*'s origins were divine—that is, that *waka* had come from the gods.[13] Some Buddhist elites found this idea convincing because it echoed esoteric Buddhist ideas about language (developed in Japan in particular by Kūkai) and because it fit with the long-standing interest in and study of Sanskrit and Siddhaṃ in the esoteric Buddhism traditions.

The idea that *waka* is the Japanese equivalent of Buddhist *dhāraṇī* became increasingly widespread in medieval Japan, in part because of its ideological implications.[14] At this time there was a growing collective identity based on the notion that Japan was the divine country (J. *shinkoku* 神国) and on the theory of a Buddhist transmission through the three "countries" of India, China, and Japan (J. *sangoku bukkyō shikan* 三国仏教史観). This triple-country construct was given further weight by two major texts: the *Sangoku dentōki* 三国伝灯記 (1173), written by the Kōfukuji monk Kakuken 覚憲 (1131–1213);[15] and the *Sangoku buppō denzū engi* 三国仏法伝通縁起 (1311) by Gyōnen 凝然 (1240–1321),[16] which identifies Japan as the legitimate successor of the Buddhist tradition after India and China.

The suggestion that *waka* is equal to or even superior to *dhāraṇī* supported the idea that Japan was in some way divine or blessed by the gods, and it also challenged the sentiment that Japan had an insignificant position within Buddhist history and within the Buddhist world. This period was also marked by a larger discourse among the literati focused on explaining the origins of Japan, a discourse that depended on a number of Shinto-Buddhist theories and myths, and that was deeply concerned with the authority and legitimacy of the royal family and lineage.[17] Japanese esoteric Buddhism recognized the potential of poetry and its aesthetics from an early period, a recognition that led to the understanding of *waka* as a uniquely Japanese expression of universal Buddhist teachings.

In medieval Japanese poetic discourse, Susanoo came to be regarded as the divine creator of *waka*. Mujū was fascinated by the idea that Sanskrit *dhāraṇī* and Japanese *waka* were equivalent. Discussing the contents of the *Kojiki*, Mujū wrote that when Susanoo built a palace for his bride Princess Kushinada 奇稲田 he composed a poem, and that this poem is the first *waka*. *A Collection of Sand and Pebbles* reads:

> The gods of our country are the traces of buddhas and bodhisattvas. They are each but one of many expedient manifestations. With his "eight-fold fence of Izumo," Susanoo

> no Mikoto originated the composition of verse in thirty-one syllables. It was no different than the words of the Buddha. The *dhāraṇī* of India are simply in the language of that country's people. Using the language of India, the Buddha expounded *dhāraṇī*. This is why the Master Yixing wrote in his Commentary on the *Dainichi Sūtra* that: "The words of the various lands are all *dhāraṇī*." If the Buddha were to appear in our country, he would surely expound *dhāraṇī* in Japanese.[18]

In this passage Mujū explains Susanno's verse as the genesis of *waka* and makes a Buddhist connection to it within the *honji suijaku* paradigm. Mujū was an erudite scholar-monk who trained in different traditions of Japanese Buddhism. Although he took an ecumenical approach to Japanese Buddhism's many divisions and sects, the identification of Susanoo as the author of the first *waka* seems to be a claim intimately associated with the Jimon and its worship of Shinra Myōjin. While the association between Shinra Myōjin and Susanoo is based on a number of perceived similarities, many of which I explore later in this chapter and in chapter 6, in the medieval mythic logic of the Jimon the two deities were in fact the same, both having returned from Silla. With the *waka* association, the two deities had another connection: Susanoo created the first *waka*, and Shinra Myōjin was the patron deity of *waka*.

By the early Kamakura period, the composition of *waka* was widely practiced in esoteric Buddhist circles, and it was commonly incorporated into Buddhist rituals and liturgies.[19] Although participation in poem composition or other artistic performances by monks and nuns was sometimes criticized as ensnaring them in the realm of the senses and the worldly quest for literary fame, these activities were also seen as being compatible with the Tendai School's teachings about original enlightenment and non-duality. As such, poetry, literature, and performing arts were fully recognized as paths leading toward spiritual attainment.

We must understand Shinra Myōjin's transformation into the patron deity of *waka* in the Jimon tradition in the early twelfth century against this backdrop. The Jimon monks believed that Shinra Myōjin supplied them with inspiration and ensured their success at *waka* competitions. The Shinra Myōjin Shrine at Onjōji began to serve as a *waka* competition venue, and Onjōji soon became famous as a nourishing environment for *waka* poets. For example, Gyōson 行尊 (1057–1135), the Tendai *zasu* from the Jimon line, was a famed *waka* poet, as well as a devotee of Shinra Myōjin.[20] Onjōji monks held a *waka* competition to which they would invite famous poets and monks, one of the biggest of which was held on the fifteenth day of the eighth month of 1176. Onjōji's temple chronicles preserve examples of *waka* poems presented at this particular competition.[21] Fujiwara no Shunzei 藤原俊成 (1114–1201), a leading *waka* poet of this time, attended the competition as a judge, which points to Onjōji's active involvement with *waka* culture.

Narratives and new myths that focused on Shinra Myōjin's role as the Jimon's *waka* patron deity soon emerged, including several stories that tell of the deity appearing to poet monks so that he might provide them with his divine guidance. For instance, the Onjōji monk Kaigaku 快學 (fl. eleventh c.) dreamed that Shinra Myōjin came to him in the form of an old man and gave him advice prior to a competition in 1076, which Kaigaku went on to win.[22] This resulted in Shinra Myōjin receiving the by-name "Poetic Immortal of Miidera" (J. *Mii no kasen* 三井の歌仙).[23] As his title suggests, Shinra Myōjin had a double role in the *waka* practices at Onjōji: he was the patron deity of *waka* as well as a *waka* poet himself, using *waka* as a way of delivering his divine messages to his devotees and answering monks' prayers in poetic form.[24]

Although Shinra Myōjin was the *waka* deity at Onjōji, Sumiyoshi Myōjin 住吉明神, the Japanese god of poetry and navigation, has traditionally been known as the patron deity of *waka* outside of the Jimon tradition. What is intriguing is that there was an intentional mixing or even merging of Shinra Myōjin and Sumiyoshi in narratives about these two figures from this period onward. In the *Kokon chōmonjū* 古今著聞集 (ca. thirteenth c.), for instance, an old man with a white beard, whom Enchin meets on his way back from China, is identified as Sumiyoshi Myōjin, *not* as Shinra Myōjin.[25] Through such stories, these two deities came to share similar functions and appearances: a seafaring deity, who is also a *waka* deity, and who appears as an old man. Regardless of which deity first borrowed from the other, this relationship helped to establish Shinra Myōjin's role as a patron deity for *waka*.[26]

While the power of the aristocracy declined during the late Heian period, *waka* culture spread to other sectors of intellectual society. Along with aristocrats, Buddhist priests and some well-educated samurai continued to compose *waka*, and it retained its value and prestige within the Japanese intelligentsia and aristocracy. In this context, Shinra Myōjin's association with *waka* increased his symbolic capital. His role as a deity of *waka* beyond the walls of Onjōji reveals the extent to which the Jimon penetrated secular elite culture and demonstrates the prominent position that this deity enjoyed within Japanese Buddhism and in Japanese intellectual culture more broadly.

MAJOR RITUALS OF SHINRA MYŌJIN

I would like now to turn to rituals associated with Shinra Myōjin that highlight his multifaceted position within the Jimon ritual tradition. Rituals for Shinra Myōjin were performed on a regular basis from the eleventh to the thirteenth centuries. One of the major ones was a series of doctrinal debates (J. *banrongi* 番論義) and a lecture series dedicated to him. Within these, the assembly on the *Daihannya-kyō* 大般若経 (Skt. *Mahāprajñāpāramitā Sūtra*) was particularly prominent. It was held four times a year and probably entailed reading the sutra in the *tendoku* 転読 manner, whereby the text is "read" by chanting the text's title while rapidly flipping through its pages.[27] The sutra was mythologically connected to Shinra Myōjin, for the deity's *honji* is the bodhisattva Mañjuśrī (J. Hannya 般若), whose name can be translated as "wisdom." Not coincidently, one of Shinra Myōjin's acolytes is called Hannya, and one of the deity's attributes is a scroll of the *Daihannya-kyō*. Another major lecture series dedicated to Shinra Myōjin was the Equinox Assemblies (J. *higan-e* 彼岸会). The ritual was held during both the spring and autumn equinoxes, although the details of the ritual are not known.

The Thirty Lectures of the Shinra (J. *Shinra sanjūkō* 新羅三十講) was another major ceremony held at the Shinra Myōjin Shrine.[28] The thirty-lecture series was inaugurated in 1202 by Kōin.[29] Because the ceremony was also called the Lectures of the *Lotus Sutra* (J. *Hokke sanjūkō* 法華三十講), it may be that the *Lotus Sutra* served as the basis for these lectures. The number thirty references the thirty days of the month, as well as the thirty masters who led the lecture series. The year 1322 was an important year for this ritual, and it was conducted for the duration of the entire year.[30]

An invocation ritual called *Shinra nenbutsu* 新羅念仏 was a ritual carried out on a more regular basis. The first *Shinra nenbutsu* was held on the ninth month of 1109.[31] The name suggests that the ritual was most likely organized around the recitation of the name Shinra Myōjin, a practice that would have been undertaken in order to invoke the deity's power of healing and granting of longevity.[32] The *Shinra Myōjin ki* provides some details about this ritual. It notes, for example, that in 1197 two Onjōji monks performed the *nenbutsu* ritual in an attempt to receive the deity's healing power. The two stayed at the Shinra Myōjin Shrine over a period of time and performed the *nenbutsu* ritual in front of the deity.[33]

The Shinra Myōjin Shrine also served as a site for the *ennen* 延年, a variety of performances of different styles that were performed at Buddhist temples and Shinto shrines. *Ennen* began some time in the late Heian period and became increasingly popular during the Kamakura period.[34] The word *ennen* means "prolonging life," and it was often held after certain events and lectures organized by student-monks.[35] Two famous *ennen* rituals were Kōfukuji's Yuima-e 維摩会 (Assembly of Vimalakīrti) and Tōdaiji's Seshin-kō 世親講 (Vasubandhu Lecture), both conducted at temples in Nara.[36] The reason why *ennen* became a major ritual at Onjōji had to do with its relationship with these Nara temples. To compete with the Sanmon, Onjōji sought alliances with Kōfukuji and Tōdaiji. Frequent contact with these temples led to the introduction of *ennen* into Onjōji circles, and Shinra Myōjin's new role as an *ennen* deity at Onjōji stemmed from these political and institutional ties.

By the Kamakura period, Onjōji had become a major temple for the performance of *ennen*. *Ennen* rituals were performed at the shrine with far greater pomp and frequency than other temples.[37] While other Nara temples used *ennen* as a reception that followed lectures, Onjōji adapted the ritual for the inauguration ceremony of the *chōri* as well as for esoteric masters' consecration ceremonies. Onjōji chronicles confirm that an *ennen* of magnificent scale was carried out at the *chōri* inauguration ceremony for the Onjōji monk Ninjo 仁助 (1214–1262) in 1246.[38] The *ennen* ritual held great political significance for Onjōji,[39] and the elevation of these rituals was an attempt to advertise the power of Shinra Myōjin and, by association, of Onjōji.

In addition to *ennen*, the Shinra Myōjin Shrine was a venue for the Shinra Myōjin festival (J. *Shinra Myōjin sairei* 新羅明神祭礼). The ritual was performed mostly between the eleventh and thirteenth centuries and was one of the largest public rituals to be carried out at Onjōji on a regular basis.[40] The Jimon records indicate that the festival was first organized in 1052 by the Onjōji *chōri* Myōson.[41] When the festival was first held, it was a small-scale ritual for high-ranking Onjōji monks; but by the thirteenth century it had grown into a major public festival. Festivals were an integral part of institutional life at temples. Not only did they create a sense of unity within the monastic community, they also attracted visitors, worshippers, and donors. The Shinra Myōjin festival served all of these basic functions. More significantly, it provided a stage and an opportunity for reenacting mythic associations between Shinra Myōjin and Susanoo.

Under the leadership of the powerful Onjōji *chōri* Kōin, the festival held in 1210 was particularly ostentatious and included eleven portable shrines (J. *mikoshi* 神輿). A description from the *Jimon denki horoku* provides us with a glimpse of that year's festival and Susanoo's role therein. Following the enactment of the narrative of Susanoo as found in early Japanese myth, the festival offered viewers a variety of parades and performances. Participants wearing lion masks led the parade, followed by eight youths portraying Princess Kushinada and eight as Susanoo. The first eight young boys, colorfully dressed as Princess Kushinada, wore red pants (J. *hakama* 袴) and their hair was adorned in the Tang style with a sacred comb (J. *yutsutsumagushi* 湯津爪櫛) on the top of their heads. The other eight boys wore a masculine costume (J. *suikan* 水干)[42] with a black-lacquered headpiece (J. *kazaori* 風折), and each carried a sword in his belt. The *chōri* followed the parade along with other high-ranking officials. Next were the portable shrines, then dignitaries, and finally, at the end, hundreds of monks and high-ranking officials with their servants. This grand procession marked the centerpiece of the first day in the two-day Shinra Myōjin festival. The second day began with a *dōji* dance (J. *budō* 舞童) in front of the Shinra Myōjin Shrine, a performance meant to honor the god. It was said that Shinra Myōjin, being greatly pleased, gave an oracle in return.[43]

Ritual items used at this festival deserve our attention. Swords played a pivotal symbolic role in connecting Susanoo to Shinra Myōjin.[44] At the very first Shinra Myōjin festival in 1052, for instance, one thousand swords were offered to Shinra Myōjin.[45] This sword recalls Totsuka-no-Tsurugi 十握剣 (sometimes written as 十拳剣), the sword that Susanoo used to slay the Eight-Headed Serpent in the myth appearing in the *Kojiki* and *Nihon shoki*. However, it still remained enigmatic (even to the Jimon monks) why not one but rather one thousand swords were offered to Shinra Myōjin. Interestingly, the *Onjōji denki* and *Jimon denki horoku* provide two different interpretations of this. The *Onjōji denki* states that the offering derives from the custom of a foreign country, which from the context seems to be a reference to Silla.[46] In contrast, the *Jimon denki horoku* denies the foreign association, arguing that this was a Japanese practice.[47] This difference in interpretation is significant because it reflects varying opinions about the connection between Shinra Myōjin and Silla. While it is not certain whether or not a thousand swords were actually offered at the ceremony, the exaggerated number as well as the sword itself represent the uncanny power of Shinra Myōjin, whose image overlapped with that of Susanoo.

The *dōji* played an essential role in a number of temple events, including *matsuri*, artistic performances, and other occasional rituals.[48] The *dōji* gave Onjōji great pride, for these divine children were thought to be intermediary beings who were able to link *kami* and humans.[49] The *dōji* also garnered highly desired public attention. For instance, the *Onjōji denki* describes: "the most magnificent spectacle was that of the splendidly decorated *dōji*."[50] Apparently the young male dancers who participated in the 1210 *matsuri* were so popular that they were later invited to a similar ceremony held at Kōfukuji.[51]

The two groups of youths in the parade correspond to the two *dōji* of Shinra Myōjin, Hannya 般若 and Shukuō 宿王.[52] The Onjōji Old Map (figure 5) includes the Shinra Myōjin Shrine, the primary venue for the festival. This fourteenth-century scroll shows the northern quarter of the Onjōji complex, with the Shinra Myōjin Shrine in the middle. On either side of this shrine are two small shrines (J. *hokora* 祠), which are for his two attendants, Hannya and Shukuō. What we see here, then, is the way in which the spiritual ties between Shinra Myōjin and his two *dōji* were expressed in the actual physical layout of the monastic complex, thus revealing the way in which Shinra Myōjin became part of Onjōji's sacred topography.

This particular layout in the map also reveals that Shinra Myōjin's two *dōji* are an extension of Shinra Myōjin, or even avatars of the deity. There are various origin stories for these two acolytes, but according to one account the two accompanied Shinra Myōjin when he came to Japan from the kingdom of Silla.[53] According to another explanation, they were born from Susanoo's halberd, which was given to him by Amaterasu.[54] Whatever the origins of these two *dōji* might be, at Onjōji they served as protectors of both the temple and its monks. It was believed that these two emissaries were the ones who protected all of those who would become monks at Onjōji from the moment those men began their existence as embryos in the womb.[55] The idea that these *dōji* are the protectors of future Onjōji monks even before they are born suggests that the bond between the *dōji* and Onjōji monks is destined from the very beginning. They are like companion spirits (J. *kushōjin* 倶生神), deities who are born at the same time as the individuals to whom they are to be companions.[56] But, if we think of a *dōji* as being an extension of the main deity, what this fateful pairing ultimately expresses is that the divine old man—namely, Shinra Myōjin—and Onjōji monks are bound together by a common destiny, just like *kushōjin*.

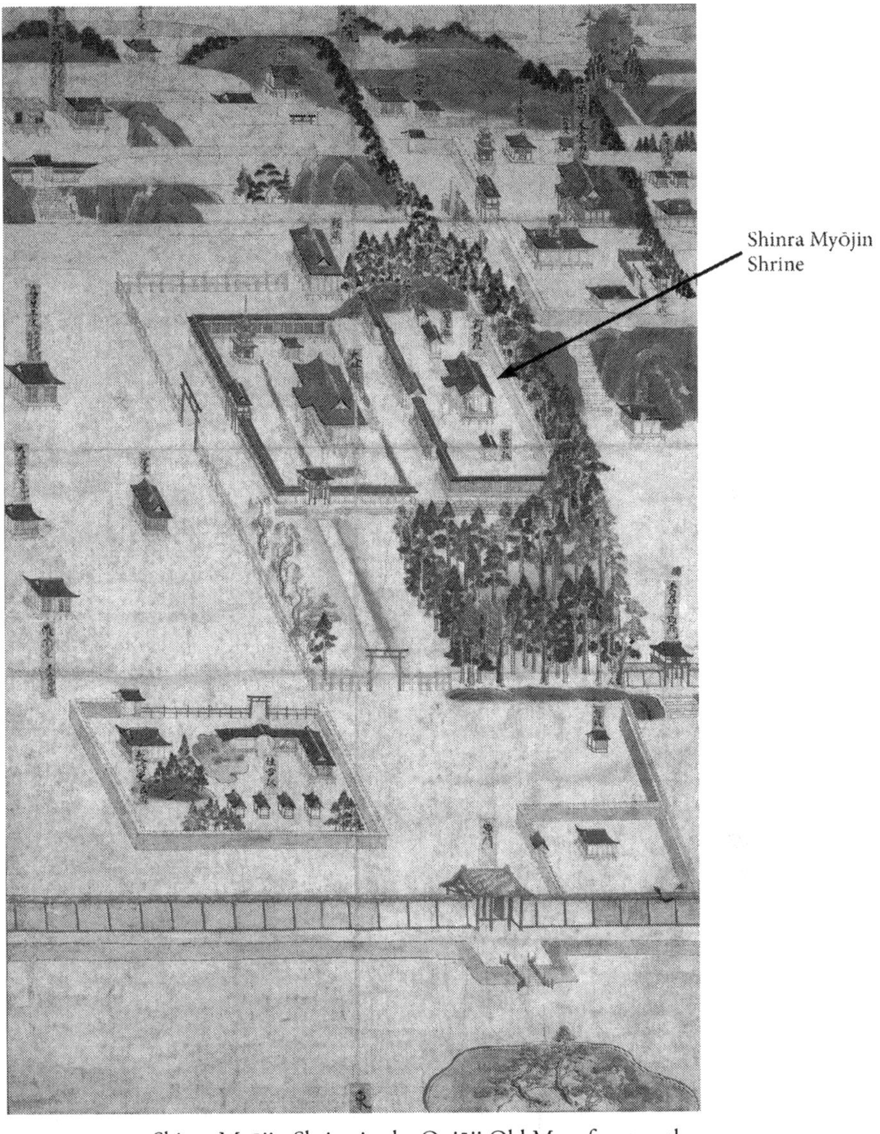

FIGURE 5. Shinra Myōjin Shrine in the Onjōji Old Map, fourteenth c., ink and colors on silk. Onjōji, Shiga Prefecture.

This chapter has examined the many facets of Shinra Myōjin as found in the Jimon's ritual space and calendar, focusing on his role in the literary tradition, performing arts, and major ceremonial events. From a *waka* deity to the main deity of the Onjōji *matsuri*, one might find Shinra Myōjin's role to be a uniquely Jimon phenomenon and practice. While this is certainly true, this chapter demonstrates that the worship of Shinra Myōjin spread far beyond Onjōji through popular literature and public festivals, a development that allowed Onjōji to extend its influence. As seen in the festival of 1210, the Shinra Myōjin festival was designed not only to maintain the worship of this deity but also to establish the mythological identification between Shinra Myōjin and Susanoo, and to advertise this mythological connection in public ritual space. The connection between Shinra Myōjin and Susanoo was ideological in nature. In the next chapter I shall explain how this association helped the Jimon to portray Shinra Myōjin as an authentic Japanese deity who was not a god of Silla but rather a god who had returned from Silla.

Part III

Restoring Fluidity

Functional and Symbolic Networks of the Silla Deities

Chapter 5

Trek for the Star Deity

Sonjōō and Shinra Myōjin

Belief that astrological events in the heavens affect human destiny and govern the lives of individuals is widespread in human societies. Observing astral bodies in the night sky helped people explain natural, social, religious, and cultural phenomena, for the night sky was not only thought to be a macrocosm of the terrestrial and social worlds, but also of each individual here on earth. This faith in the stars was even more important for those who held political power. In the case of Japanese history, we see that in some cases heavenly bodies could be manipulated or petitioned in order to secure the longevity of the emperor and ensure the stability of the political and social orders.

There were many star deities in the medieval Japanese Buddhist pantheon, and in this chapter I deal with Sonjōō 尊星王, who is one of the least known but arguably the most esoteric and powerful of these astral deities. His relevance to the study at hand stems from the fact that within the Jimon tradition Sonjōō was believed to be a manifestation of Shinra Myōjin. Sonjōō came to be a symbol and expression of the Jimon's attempt to create a powerful, legitimate Tendai tradition and played a key role in the "esotericization" (J. *mikkyōka* 密教化) of the Jimon's ritual realm, representing one of the clearest examples in Japanese medieval Buddhism of a body of foreign, celestial knowledge being used to exert religious and political influence.

The Sonjōō ritual was known as the most esoteric of the star rituals. Before discussing it, I want to briefly explain what I mean by "esoteric" in this case, as this concept is central to understanding Sonjōō worship as practiced in medieval Japan. There have been many debates about the term "esoteric" in the field of Buddhist studies, none of which has led to a consensus about its definition; general confusion has been the result. Recent research about how the term has been used historically, however, has brought some clarity to the matter.[1] Its historical use aside, it is important to remember that this term is partly a product of modern academic imagination and interpretation.[2] With this in mind, in addition to its use to designate a particular kind of Buddhist tradition that began in India and then spread throughout South, Southeast, and East Asia, here I use "esoteric" to refer to a polemical strategy that was used extensively within Tendai and Shingon ritual discourses during the Japanese medieval period.[3] In this context, "esoteric" can also mean secret, superior, or both.[4]

Highly sophisticated Chinese theories about astral movements and a Chinese divinatory system served as a basis for Japanese Buddhist monks' own development of astrological rituals and iconography. Images of star deities appear in Japan as early as the eighth century, these being based on continental precedent.[5] Later on, star rituals were executed primarily in the Tendai and Shingon traditions, although there were some other religious professionals (e.g., *onmyōji* 陰陽師, who were experts in the so-called Way of Yin and Yang, Onmyōdō 陰陽道) who also dealt with interpretation and manipulation of stars and star deities. In the eleventh and twelfth centuries, new forms of star rituals and new star divinities emerged. Many of these were aimed at ensuring the longevity of the emperor and the stability of the realm, and esoteric ritual specialists competed with each other for court patronage. Each specialist argued for the superior efficacy and power of his deity or ritual.[6]

One of the most popular star deities during the medieval period was Myōken 妙見 (lit. "mysterious sight," Skt. *sudarśana*), also known as the bodhisattva Myōken (J. Myōken bosatsu 妙見菩薩).[7] Worship of this deity can be traced back to the eighth century. Myōken is the deification of Polaris (the polestar, J. *hokushin* 北辰), being a star in the constellation Ursa Minor (the Little Dipper, or Little Bear), but is also the deified form of the constellation Ursa Major (the Big Dipper, Great Bear, or Northern Dipper, J. *hokuto* 北斗). Following Chinese astrology, the Japanese believed that the polestar corresponds to the *tennō* 天皇 (the Japanese emperor), the highest order in the cosmos.[8] Accordingly, originally Myōken worship was dedicated to the veneration of the *tennō*, although later on Myōken acquired a diversity of roles and personality traits as he became more popular and as Myōken worship spread to other social strata.

Sonjōō and Myōken developed very similar functions. Both were associated with prolonging the life of the emperor, guarding against natural disasters, and protection of the nation.[9] But the Jimon's assertion of Sonjōō's superiority was based on its own unique arguments.[10] For instance, it asserted that Sonjōō was transmitted exclusively to the Jimon, seeing that it was Enchin, and Enchin alone, who encountered Sonjōō in China.[11] The Jimon also came up with explanations about the relationship between Myōken and Sonjōō. According to the Onjōji monk Keihan 慶範 (1155–1221), Sonjōō is called Myōken when he appears on earth, and Sonjōō when he appears in the heavens.[12] Emphasizing Sonjōō's uniquness, the Jimon asserted that he is not just the polestar but represents the entire cosmos. In other words, whereas other star cults focused on the polestar as the center of the universe, Sonjōō contains more than the polestar, extending the center in every direction. In this new configuration in which the polestar became one of the directional points, Sonjōō occupied the central position. According to this logic, Sonjōō stands at the center of the entire cosmos, and thereby becomes the *axis mundi*. This idea is also expressed in the rite of the deity in which the ritual combines a number of celestial deities into a single visualization of Sonjōō.[13]

Sonjōō's composite nature was due in part to this deity's role in sectarian rivalries and in part to the Jimon's strong ties with continental culture. As I explain later, rituals and iconography associated with Sonjōō contained elements from Onmyōdo and other Chinese religious traditions.[14] His identity was made even more complex by his identification with Shinra Myōjin.[15] The result of this accretion and transformation, driven by Jimon ritual specialists, was a composite deity whom the Jimon could claim as unique and superior to most other deities.

Echoing the emergence of Shinra Myōjin, scholars have suspected that the origins of Sonjōō are to be found in the Sanmon-Jimon split and the contentious rivalry that followed.[16] For example, Misaki Ryōshū argues that the Sonjōō ritual may have been created as a response to the Sanmon's development of a star ritual called the *Shijōkō hō* 熾盛光法 (Ritual of Blazing Lights). In a similar vein, Tsuda Tetsuei suggests that the Jimon monk Yokei was in part responsible for the creation of Sonjōō icons, and that Yokei was attempting to create a star deity for the Jimon.[17] Originating in Chinese Buddhism, the *Shijōkō hō* was the Sanmon's main star ritual, and it was first performed in Japan in 850 by Ennin, who conducted the ritual for Emperor Montoku 文徳 (r. 850–858). Just as the star ritual in China was performed for the longevity of the emperor, the *Shijōkō hō* in Japan started as a ritual for the same purpose. However, beginning around the time of the monk Ryōgen, use of this ritual expanded to the aristocracy, among whom it was used to cure illnesses and bring about a host of mundane benefits.[18] The Sonjōō ritual uses different symbols and deities but is very similar in function to the *Shijōkō hō*.[19] However, in what may have been an attempt to win patronage, the Jimon claimed that the Sonjōō ritual incorporated unique iconography and doctrinal interpretations. In the following section I turn to the details of the Sonjōō ritual.

THE RITUAL OF SONJŌŌ

From the eleventh to the thirteenth century, the ritual of Sonjōō thrived in the Jimon.[20] The earliest record of Sonjōō is found in the *Gonki* 権記, the diary of Fujiwara no Kōzei 藤原行成 (972–1028). Entries from 1006 and 1008 mention the performance of a ritual dedicated to Sonjōō that was called the *Sonjōkō hō* 尊星光法, a name very similar to that for the Sanmon star ritual.[21] Initially, the Sonjōō ritual was not exclusive to the Jimon but can instead be traced to Mt. Hiei. For instance, in 1093, the ritual was performed by Ryōi 良意, a priest of the Sanmon branch, suggesting that at the end of the eleventh century there were still at least some cases in which non-Jimon monks performed it.[22]

However, this example may be the exception that proves the rule, for the Jimon was already developing a monopoly on the ritual in the early eleventh century, and by the middle of the same century Sonjōō was associated almost exclusively with the Jimon and was thought of as a Jimon deity. Subsequent interest in Sonjōō and associated rituals on the part of retired emperors led to Sonjōō's rise and development into one of the Jimon's most prominent astral deities. The first shrine dedicated to him was built in 1080 in the northern quarters of the Onjōji complex, near the Shinra Myōjin Shrine. The Fujiwara descendant and Onjōji monk Ryūmyō 隆明 (1020–1104) then secured for the shrine the status of imperially designated temple (J. *goganji* 御願寺) from the emperor Shirakawa.

Sonjōō helped the Jimon strengthen its ties with the retired emperors. Retired emperors Gotoba 後鳥羽 (r. 1183–1198) and Goshirakawa (r. 1155–1158) turned to the Jimon's star ritual after prayers to Myōken were not successful. For example, according to the *Asabashō*, a Tendai ritual compendium, the Gotoba made an offering to Myōken at Byōdōin 平等院 of Onjōji (currently Enman'in 円満院) and had Buddhist masters perform a ritual in which Myōken was asked to cure the emperor's eye disease.[23] Initially a monk from Enryakuji performed the rite. However, halfway through, the emperor had the Enryakuji monk terminate the Myōken ritual prematurely and replaced him with an Onjōji monk, who proceeded to perform a Sonjōō ritual. The shift from the Enryakuji monk's Myōken ritual to the Onjōji monk's Sonjōō ritual was a defining moment for the ritual's acceptance as an imperial rite.

One figure central to the development of the Sonjōō ritual was the Onjōji monk Keihan. Initially the ritual was transmitted orally as a sort of secret transmission (J. *kuden* 口伝).[24] Keihan, however, recorded the details of the Sonjōō ritual as he had learned it from his master, Shin'en 真圓,[25] and included this account in the *Secret Record of Treasure* (J. *Hōhiki* 宝秘記, early Kamakura period).[26] Keihan's knowledge of Sonjōō was known outside Onjōji circles as well. A Shingon Buddhist text called the *Myōken zasshū* 妙見雑集 included the following passage, in which Keihan explains Sonjōō's identity, function, and iconography.

> According to Keihan: "Someone says that every school has its own secret rituals. Each one has a secret oral transmission and secret mudras. But why do the followers of this particular ritual [of Sonjōō] claim that it is superior to others? . . . I [Keihan] am the one who inherited the ritual that the master Enchin transmitted. Other sects do not know it and therefore this is a secret ritual of the [Jimon] school. First of all, Sonjōō is Myōken. Myōken is enshrined because [this deity] illuminates the four cardinal directions of the capital. . . . When Myōken appears in the heaven he is called Sonjōō, whereas when he

> appears [not in the heavens], he is called Myōken. . . . The master Enchin learned about Sonjōō when he was studying in Tang China. The knowledge was only transmitted to the master. This is why the Sonjōō ritual surpasses other schools' [rituals]. Sonjōō means that the deity is the Revered King among all stars: the Seven Stars, the Nine Luminaries, the Twenty-eight Lunar Mansions, and the Twelve Zodiacal Constellations. The deity is called 'Sonjōō' because it includes every star. When the deity appears in the sky, it is astral, but when it appears on the earth, it is the Five Elements: Wood, Fire, Earth, Metal, and Water. The Sixty Deities of the sexagenary cycle and the Four [Cardinal] Deities (the Blue Dragon, the White Tiger, etc.) are all Sonjōō. This is why during the ritual, one can see the four groups of deities, the sixty deities, and so on. Sonjōō manifests in different forms. Therefore, the deity is flanked by the White Tiger on his right and the Blue Dragon on his left, while standing on the Tortoise."[27]

As the ritual of "pacifying and protecting the nation" (J. *chingō kokka* 鎮護国家),[28] as it is called in the *Myōken zasshū*, the Sonjōō ritual was performed for various reasons, such as for the emperor's longevity, recovery of ill court members, and safe childbirth for the women of the Fujiwara family. The earliest record of a link between Sonjōō and childbirth dates to the Fujiwara empress's delivery of the future emperor Goichijō 後一条天皇 (r. 1016–1036) in 1006.[29] The *Sanchōki* 三長記, the diary of Fujiwara no Nagakane 藤原長兼 (fl. twelfth c.), records an occurance of the ritual in 1195. It was performed for the safe childbirth of Emperor Gotoba's pregnant consort Kujō Ninshi 九条任子 (1173–1239). In the ritual, the *Heart Sutra* and the *Sutra on the Comparison of Life Spans* (J. *Kakuryō jumyō kyō* 較量壽命經; Skt. *Āyuṣparyanta Sūtra*) were recited. After that, Sonjōō was invoked and other esoteric rituals were also performed, including the ritual for the Five Wisdom Kings (J. *Godan hō* 五壇法); the ritual for the Seven Medicine Buddhas (J. *Shichi butsu Yakushi hō* 七仏薬師法, which was a specialty of the Sanmon); the ritual for Aizen (J. *Aizenō hō* 愛染王法); the ritual for Aizen and the wish-fulfilling jewel (J. *Nyohō Aizenō hō* 如法愛染王法); and the ritual for the *Kujaku-kyō* 孔雀經 (J. *Kujaku-kyō hō* 孔雀經法).[30]

The Kujō women continued to be the main sponsors and beneficiaries of the Sonjōō ritual when it was performed for ensuring safe delivery. In 1218, for example, the Onjōji monk Kōen 公縁 (1174–1261) received the support of empresses from the Kujō family to make copies of the *Hōhiki*, which were then presented to Kujō Ninshi 九条任子 (1173–1238, the empress of Emperor Juntoku 順徳, r. 1210–1221), and Kujō Ryūshi 九条立子 (1192–1248).[31] The ritual was also performed for the young children of the Kujō family. In 1227, for instance, the Sonjōō fire ritual (J. *goma* 護摩) was performed for the nine-year-old Fujiwara no Yoritsune 藤原頼経 (1218–1256) when he became ill.[32]

Because of Sonjōō's association with females and childbirth, this deity was often perceived as female. The *Hōhiki* states that as Sonjōō is a female deity, a mirror was used for her ritual just as a mirror is used for the Kichijōten 吉祥天 ritual.[33] During the ritual, musk was placed next to the mirror.[34] This information was known to the Shingon masters as well. In the *Kakuzenshō* 覚禅鈔 (1198), for instance, it states: "Sonjōō is a female deity (J. *nyoten* 女天). Therefore, a mirror and musk are offered to the deity."[35]

Further strengthening this female identity is the identification of Sonjōō as Kannon 観音.[36] In the *Hōhiki*, we find a passage in which the powerful Fujiwara aristocrat Kujō Kanezane 九条兼実 (1149–1207, also known as Fujiwara no Kanezane) asks the Onjōji monk Shin'en about Sonjōō's identity and this deity's relationship to Kannon. The conversation between Kujō Kanezane and Shin'en occurred in 1195, around the time when Shin'en was invited to perform the ritual:

Kanezane's question:	"Which bodhisattva is Sonjōō?"
Shin'en's answer:	"It is Kannon."
Kanezane:	"Why Kannon? . . . Why is the deity also known as Fukūkensaku 不空羂索?"
Shin'en:	"It is because Sonjōō wears a deer-crown. It matches perfectly with Fukūkensaku, who wears the skin of deer."
Kanezane was deeply satisfied and commented:	"I realize that the *dhāraṇī* of [Fukūkensaku] Kannon is used because Fukūkensaku protects the Fujiwara family."[37]

There are two points to note in this dialogue. One is Sonjōō's identification as Fukūkensaku Kannon (the Bodhisattva of Compassion with the Never-empty Noose), and the other is the ritual's symbolic connection to the Fujiwara family. The Jimon had developed a long-standing tradition of the cult of the bodhisattva Kannon.[38] The Kannon cult was adopted very early on at Onjōji. The Jimon monks also played an essential role in the creation of a pilgrimage circuit for Kannon in the Saikoku 西国 region after Kannon pilgrimages increased in popularity in the tenth century.[39]

In addition, Sonjōō's identification with Fukūkensaku Kannon reflects the Jimon's aspiration to retain close political ties with the Fujiwara clan. This identification, and the inclusion of a deer-crown in Sonjōō's iconography, are not accidental, but a strategic and politically charged depiction.[40] As Shin'en explains, the deer represents the manifestation of Kasuga 春日 Myōjin, the patron deity of the Fujiwara clan. Fukūkensaku Kannon is also known to protect the Fujiwara clan. It is because of this relationship that the Fujiwara promoted Fukūkensaku Kannon's association with the deity of the Kasuga Shrine in Nara.[41] The deer is ever-present in the iconography of Fukūkensaku Kannon; Fukūkensaku Kannon is often portrayed seated on a deer or with a deerskin covering her shoulders.[42] The mythological and iconographical association between Sonjōō and Fukūkensaku Kannon suggests that the Jimon's creation and development of Sonjōō was done in part for the Kujō clan, and that in making this move the Jimon hoped to maintain the strong ties between the Jimon and the Kujō family.[43]

THE ICONOGRAPHY OF SONJŌŌ

Images of Sonjōō exhibit interesting aspects about the deity. The Jimon's legend traced the origin of the icon to Enchin, who is supposed to have acquired the statue of Sonjōō from Faquan at Qinglongsi in China. Along with many other items, he stored the statue in the Tōin at Onjōji.[44] Although it shows strong Chinese influence, some scholars have suggested that the image is in fact a Japanese invention.[45] One problem is that it is not known when the image was first created.[46] The oldest extant example of the Sonjōō mandala (J. Sonjōō mandara 尊星王曼荼羅) is a monochrome drawing from the late Heian period that appears in the *Besson zakki* 別尊雑記 (Miscellaneous notes on Buddhist images other than the Buddha), a twelfth-century collection of Buddhist iconography compiled by Shinkaku 心覚 (1117–1180) (figure 6).[47]

In this mandala, Sonjōō appears with different animals, constellations, and talismans. As the polestar, he occupies the center, riding on a dragon, an animal that symbolizes the emperor. Surrounding Sonjōō in the outer of the three circles are seven animals representing the stars of the Big Dipper. While Sonjōō symbolizes the emperor, these seven animals or stars behind the deity represent his consorts.[48] The animals include an elephant, a white fox, and numerous three-legged black crows. Each animal is paired with either the sun disc (e.g., with the three-legged crows) or the moon disc (e.g., with the three rabbits), indicating their astral functions. In this and other images, Sonjōō holds the sun and the moon, one in each hand. This composition—the stars (the Big Dipper), the sun, and the moon—is a recurring visual pattern found in other star rituals.[49] Here, the star represents the celestial power of the sovereign,[50] while the Big Dipper signifies his symbolic role as the cosmic axis. The Sonjōō ritual incorporates this idea by including three types of mudra (J. *san'in* 三印), or hand gestures: the mudra of Sonjōō and the mudras for the sun and moon.[51]

In between these animals there are six talismans suggesting the influence of the worship of Chintaku reifujin 鎮宅霊符神, the astral deity who was said to transmit the seventy-two astral talismans to Japan.[52] In the middle circle different constellations are depicted, and in the inner circle we see another set of six talismans. If we count the total number of talismans—six on the outermost rim, and another six small ones in the center—we have twelve in all. The twelve talismans very possibly symbolize Sonjōō's power of expelling demons over the course of the twelve months, that is, during the entire year.

Figure 7 is a Kamakura-period representation of Sonjōō in which he and various animals are presented in a more enigmatic manner. Similar to the earlier Heian-period example, Sonjōō is situated in the middle, in front of three concentric rings.

FIGURE 6. Sonjōō (Myōken), *Besson zakki*, late Heian period, ink, color on paper. Ninnaji, Kyoto.

The deity has four arms, and each arm holds a different attribute: his upper-right hand holds a sun disc with a three-legged black crow inside; his upper-left hand holds a moon disc with a rabbit and frog inside; his lower-right hand holds a trident (J. *gekihoko* 戟鉾); and finally, in his lower-left hand, he holds a staff with metal rings (J. *shakujō* 錫杖). As the supreme star in the sky, he wears a crown that is embellished with a deer head complete with antlers. He stands on a moon disc and a dragon. The shape of the dragon's body mimics the Big Dipper, with Sonjōō representing the polestar at the center of the three concentric circles. Taken together, this presents us with a mandalic vision of the entire cosmos.

The symbolism of the animals that appear in the outer rim is perhaps the most perplexing element. These animals are a panther (or leopard), a tiger, a white fox, an elephant, and a deer. The first three animals—panther, tiger, and fox—represent

FIGURE 7. Sonjōō mandara, Kamakura period, colors on silk. Hōmyōin, Onjōji, Shiga Prefecture.

three constellations that protect the northeast: Kishuku 箕宿, Bishuku 尾宿, and Shinshuku 心宿, respectively.[53] The northeast is commonly referred to as the demon gate (J. *kimon* 鬼門), the direction from which the most harmful spirits come, and the aforementioned three divinities were thought to protect humans from this menacing direction. After the transmission of Indian astrology and Chinese geomancy to Japan via esoteric Buddhism, it came to be popularly believed that foxes are particularly adept at protecting one from the evil influences of the northeast. The elephant is included here due to its association with the bodhisattva Fugen 普賢. Fugen is often associated with the northeast and is commonly depicted atop an elephant.[54] Indeed, Fugen is invoked in the mantra known as Long Life Fugen (J. *Enmei Fugen* 延命普賢), which is recited during the Sonjōō ritual.[55]

To complete our understanding of the visual program presented here I want to explain the deer depicted above Sonjōō, as well as above a sun and a moon disc at the very top. As mentioned previously, the deer is a messenger of the Fujiwara clan's tutelary deity (the Kasuga deity), and is thus a symbol of the Fujiwara clan itself. Here the deer may also be a symbol for the Daoist quest for immortality. One of the ways to achieve immortality was to obtain the mushroom of immortality, the so-called marvelous fungus (Ch. *lingzhi* 靈芝), which can take all kinds of extraordinary forms and which is closely associated with the deer.[56] Another possible link is seen in the *Nihon ryōiki*, a collection of Buddhist tales.[57] Three of the tales concern Myōken, and in two of these Myōken transforms himself into a deer.

All of these suggest that in the Sonjōō mandara the deer operates at different yet related levels of symbolism. On the one hand, it points to the Sonjōō ritual's role in creating a political tie to the Fujiwara clan, while on the other it suggests longevity and immortality, both of which are broader symbolic associations with the deer and both of which are results that the Sonjōō ritual is supposed to bring about.

I now want to analyze another Sonjōō image in the *Zuzōshō* 図像抄 (figure 8), the encyclopedia of Buddhist icons edited by Ejū 恵什 (1060–1145) at Ninnaji 仁和寺. There are a few noticeable differences between the first two types of Sonjōō images I have already discussed and this image. In this example, Sonjōō's two upper arms hold the sun and the moon discs, which suggests his role as a cosmic lord. In his two lower arms, however, the deity holds a brush and a karma record book, emphasizing his function as a god of destiny who records people's deeds and governs one's life span. This role of Sonjōō is duplicated in the representation of his two acolytes: one with a benevolent appearance, almost identical to Sonjōō, and the other with a wrathful appearance, both of whom possibly suggest their role as emissaries who report good and evil deeds. Indicating their role as assistants to Sonjōō, the one on the right holds a paper and the one to Sonjōō's left holds an inkstone. The most unfathomable feature in both types of Sonjōō icon that I have discussed so far is the position of his legs and feet: standing on one leg on the moon disc or sometimes just being carried by a dragon. In the next section I turn to these postures and their cross-cultural significance.

SKYWALKER: THE RITUAL STEPS OF SONJŌŌ

Chinese astrological knowledge played a key role in shaping the ritual symbolism of Sonjōō. The Big Dipper, which occupies the highest order in Chinese astrological theories, is central in this process of transforming Sonjōō into the ruler of human destiny.[58] The Big Dipper is composed of nine stars: the visible seven and two minor or invisible ones: Auxiliary Star (the eighth, Ch. Fuxing 輔星) and Adjuvant Star (the ninth, Ch. Bixing 弼星). While the seven stars of the Dipper are known to govern prenatal life,[59] the two minor stars were perceived as equally powerful in the Japanese esoteric Buddhist tradition, as they were thought to be the hidden source of longevity.[60] The eighth and ninth stars are essential elements for the Daoist ritual of "walking on" (or "walking among" or "strolling among") the stars of the Big Dipper (Ch. *bugang tadou* 步罡踏斗) as well.[61] It was believed that if the person performing this Daoist ritual dance saw these invisible stars then his or her life would be prolonged by three hundred or even six hundred years.[62]

This idea of the Daoist ritual dance (Ch. *bugang* 步罡) seems to be closely related to Sonjōō's leg posture, which mirrors a Chinese ritual called the Pace of Yu (Ch.

FIGURE 8. Sonjōō in the *Zuzōshō*, thirteenth to fourteenth c., colors on silk. Kanazawa Bunko (Shōmyōji), Yokohama.

yubu 禹歩). The Pace of Yu can be traced back to the legendary Chinese ruler Yu the Great (Ch. Dayu 大禹) of the Xia 夏 dynasty (ca. 2070–ca. 1600 BCE). In Chinese myth Yu is credited with taming a flood, and his ability to control water was further reinforced by his close association with dragons.[63] There are several stories in which dragons assisted Yu, either by dredging out river channels with their tails or by carrying him across rivers.[64] The reason why Yu stands on one leg—later known as the Pace of Yu—is because during the battle in which he tamed the flood, he was paralyzed on one side (Ch. *pianku* 偏枯). After this, it is said that he was only able to move with a hopping gait. The Nine Steps of the Pace of Yu, as found in Daoist tradition, entails a sort of hopping. The ritual was performed to protect travelers and to cure diseases. The instructions state that the ritual must be performed using a specific and different *dhāraṇī* for each step, while the practitioner stands on the left leg with the right foot raised behind the left knee.[65] It was thought that when enacting Yu's steps, the performer's body transformed into a point of contact with Yu and merged with both Yu and the Way (Ch. *dao* 道).

In the Japanese Onmyōdō tradition Yu's Steps are known as *uho* 禹歩, or sometimes *henbai* 反閇, which indicates the trampling of the ground in order to drive off evil.[66] The prescribed steps of this ritual were transmitted to Japan and became particularly popular in the Japanese Onmyōdō tradition during the late Heian period.[67] This Onmyōdō practice was then incorporated into images of, and rituals focused on, Sonjōō. According to the *Asabashō*, "There is a secret ritual of Miidera known as the Sonjōō ritual. . . . It is not performed in Shingon. Its technique relies on the Onmyōdō."[68] The Onmyōdō technique that *Asabashō* is referring to here seems to be the ritual steps of Sonjōō.

Besides the ritual steps, other religious symbolism of Sonjōō clearly drew on the legends of Yu. For instance, in China myths about Yu led to the so-called Yu's placenta burial method, or *yuzang* 禹藏. This practice entailed burying a newborn's placenta in a certain direction so that the child would enjoy a long life, and its existence is confirmed by a discovery at King Ma's Mound (Ch. Mawangdui 馬王堆), an early Western Han archeological site.[69] According to the archeological findings, before burying placentas, people consulted a diagram that showed different positions and directions in which it could be buried, each of which corresponded to an astrological birth star.[70] The underlying idea here was that the placenta is a newborn baby's double. An auspicious positioning of the placenta would ensure that the related constellation would protect the child.[71] This emphasis on protecting newborn children is found in the Sonjōō ritual, for the latter is also concerned with the protection of children insofar as Sonjōō is prayed to for the safe delivery of the imperial prince and for the longevity of the future emperor. While the Sonjōō ritual developed far from China and much later, its use of the Pace of Yu indicates that the two rituals are functionally related to each other.

Sonjōō's association with continental religious symbolism can also be seen in the identification of this deity with Shinra Myōjin. In the Jimon tradition, Shinra Myōjin is said to have come to Japan to safeguard the Sonjōō ritual. According to the *Onjōji denki*:

> In the [*Lotus*] *Sutra*, Senju Kannon entered the ocean. The bodhisattva preached to the Nāga girl and named her Bodhisattva Suisei 水精. The secret mantra of Bodhisattva Suisei is (This is the very mantra of Kudokuten [i.e., Kichijōten]. This is also the mantra of Sonjōō): "*Maka shiri-ei chiri-bei sowaka.*" The deity [Shinra Myōjin]'s *honji* is Mañjuśrī. He is the third prince of the Nāga King Sāgara 娑竭羅, as well as the brother of the Nāga girl. This explains why Shinra Myōjin manifests himself for the ritual of Sonjōō. It is why the master, Enchin, transmitted the ritual of Sonjōō. . . .
>
> According to the opening chapter of the *Lotus Sutra*, Bodhisattva Mañjuśrī is in fact the Bodhisattva Avalokiteśvara. These two correspond to Shinra Myōjin and Sonjōō, respectively. When Shinra Myōjin and Sonjōō are put in a line, the shape of the two matches perfectly. This is why Shinra Myōjin and Sonjōō are identical. Sonjōō is in fact none other than the female deity Kichijōten. When [the two deities] are put back to back, [Sonjōō] is none other than Senju Kannon and [Shinra Myōjin] is the Tenbōrin 轉法輪 bodhisattva. Therefore, the *mudrā* of the Senju [Kannon] is performed. In this back-to-back form, Shinra Myōjin holds his staff in his hand and Sonjōō holds a staff while Kudokuten 功德天 [or Kichijōten] holds her one-thousand-hands *mudrā*.[72]

This text provides a doctrinal link between Sonjōō and Shinra Myōjin by applying a loose interpretation of Avalokiteśvara as he appears in the *Lotus Sutra*. The passage explains that Shinra Myōjin is the protector of the Sonjōō ritual while he is also none other than Sonjōō. This association consolidates each deity's esoteric power through mutual promotion. Shinra Myōjin's identification with Sonjōō suggests the Jimon's desire to appropriate continental religious symbolism and ritual knowledge in their own way. This is how Sonjōō reveals the medieval Jimon monks' rediscovery of continental mythology and astrological knowledge, and their adoption of existing local practices from the Myōken cults of other esoteric Buddhist schools, Onmyōdō, and the worship of Shinra Myōjin.

By unpacking the symbolism of Sonjōō, we see that the case of Sonjōō exemplifies how new esoteric deities were created through the reimagining and reorganizing of ancient continental mythology that circulated among Japan's religious elites. As many scholars have noted, from the Insei period onward, secrecy was a central element of Japanese religion.[73] In the case of the Sonjōō ritual, the Jimon used secrets as a form of symbolic capital; secrecy can be "best understood as a strategy for concealing and revealing information," an approach that makes that information scarcer and thus superior.[74] Mark Teeuwen has suggested that, when it comes to "knowing versus owning a secret," what matters is not the content of the secret, but rather possession of the secret. According to this view, the ownership of secrets can be secured through formal transmission, a system that allows for control of both the production and the management of secrets.[75] This use of secrecy helps to explain how Jimon ritual specialists managed the secrets and power of the Sonjōō ritual. Due to the nature of secrecy in esoteric ritual, the ritual's details were not known outside of the Jimon circle, although Jimon clerics were tactful enough to let others be aware of the existence of the ritual as a way to acquire social capital.[76] The paradox of non-secret secrets allowed the ritual to become known as the Jimon's most secretive star ritual.

The Sonjōō ritual enjoyed significant popularity, especially during the Insei period, when this culture of secrecy began to take hold in both the religious and the secular domains.[77] This period witnessed an increased interest in esoteric rituals on the part of courtiers, and esoteric Buddhist schools developed secret oral transmissions as a way to build their authority, distinguish themselves from one another, and build their symbolic capital. The case of Sonjōō specifically demonstrates how a specialized ritual and celestial knowledge came to be used as a way of negotiating and extending religious authority. Ultimately, devotional practices focused on Sonjōō and Shinra Myōjin were aimed at meeting the Jimon's need for political leverage and institutional independence.

This chapter has illustrated the development of the Sonjōō ritual in the Jimon. Sectarian rivalry partly provided an impetus for the growth of the deity. However, the creation of Sonjōō itself was a direct response to the complex political, social, and religious situations that the Jimon faced during the Insei period. Unlike Myōken, whose cult was open to believers of all stripes, Sonjōō was confined to imperial rites. The narrowly confined role that this deity played and the secrecy surrounding his ritual explains in part why Sonjōō enjoyed such immense power. But because of its exclusive focus on the imperial line, the deity was destined to be short-lived and did not spread beyond the Jimon circle.

More broadly, Sonjōō worship at Onjōji demonstrates the Jimon's position in the process of "esotericization" that transformed Japanese Buddhism. By using continental religious elements, the Jimon was able to eventually establish Sonjōō as one of the most distinctive and esoteric star deities of medieval Japanese Buddhism. In the development of Tendai esoteric teachings (J. *taimitsu* 台密),[78] the significance of the Jimon has been overlooked in previous scholarship. Incorporating more esoteric doctrinal interpretations, rituals, and iconography, the Jimon managed to create a symbiotic relationship with the regime in power and therefore enjoyed great political influence.

Chapter 6

Shinra Myōjin as a Pestilence Deity

Susanoo and Shinra Myōjin

This chapter examines Shinra Myōjin's association with Susanoo and, more broadly, with epidemics. The transmission of infectious diseases was one of the downsides of exchange between human populations in the East Asian Mediterranean. Devastating and mysterious, epidemics have helped shape religious, political, social, and mythological thought, and indeed they were a central feature of the long history of exchange, especially between Korea and Japan. From early on, the Japanese regarded Silla as the country from which pestilence came.[1] It was due to this association between Silla and disease that during the medieval period Shinra Myōjin came to be a deity of pestilence within the Onjōji tradition. The link between Shinra Myōjin and epidemics persisted in collective memory but remained unexpressed as a sort of "latent reserve,"[2] which somehow reemerged in the form of myth, and eventually materialized as devotional practices focused on the deity of Silla. The outcome was the belief that Shinra Myōjin could control epidemics. But how did the association between Silla and epidemics become a subverting force with regard to Shinra Myōjin? How do different layers of mythological narrative invent, appropriate, and contest the historical "reality"?

The concept of *imaginaire* provides a useful framework for helping us understand how the Japanese image of Silla evolved and influenced the cult of Shinra Myōjin. Jacques Le Goff suggests that *imaginaire* can be applied as a category of historical inquiry for the study of medieval culture.[3] Building upon his idea and following Bernard Faure's use of this concept for the study of religion,[4] I here define *imaginaire* as a large network of images comprising two modalities that vacillate between resilient, perceived images and fluid perceptions. Shinra Myōjin emerged from this imagined perception of Silla, complete with a central contradiction: on the one hand he is a deity who can cure pestilence, but on the other he is a deity who causes it.

In trying to understand the complex relationship between Shinra Myōjin and Silla in the Japanese medieval *imaginaire*, studies on cultural memory and its derivative concept, cultural imagination, provide valuable insights.[5] While Jan Assmann's treatment of "cultural memory" deals with actual vestiges and historical dimensions of memory, an invented or imagined deity like Shinra Myōjin requires us to look at another dimension of memory, namely the *imaginaire*, in the collective sense. Recent studies in cultural anthropology have focused on the role of *imaginaire* in diverse social and cultural contexts—from the intimate arenas of subjective experience to the more encompassing vistas of cosmological contemplation. In a similar fashion, looking at myth can shed new light on the way in which people express the *imaginaire*. The association between Shinra Myōjin and epidemics was established through the use of texts, icons, rituals, and, more than anything else, myth. Myths serve as cultural repositories not only by preserving specific ideas and practices but also by providing a wider scope for the evolution of imagination.

Deities associated with Silla were often identified as gods of pestilence, Shinra Myōjin, Susanoo, and Gozu Tennō 牛頭天王 being three such examples. Susanoo, one of the major *kami* from classical Japanese mythology is another "Silla" god who played a pivotal role in cementing the association between Silla and pestilence. The pairing between Shinra Myōjin and Susanoo was carefully chosen during a period characterized by new configurations of and connections between buddhas and *kami*. According to the *Onjōji denki*, "Shinra Myōjin became a king of Silla in order to wield Japanese power all over the world."[6] This passage displays an interesting ideological twist, for here Shinra Myōjin is not a god from Silla but a god who manifested himself in Silla in order to exercise Japanese power. With the connection between Shinra Myōjin and Susanoo established, Shinra Myōjin could become an autochthonous deity who appeared in Silla in order to conquer the kingdom. Shinra Myōjin's identification with Gozu Tennō, the archetypal pestilence god of the medieval Japanese pantheon, was part of a complex web of historical consciousness and cultural imagination.[7] What is significant in the network of "Silla gods" is that, through their individual connections to Silla, they reinforced each other's association with it and strengthened the perception of Silla as a land of pestilence.

SILLA IN THE MEDIEVAL JAPANESE BUDDHIST CONTEXT

Before I turn to medieval Japanese perceptions of Silla, I first want to spend a moment on the Buddhist transmission through the three kingdoms (J. *sangoku bukkyō shikan*), for by the Kamakura period this model had become the dominant view of history and of the known world, and it is of central relevance to our understanding of Shinra Myōjin.[8] This model identified India, China, and Japan as the three sacred Buddhist lands.[9] Here, "India" (J. Tenjiku 天竺) referred originally to the land of the Buddha, but also to the world outside the Sino-Japanese sphere. "China" (J. Shintan 振旦) was the Chinese cultural world, including Korean kingdoms; and "Japan" was referred to as "our court" (J. *honchō* 本朝).[10]

The marginalization of "Korea" in this model is key to understanding the ambivalent character of Shinra Myōjin. By intentionally eliminating Korean Buddhism, Japan could position itself as the apex of Buddhism's development and secure a position of greater legitimacy. The adoption of this model was, in fact, both a result of and a response to the tensions involved in overcoming the cultural complex that resulted from existing at the geographical margins of the Buddhist world and of Chinese civilization. On the one hand, Japanese clerics were aware of how far they were geographically from India, the original land of Buddhism, while on the other hand the Japanese had always existed in the shadow of China and its technological and cultural achievements.[11]

From the latter half of the Heian period onward, Japanese Buddhists tended toward a pessimistic view of Japan as being distant in both time and space from Buddhism's source, the historical Buddha who had lived in India. By the Kamakura period, it had become widely accepted that Japan was a marginal country on the outskirts of the Buddhist world. Whereas India and China were clearly defined by the three-kingdoms model, Silla and the other Korean kingdoms were not. This made Silla both a problem and a solution. By folding Silla into the Sinitic world, Japan could not only reduce the physical and temporal gap between itself and China, but also conveniently forget the fact that the Japanese had received Buddhism and continental culture in large part from Korean kingdoms. Furthermore, this exclusion allowed Japan to be depicted as the orthodox center of Buddhism. As such, they vacillated between being "equal" and "superior" to China and India. With their comprehensive knowledge of the transmission of Buddhism and about the world in general, scholar-monks were active in promoting this idea from a relatively early period, as is evident in the writings of the monk Gomyō 護命 (750–834) from the Hata clan (ironically, the immigrant clan from Silla) and those of the Tendai priest Annen 安然 (841–?).[12]

The three-kingdoms model held sway not only in the quasi-historical writings of Buddhist ideologues but also in the realm of mythology in connection with the *honji suijaku* ideology.[13] The phrase "manifestations of the three kingdoms" was used to explain the origins of foreign deities by anachronistically dissolving the temporal and spatial distances between India, China, and Japan. By using stories that linked Japanese deities to China and India, this model made those deities legitimate in Buddhist eyes. Though this model drew a distinction between foreign and indigenous, it also conveniently blurred and even dissolved it, as seen in the case of Shinra Myōjin.

A key concept in the transformation of seemingly foreign deities (J. *ikoku no kami* 異国の神) into native ones was the notion of "landlord deity" (J. *jinushigami*). *Jinushigami* is a deity born from the soil, an autochthonous god associated with a particular area or piece of land. In Japanese religions, it is not uncommon for a deity of foreign origin to become the landlord deity of a certain place, which can take the form of a replacement or an "upgrade." In this ideological twist, gods of seemingly foreign origin, such as Shinra Myōjin, became landlord deities who were then depicted as having been there from time immemorial. Their apparent foreignness was explained by stating that they had traveled or temporarily manifested themselves in foreign lands, such as Silla. According to this logic, Shinra Myōjin—who did not fit neatly into in the three-kingdoms model—became a legitimate Japanese deity who, like Susanoo, traveled to Silla in order to exercise Japanese power.[14]

Even employing this logic, Jimon monks were still hard-pressed to explain Shinra Myōjin's association with Silla. To solve the dilemma, they first attempted to explain why Shinra Myōjin contained "Silla" in his name. The very beginning of the *Jimon denki horoku* states that Silla is the country from which Shinra Myōjin came:

> Silla is the name of a vassal country (J. *hankoku* 藩国). It is located to the northwest of Japan (J. Wa 倭). It is one of the Three Han States. . . . Among the three Han states there is Ma Han 馬韓 located in the west and consisting of fifty-four tribes. On the northern frontier, it adjoins Nang'rang 樂浪, and on the south it shares a border with Japan. The other one is Jin Han 辰韓, located on the eastern side. It comprises twelve tribes. Its northern side borders Yemek 濊貊. It is also called Jin Han 秦韓, because Jin 秦 (J. Hata) people fled to Silla and integrated. The last one is Pyŏn Han 辨韓. This state is next to Jin Han, and it consists of twelve tribes. Its southern part borders Japan. . . . Silla used to be Jin Han.[15]

This passage seems to be in accord with the history and geography of the Korean kingdoms.[16] It is interesting to see this compiler's attempt to establish a historical connection between Shina Myōjin and the ancient Korean kingdom of Silla. What is more intriguing is the way in which the position of Silla in the traditional three-kingdoms model was negotiated. On the one hand, Silla is merely a foreign vassal country; but, on the other, it has to be more significant as Shinra Myōjin is associated with it. To solve the dilemma, the Jimon theorists altered the traditional India-China-Japan framework by inserting Silla, all the while emphasizing that it is not the "foreign" Silla but the "familiar" Silla that the Japanese deity Susanoo visited.

This idea is also found in the following passage, in which Shinra Myōjin's various names are explained in the *Onjōji denki*. According to the text, Shinra Myōjin is also called Sūgoku 崧嶽 (var. Sūkaku takaki), Sūshisu 菘崧, Shusan'ō 朱山王, Shitenfujin 四天夫人 (or 天夫人), and Suhatsu hoshikashi 素髮ホシカシ (possibly a misspelling of *hoshikami* 星神, meaning "star deity").[17] Concerning the five different names for Shinra Myōjin, the *Jimon denki horoku* expounds that "The name Sūgoku was the name of the deity when it resided at Mt. Song in China, and Sūshisu was its name when it resided in Silla. As for the peculiar name Shitenfujin, it corresponds to the name Mikō 未考 (Kor. Migo) and the deity was called by this name when it was in Silla. Finally, the deity was called Suhatsu when it appeared at sea, and in such instances the deity was in fact a *suijaku* or provisional manifestation of Susanoo."[18] The passage does not include Shinra Myōjin's manifestation in India. However, another section in the *Onjōji denki* recounts that Shinra Myōjin appeared in India in the guise of Benzaiten.[19]

Significantly, all of Shinra Myōjin's names are phonetic variations of Susanoo—that is, they are semiotic operations meant to establish a strong mythological connection between Susanoo and Shinra Myōjin. In the world of medieval mythology, a typical way to create an association between two deities was to introduce the hidden name of one of them. Using this logic, Shinra Myōjin became both a foreign and a native god, with the "Silla" in the deity's name no longer being a problem. I shall next delve into this mythological equation between Shinra Myōjin and Susanoo, as it proves crucial for understanding Shinra Myōjin's association with epidemics.

FROM "A GOD OF SILLA" TO "A GOD WHO CONQUERED SILLA"

Japan's ambivalent attitude toward Silla can best be described as an oscillation between reverence and reaction. Throughout the medieval period, Silla remained the "closest other" in Japanese historical consciousness from as early as the emergence of legends of the female ruler Jingū kōgō's 神功皇后 invasion of Silla. In contrast to this, Paekche, another Korean kingdom from the period and a political rival of Silla, was an ally of the Yamato court.[20] Silla's conquest of Paekche in 660 CE, and the Yamato court's failure to aid Paekche, caused further tension between the now-unified Korean Peninsula and the Yamato court.[21] Japan's aversion toward Silla was not only politically motivated but was also partially a matter of culture. After absorbing continental civilization and advanced technologies transmitted through Paekche, the Yamato court was faced with the task of establishing its own political stability and cultural identity.

The ninth century was a turning point in cementing Japan's image of Silla as a place of disorder. During this period, the unified Silla kingdom started to wane, and the Korean Peninsula entered a new period of transition known as the Later Three Kingdoms (892–936 CE). Because of unrest during this time, Silla pirates flourished, and piracy on the Japanese coast—particularly in northern Kyushu—increased dramatically, which consequently led to intense Japanese animosity toward Silla pirates. This negative perception was further exacerbated by a series of events, including a Silla immigrant uprising in 820 and its attempt to attack Tsushima.[22] At this point Japan halted all formal relations with Silla. A series of epidemics that broke out following contact with Silla merchants was another major factor leading to the cessation of diplomatic relations and to the negative perception of Silla.[23] Japan further blamed Silla for various calamities: natural disasters such as earthquakes came to be linked with Silla piracy, and the Silla pirates were even blamed for volcanic activity in Japan. In this way, foreign threats were placed in the same class of phenomena as natural calamities, and both were viewed as being dangerous eruptions of chaos.

Japanese anti-Silla sentiment, which was widespread in the ninth century, re-emerged on a larger scale and in a different form in the thirteenth century. Military encounters with Yuan China such as the Battle of Bun'ei (J. Bun'ei no eki 文永の役) in 1274 and the Battle of Kōan (J. Kōan no eki 弘安の役) in 1281 provided the impetus for Japan to remain vigilant and reaffirm its collective resentment toward foreign invaders.[24] These battles were initiated by the Mongols. But as the Koryŏ dynasty (918–1392) was under the control of the Mongols and the Korean naval forces were mobilized against Japan at this time, the Korean kingdom was seen as threatening the divine kingdom (J. *shinkoku*) of Japan.[25]

The notion of Japan being a *shinkoku* first surfaced during the early Heian period and matured in the medieval period. The idea was that Japan is a sacred land and that its inhabitants share the divine nature of both their emperor and the *kami* protecting the country. The belief that Japan is the land of *kami* goes back to the reign of Emperor Seiwa (r. 858–876), when two ships from Silla landed in Kyushu and devastated areas of the island.[26] Envoys were dispatched by the emperor to Ise 伊勢, Iwashimizu 岩清水, and Usa Hachiman to petition the deities to restore peace to the country. In these prayers, expressions referring to Japan as the divine nation blessed with the gods' protection (J. *shinmei no kuni* 神明の国) appear. Although the medieval *shinkoku* idea was different from that which appeared in the *Nihon shoki*, this self-conceit and emphasis on Japan's divinity was used in the medieval period as a form of political ideology and to create a sense of cultural superiority.[27]

Considering the prevailing *shinkoku* ideology during this period, how can we make sense of the worship of a Silla deity? And what did it mean to worship Shinra Myōjin? It seems fair to say that medieval Japanese Buddhists were inspired by Silla as much as they were haunted by it—inspired because Silla was closer to the sacred land of the Buddha and to Chinese civilization both geographically and culturally, but haunted because this country had actually threatened the Japanese politically and epidemiologically. However, Jimon monks found a way to avoid dealing with the Silla problem when they theorized the origin of Shinra Myōjin. Like Susanoo and Jingū, Shinra Myōjin visited Silla only temporarily, and did so in order to exert Japan's power, as elaborated in the *Onjōji denki*: "Concerning Shinra Myōjin's becoming the king of a foreign country to display Japan's power: The first human ruler, Jinmu 神武, transmitted three swords and three mirrors. . . . One thousand years later, Jinmu was reborn as the great king of Silla. Why is it so? It is because Japanese is the land of *kami* (J. *shinkoku*), and is superior to other countries."[28] As seen here, Shinra Myōjin is no longer a deity associated with Silla immigrants in Ōmi. Just like past emperors, he is the god who gloriously conquered Silla. The transformation of Shinra

Myōjin from a god of or from Silla to a god who subjugated Silla resonates with the story of Jingū in the *Nihon shoki*. The myth of Jingū is crucial for our discussion because it helps to explain the ambivalence of Shinra Myōjin.[29] The legend served a political purpose and told a historically dubious story in which Silla paid tribute to Japan. Putting aside the historical accuracy of this story, what is significant is that Jingū was a cultural symbol that was a powerful Japanese self-image, and accounts of the semilegendary figure's victory over Silla continued to be reproduced, circulated, and interpreted throughout the medieval period. This legend helped Japan regain confidence, feel superior, and carve out a cultural identity separate from Korea and China. With the Mongol invasions serving as a catalyst, the Jingū legend reemerged during the thirteenth century and appeared in *setsuwa* collections as well as temple and shrine chronicles.[30] The ideological nature of Jingū's myth and its continuous reproduction of the story throughout the medieval period suggest that Silla was perceived as a hostile enemy to be subdued.

Shinra Myōjin's association with pestilence emerged against this backdrop of a long-standing fear of Silla. The logic behind the worship of Shinra Myōjin was to redirect the foreign deity's power and protect Japan. With the continuation of hostile interactions with Silla, and with the rise of proto-national identity around the time of the Mongol invasions, however, Shinra Myōjin evolved from a deity who came from Silla into a "Japanese" deity who went to Silla in order to exert Japanese power; this is the same rhetoric found in the legend of Jingū. In the narrative of both Shinra Myōjin and Jingū, Silla was imagined as a space where desire and fear intersected: desire to conquer, and fear of being contaminated. In the next section, I focus on this fear of contamination, explain the ways in which Silla was identified as a source of pestilence, and discuss how Shinra Myōjin came to be a god who controls epidemics.

SILLA AS THE SOURCE OF PESTILENCE

When it comes to understanding how ancient and medieval Japanese distinguished between the space in which they lived from the space where others lived, the idea of a boundary is more useful than that of a territory.[31] During the early Heian period, while the court was attempting to centralize the government, a series of epidemics swept through Japan.[32] As the elite Japanese saw it, the pure space, where Japan was located, had to be protected from the polluted outer spaces, which included Silla. This idea explains why one of the earliest Buddhist cults in Japan, that of the Four Heavenly Kings (J. Shitennō 四天王), was initially thought to be a powerful means for preventing plagues coming from Silla, though worship of these deities certainly had other benefits as well.[33]

Likewise, the idea of disease or, more specifically, pollution, was understood spatially—in terms of an inside-outside dichotomy.[34] Diseases were a form of pollution that came from the "outside." Given Japan's geographical position, epidemics came from the continent, and the Korean Peninsula, as the closest neighboring kingdom, was singled out for blame.[35] Silla's association with epidemics in Japan was formed over several centuries, during which time there were numerous epidemic outbreaks.[36] One of the most fatal diseases in premodern Japan was smallpox.[37] In fact, the first outbreak of smallpox in Japan may very well have been brought there from the Korean Peninsula. The Paekche envoys were accused of bringing it to Kyushu, the major contact point between the continent and the Japanese islands, in 552.[38] Notorious for its high mortality rate, it was thus seen as being the most powerful punishment that a pestilence deity could unleash. It is intriguing to note that it was not until the medieval period that Silla, or the Korean Peninsula in general, was blamed for being the origin of epidemics. For example, Heian-period texts describing the Great Smallpox Epidemic of the Tenpyō 天平 era (729–749) used vague terms such as "barbarians" or "barbarian ship" to refer to the people or vessels that introduced the disease to the islands.[39] It was only in the medieval period that sources began to insist that the barbarians were men from Silla, and from the thirteenth century on this came to be the accepted view.[40]

Silla's association with pestilence was central to the process by which Shinra Myōjin came to be seen as a god of pestilence. When epidemics occurred, purification rites addressed to the pestilence deities were frequently made to subdue the unwelcomed outsider.[41] As Michael Como has shown, several deities from the Korean Peninsula (or perceived to be of Korean origin) were associated with disease in the Nara and early Heian periods, and some of them were even incorporated into the royal court as a way to tame those foreign demons.[42] The case of Shinra Myōjin was similar. His association with pestilence was grounded in deep-seated antagonism shaped by historical experiences and lingering cultural memory. We can find numerous legends in the *Jimon denki horoku* in which Shinra Myōjin is described as a god who both causes and expels pestilence. In one example, the Jimon's record claims that when the court prayed to Shinra Myōjin during an outbreak of a disease in 1084 the epidemic immediately stopped.[43]

In the Jimon tradition Shinra Myōjin's role as a pestilence deity took another interesting turn when he came to be associated with the Chinese memory of a particular epidemic that occurred around Mt. Song.[44] The *Onjōji denki* explains that the deity was already a god of pestilence in China:

> During the time of Śākyamuni Buddha, Shinra Myōjin made a vow that he would appear as Myōon 妙音 to protect Buddhist teachings and Buddhist halls. This is the reason why all the temples in India and China venerate him. On Mt. Tiantai in China, he manifested himself as Shusan'ō 朱山王 to protect the sovereign and to expel pestilence. At times, he appeared on Mt. Song; at other times, he appeared on Mt. Tai 太. Likewise, he watched over every nook and cranny of the land. In Japan, he manifested himself as Susanoo 素戔嗚. From the Hi 簸 River in Izumo he went to

> Soshimori 曽尸茂梨 in Silla. There he supported the king and also preached to both the monks and the laity. Afterwards, in the twelfth year of the Tang Emperor Dazhong's 大中 reign (857), the deity appeared to Enchin on the boat during his return trip to Japan and became a protector deity of Miidera.[45]

One of the interesting points here is the way in which Chinese sacred Buddhist topology was used to create a mythic link between Shinra Myōjin and Mt. Song. Mt. Song occupies a special place in the beliefs of East Asian Buddhist followers, as the mountain is the site where Bodhidharma (the first patriarch of Chan/Zen) allegedly sat for nine years in meditation. The *Jimon denki horoku* interestingly notes that Mt. Song is the sacred place of Bodhidharma.[46] What is relevant for our discussion is Bodhidharma's association with smallpox. The association between Bodhidharma's Mt. Song and his later transformation into the god of smallpox in Edo-period Japan is not a coincidence, as the imagery of Mt. Song as the dwelling-place of the god of pestilence is already found in the medieval period.[47] By replacing Bodhidharma with Shinra Myōjin, Mt. Song becomes the most suitable spot for nurturing the power of the pestilence deity.

Another intriguing point from the above excerpt is Shinra Myōjin's other Chinese name, Shusan'ō, which indicates a close connection to Susanoo. The passage further states that Shinra Myōjin is none other than Susanoo when the deity manifested himself in Japan. I now want to further examine how the equation between Shinra Myōjin and Susanoo was rationalized in the Jimon circle.

SUSANOO AND SHINRA MYŌJIN IN THE JIMON

Shinra Myōjin's identification with Susanoo is one of the most peculiar mythological associations in medieval theories of the amalgamation of buddhas and *kami* (J. *shinbutsu shūgō* 神仏習合). Susanoo is a complex god whose character is rarely easy to discern.[48] While he plays a prominent role in the creation mythology found in the *Kojiki* and *Nihon shoki*, the Izumo 出雲 tradition transmits a different mythological tradition and ritual practice regarding Susanoo. In Izumo, for instance, he is regarded as the supreme god, whose status is even higher than that of the Sun Goddess Amaterasu.[49] In his medieval transformations, Susanoo also becomes a major pestilence deity.

The most obvious similarities and links between Shinra Myōjin and Susanoo are found in the *Nihon shoki*. In the Age of the Gods section, Susanoo is said to have gone to Silla after he was expelled from the Plain of High Heaven (J. Takama-ga-hara 高天原), although he soon made a boat and came back to Izumo.[50] This passage served as the locus classicus for the association of Susanoo with Silla in the medieval mythological literature. We see a paraphrasing of this idea in a passage in the *Jimon denki horoku*, a passage that exemplifies how a new mythic association is made through the rewriting and reinterpretation of a particular myth: "Shinra Myōjin is none other than Susanoo, the son of Izanami 伊弉册. Once upon a time, his parents expelled him to the underworld (J. *ne no kuni* 根の国). But he went to the Plain of High Heaven. After meeting his sister, the Sun Goddess, he went to Soshimori in Silla with his fifty sons."[51]

It is not entirely clear when the association was made, but the identification of the two was firmly in place in the Jimon tradition by the thirteenth century at the very latest. The Jimon's description of the Shinra Myōjin festival and its organizational framework around the theme of Susanoo confirms this point. As I explained in chapter 4, the 1210 festival of Shinra Myōjin focused on Susanoo's legend, and its climax was the parade of children impersonating Princess Kushinada (Susanoo's bride) and Susanoo. The parade in the festival was in a way a public display of this mythic association between Susanoo and Shinra Myōjin.

Intriguingly, Susanoo's link with Gozu Tennō, the quintessential pestilence god of Japanese mythology, was also established around the thirteenth century. One of the earliest texts to present this relationship is the *Commentary on the Chronicle of Japan* (J. *Shaku Nihongi* 釈日本紀) compiled by Urabe Kanekata 卜部兼方 (fl. late-thirteenth c.) between 1274 and 1301. Herein, we find a passage in which Ichijō Sanetsune 一条実経 (1223–1284), the formal imperial regent, poses a question to Urabe Kanefumi 卜部兼文 (fl. mid-thirteenth c.)—a court priest as well as the compiler Kanekata's father—asking whether or not Susanoo is a Silla deity:

> [Sanetsune's] Question: Isn't the main deity of Gion 祇園 Shrine a foreign deity?
>
> [Kanefumi's] Answer: According to a record, Susanoo first crossed the sea and arrived in Silla and then came back to Japan. Because of this, some people think that Susanoo is a foreign deity. But people all know that Mutō Tenjin 武塔天神 is the name of a god of pestilence worshipped as the main deity of Gion. When the god of a pestilence says that "I am Haya Susanoo no Mikoto," it means that the deity's name is Susanoo no Mikoto. The deity's other name, Haya Susanoo no Mikoto, and the origin of the deity is found in the *Nihon shoki*.[52]

Although Urabe Kanefumi's answer is rather evasive, he makes the point that Susanno is not necessarily a foreign deity but surely a god of pestilence. As seen in the link between Susanoo and Gozu Tennō, as well as that between Susanoo and Shinra Myōjin, it is noteworthy that the Silla connection was the only common denominator that brought these two very different deities together. The initial connection between Shinra Myōjin and Susanoo may have started with a toponymic confusion, both being referred to as a god of "Silla" or as a god who returned from "Silla," respectively. But as seen in later Yoshida Shinto texts,[53] the identification between Shinra Myōjin and Susanoo was well received and widely known even beyond the Jimon.[54]

Focusing on the medieval identification of Shinra Myōjin and Susanoo, I have explained how the perception of Silla in the Japanese *imaginaire*, in which history and myth are interwoven, led to the belief that Shinra Myōjin was a god of pestilence. Silla, as I have discussed, was part of an imagined geography. Here, "imagined" does not mean false or fabricated but rather "perceived." As a form of social constructionism similar to what Benedict Anderson has called "imagined communities," imagined geographies are spaces created through the use of images, texts, and discourses.[55] While imagined geographies are often seen as being a tool or means of controlling and subordinating areas in a postcolonial context, here I do not mean to critique "imagined geography" but simply to show it as an integral part of cultural imagination.

In the case at hand, Shinra Myōjin was not only the object of imagination and re-creation; he also served as the medium for the medieval imagining of Silla. Through the production and dissemination of narrative, the imagined geography of Silla was actively perceived as being the land of the Silla deity as well as the land of pestilence. Furthermore, although the myth of Shinra Myōjin circulated primarily in the Jimon tradition, the Silla god enjoyed wide, transinstitutional popularity because of his association with Gozu Tennō. This reflects the Jimon's strategic decision to deal with pestilence while establishing another powerful facet of Shinra Myōjin, which helped the institution grow and the deity develop.

In short, Shinra Myōjin's association with Susanoo highlights the interactions among historical perception, religious imagination, and actual practices on the ground, and how each of these elements reinforces one another. It further points to the way in which the medieval Japanese perception of Silla was encoded in the Japanese religious landscape and how far the image of Silla in the Japanese *imaginaire* penetrated the Tendai esoteric tradition and extended beyond it.

Chapter 7

Shinra Myōjin as Part of the Network of the Divine Old Man

This chapter looks at possible origins of Shinra Myōjin iconography and explains the significance of the deity's visual representation in the context of the East Asian Mediterranean.[1] Shinra Myōjin was often depicted as a divine old man (J. *okina* 翁), but precisely why this was the case has proven to be a vexing question for scholars of Japanese religion. To begin to answer this question we must first examine Shinra Myōjin in the context of Silla deities in Japan, all of whom are usually portrayed as old men with white beards or white hair. Shinra Myōjin's depiction as an old man can be best understood as the result of a meeting of deities that shared a similar mythological origin but that drew on different symbolism. In this chapter I argue that cross-cultural transmission shaped Shinra Myōjin's iconography as a divine old man, which is consistent with the way in which other Silla-related deities were viewed and depicted in Japan.

Interestingly, the individual gods within this network of old-man deities are almost all connected to Korean immigrants, the best-known examples being Inari Myōjin, Sekizan Myōjin, and Shirahige Myōjin 白髭明神. It is not true that all old-man deities in Japan were brought there by Korean immigrants or worshipped exclusively within Korean religious traditions.[2] What is true, however, is that these divine old-man gods were in most cases thought to have connections to Silla/Korea. This type of deity was a prominent archetype in the Japanese Buddhist pantheon, and it was shaped by (and in turn influenced) Tendai Buddhist visual culture. Examining the image of Shinra Myōjin thus alerts us to a significant element of Japanese religiosity (the old-man deity) and to the way in which this element was part of the broader East Asian Mediterranean.

Studying the main Shinra Myōjin icons and then seeking to understand the tradition of the worship of Mañjuśrī at Mt. Wutai in China are important for making sense of Shinra Myōjin, for they paved the way for the depiction of him as an old man, and he had close doctrinal links to Mañjuśrī. Here I further explain the old-man deity archetype and show that Shinra Myōjin's portrayal indicates he was part of a larger network of Silla-affiliated gods. A visual analysis of Shinra Myōjin allows us to understand how this particular visual form reflected deep-rooted cultural symbolism that enriched the medieval Japanese religious landscape.

THE DIVINE OLD MAN: FROM MT. WUTAI TO ONJŌJI

In the year of 1072, Jōjin 成尋 (1011–1081), a Japanese Buddhist monk from Daiunji 大雲寺 in Kyoto, began his pilgrimage to Mt. Tiantai and Mt. Wutai, the latter being the sacred dwelling-place of Mañjuśrī. In the travelogue that he wrote upon his return (the *San Tendai Godaisan ki* 參天台五臺山記, covering the years 1072 to 1081), Jōjin related his experience of meeting an old man begging for food at the refectory of a monastery on Mt. Wutai; Jōjin immediately recognized that the old man was a manifestation of Mañjuśrī.[3] This miraculous story of Jōjin's encounter with Mañjuśrī disguised as an old man at Mt. Wutai was not, however, unique.[4] What is intriguing is that the story of encountering an old man suggests a legitimate transmission of Buddhist teachings from China to Japan.

As the dwelling-place of the bodhisattva Mañjuśrī (J. Monju 文殊), Mt. Wutai had a unique status in the Buddhist world.[5] Partially due to Mañjuśrī's prominent role in the *Lotus Sutra*, the central scripture of Tendai, early Tendai masters such as Saichō, Ennin, and Enchin were interested in the Chinese cult of Mt. Wutai.[6] The Tendai tradition on Mt. Hiei recognized Ennin as the one who introduced the cult of Mañjuśrī to Japan, as it was he who visited the sacred mountain during his travels in China (838–847). After his return, Ennin had a group of Mañjuśrī statues carved and installed in a newly built structure on Mt. Hiei, the pavilion of Mañjuśrī (J. Monjurō 文殊樓). He is said to have subsequently performed the eight-letter ritual dedicated to Mañjuśrī in this building for the purpose of averting disasters and promoting good fortune.[7] He also supposedly bought several images of Mañjuśrī during his trip, and one of them is said to be the Mañjuśrī Pentad.[8] Ennin's familiarity with the Mañjuśrī tradition on Mt. Wutai was crucial for the successful re-creation of the cult on Mt. Hiei in Japan, and soon after the cult's introduction it became an integral part of the Tendai's devotional practices.[9]

As part of the greater Tendai tradition, the Jimon followers also had a deep interest in Mañjuśrī and sought to bring the cult to Onjōji. In the Sanmon's records, it is Ennin who first invoked Mañjuśrī at Mt. Wutai and who introduced the esoteric cult of Mañjuśrī to Japan.[10] However, the Jimon sources assert instead that it was Enchin who brought the "authentic" Mañjuśrī cult from Mt. Wutai to Japan.[11] The Jimon imagined Onjōji as the sacred dwelling-place of Mañjuśrī and tried to incorporate Mañjuśrī into their legends, doctrines, and iconography. The Jimon Buddhists found a doctrinal means of cementing the association between Mañjuśrī and Shinra Myōjin: using the *honji suijaku* paradigm, they identified Mañjuśrī as Shinra Myōjin's original ground, as is explained in the *Onjōji denki*.[12] With the link between Mañjuśrī and Shinra Myōjin thus established, Shinra Myōjin gained canonical status in the Jimon tradition. While this doctrinal claim was based on the *honji suijaku* framework, it was further reified though iconography. This becomes clear when we compare the image of Shinra Myōjin with that of the old man found in the Mañjuśrī Pentad (J. *Monju gosonzō* 文殊五尊像). Before discussing this in detail, however, I want to turn to descriptions of the oldest and the most iconic image of Shinra Myōjin.[13]

The statue in question is currently stored in the shrine of Shinra Myōjin in the northern part of Onjōji's grounds. This wooden statue of Shinra Myōjin is known to be the oldest extant image of a dharma protector deity (J. *gohōjin*), and has been recognized as one of the most enigmatic pieces of Shinto-Buddhist art in Japan.[14] The statue is also one of the most secret of the "secret buddhas" (J. *hibutsu* 秘仏), which are statues that are kept hidden from the public because of their uncanny powers.[15] The temple maintains that it can only be viewed by ordained monks of the Jimon. The *Onjōji denki* claims that "the master Enchin made [the first statue of Shinra Myōjin] during the Jōgan 貞観 period (859–879),"[16] though it is difficult to take this claim at face value. Although chronicles do not specify the date of dedication for this statue, it has been suggested that it was created for the first official ceremony of the deity in 1052.[17]

An interesting link between graphic puzzles and religious secrecy is found in the enigmatic statue of Shinra Myōjin. Tendai doctrine provides hints about the symbolism of this piece. The triple-pointed cap atop Shinra Myōjin's head is one of the statue's most conspicuous features. The contour of the cap is in the shape of a mountain—*san* 山—with three peaks. The phonetic resemblance, however, results in a play on words. In Japanese, the Sino-Japanese reading of "three" is *san*, and the number three is a particularly important number in Tendai. This kind of pun, combined with graphic puzzles, is quite common in Tendai hermeneutics, as well as in medieval Japanese culture.[18] Allan Grapard calls linguistic games such as the one found here "linguistic cubism."[19] According to him, they were often used to create meanings, provide new interpretations, and link those interpretations to central Tendai teachings. While it may be impossible to retrieve all of this statue's hidden meanings, this linguistic cubism provides one possible interpretation of the statue's triple-pointed cap.

Below the cap, the statue exhibits a distinctive facial expression, as well as a peculiar white face. Using various plays on words, the *Onjōji denki* explains Shinra Myōjin's facial expression as follows:

> On the forehead [of the deity] there are five wrinkles, which is a reference to the character for five (五). On each cheek, there are four wrinkles, which together create the character for eight (八). Five [times] eight (*gohachi* 五八) [meaning, multiply five by eight to get forty 四十] refers to the name of the well [of the temple]. If you break the character 井, there are four tens (十). If the four tens (十) are aggregated, they become the well (井). Therefore, [we know that the deity] dwells in this well.[20]

According to this interpretation, each feature of the statue is a manifestation of the deity's higher reality, and all of the visual representations are deeply intertwined with the sanctity of Onjōji. This passage also provides a clue as to how Shinra Myōjin's iconographic details can be decoded, deconstructed, and reconstructed through linguistic strategies. The decoding process proceeds from the top of the statue to the bottom, beginning with the forehead wrinkles and then moving on to the middle of the face, and then the lines around his smile. And when it reaches the third point (again, the number three being Tendai's magic number) at the bottom, which is the deity's mouth, we come to the most mysterious and transcendental meaning of the whole scheme, which is a cryptic representation of the sacred well of Onjōji, from which the temple gets its popular name, Miidera. The face is thus seen as a sacred map that contains hidden meanings. What is also interesting is that while this passage appears to be concerned with minor details and with creating a self-contained world of significance, it actually connects all this to the broader Tendai semiotics.

While this image is the best-known Shinra Myōjin image, there are others in which Shinra Myōjin is combined with other deities or accompanied by his acolytes. The painted image of Shinra Myōjin (figure 9) is from the thirteenth century and has the same triangular composition as the previous image. With the help of a description found in the *Onjōji denki*, we can identify all the characters in this Shinra Myōjin hanging scroll. On the far right is a seated acolyte called Hannya 般若 Bosatsu (Bodhisattva Hannya), and next to him we find Shukuō 宿王 Bosatsu (Bodhisattva Stellar King). On the opposite side from the two *dōji* there is an old-man deity known as Hi no miko 火御子 (August Child of Fire), who is an Onjōji earth-deity (J. *jinushi*).[21] Shukuō and Hannya are the two main acolytes of Shinra Myōjin, and they appear in numerous miracle stories about this deity. The two often accompany him, and the physical manifestation of the triad is also found in the Old Map of Onjōji produced during the Kamakura period (figure 5). In the map, we find the shrine of Shinra Myōjin in the northern part of the temple complex, and two smaller shrines—one for Hannya and the other for Shukuō—on either side of the Shinra Myōjin Shrine.

Mañjuśrī appears prominently in the iconography of Shinra Myōjin. In the painting of Shinra Myōjin here, Mañjuśrī is depicted with a golden mandorla above Shinra Myōjin, indicating that the Silla deity is in fact a manifestation of Mañjuśrī. The

FIGURE 9.
Shinra Myōjin, his acolytes, and Mañjuśrī, thirteenth c., colors on silk. Onjōji, Shiga Prefecture.

identification of Shinra Myōjin and Mañjuśrī was achieved through both doctrinal and iconographic interpretations, with the former often serving as a reference to the latter, and vice versa. The following passage from the *Onjōji denki*, which focuses on the staff and sutra held by Shinra Myōjin, is one such example.

> Shinra Myōjin is the god of meditation and wisdom, which are expressed by the two *mudras* of his right and left hands: the hand of meditation holds a staff, and the hand of wisdom holds a *sutra*. Meditation and wisdom are non-dual. *Śamatha* (cessation) and *vipaśyanā* (observation) are of a single essence. This is the reason why there are two *dōji* on [the deity's] right and left sides. Hannya signifies wisdom and he has Mañjuśrī as his *honji*. Shukuō symbolizes correct virtue and he has Samantabhadra as his *honji*. Samantabhadra and Mañjuśrī correspond to meditation and wisdom, respectively.[22]

There are several interesting points in this passage. First of all, one of the attributes of Shinra Myōjin is a staff, which is also true of Mañjuśrī when the bodhisattva is portrayed as an old man in the Mt. Wutai cult. Furthermore, a scepter (J. *ruyi* 如意) often appears as one of Mañjuśrī's attributes, symbolizing his wisdom and eloquence.[23] Mañjuśrī often holds a Buddhist sutra in his hand, which is possibly meant to symbolize the *Perfection of Wisdom Sutra* (Skt. *Prajñāpāramitā Sūtra*) in which Mañjuśrī plays a prominent role. Last, as the passage illustrates, the association between Shinra Myōjin and Mañjuśrī is further strengthened by the presence of one of Shinra Myōjin's acolytes, Hannya. Hannya is the Japanese pronunciation of the Sanskrit word *prajñā*, meaning "wisdom." Having Mañjuśrī as his *honji* and Hannya as his acolyte, Shinra Myōjin indeed becomes the embodiment of wisdom, that is, of *hannya*.

The Jimon's soteriological scheme of establishing a firm association between Shinra Myōjin and Mañjuśrī also created a link between Shinra Myōjin and Vimalakīrti, the elderly bodhisattva from the *Vimalakīrti-nirdeśa*. In the *Vimalakīrti-nirdeśa* Mañjuśrī serves as Vimalakīrti's main interlocutor.[24] Just as doctrinal and visual interpretations within the Jimon tied Shinra Myōjin to Mañjuśrī, so did such interpretations link Shinra Myōjin to Vimalakīrti.[25] In the *Jitokushū*, for instance, Vimalakīrti is identified as one of the three *honji* of Shinra Myōjin (Mañjuśrī and Sonjōō being the other two).[26] In the *Mii zokutōki*, applying the combinative pairing of *prajñā* and *upāya* (method, J. *hōben* 方便) from the *Vimalakīrti-nirdeśa*, at the end of a prayer performed for the deity in 1202 it states that Enchin is the father of *upāya* and Shinra Myōjin the mother of *prajñā*.[27] In the *Onjōji denki* we find a passage that reads: "The master said that 'If the body [statue] of Shinra Myōjin gets lost, it can be replaced with that of Vimalakīrti.'"[28] The text does not explain the reasoning behind this assertion, but it is possible the two were associated in part due to the fact that they were both portrayed as elderly laymen.

SHINRA MYŌJIN AS MAÑJUŚRĪ, MAÑJUŚRĪ AS SHINRA MYŌJIN

Shinra Myōjin was at the center of the Jimon's scheme of establishing the cult of Mañjuśrī at Onjōji. At the same time, the cult of Mañjuśrī, especially the tradition from Mt. Wutai, shaped the worship of Shinra Myōjin at Onjōji, particularly in the way the deity was depicted in visual representations. In this section, I would like to turn to possible visual associations between the Mañjuśrī Pentad and Shinra Myōjin. More specifically, Mañjuśrī's two acolytes in the Mañjuśrī Pentad—an old man holding a staff and an old monk with a monk's staff (J. *shakujō*)—are strikingly similar to the image of Shinra Myōjin. In a variant that modern scholars call "Mañjuśrī crossing the sea" (J. *tokai Monju* 渡海文殊), Mañjuśrī and his entourage are depicted traversing the sea on clouds, heading in the direction of Mt. Wutai.[29] The earliest such image dates to the Tang period, and this format was popular in China until the Song dynasty. It also enjoyed wide popularity in central Asia, as well as in Xixia 西夏 (1038–1227 CE), the Tibetan-speaking Tangut kingdom. In Japan, this type of image first appeared during the late Heian period and reached its pinnacle of production during the Kamakura period. It is difficult to pinpoint the earliest transmission of the image to Japan, although among the ten extant sets of the Mañjuśrī Pentad, three are from the late Heian to early Kamakura periods.[30]

In the Mañjuśrī Pentad, Mañjuśrī is often accompanied by four acolytes (J. *kenzoku* 眷屬) while figure 10 shows two additional attendants, a slight variation. There is no scriptural basis for this combination of the four acolytes, which makes it very difficult to identify its origins. However, the visual representation itself reflects an amalgamation of various Buddhist legends related to Mañjuśrī. Among the acolytes appears the youth Sudhana (J. Zenzai dōji 善財童子), usually in the front, whose pilgrimage in search of the Dharma is described in the *Avataṃsaka Sūtra* (J. *Kegonkyō* 華厳経). Another figure is the king of Khotan, Udayana (J. Utennō 優填王), who is traditionally credited for commissioning the first image of the Buddha. The other two figures—the monk Buddhapāli (var. Buddhapāla, Buddhapālita; J. Butsudahari 仏陀波利; fl. late seventh c.) and another elderly figure known as Taishō Rōnin 大聖老人 (var. Saishō rōnin 最勝老人)—were added later, around the mid-ninth century.[31] These first two acolytes deserve special attention, for they echo Shinra Myōjin, with regard to both doctrinal symbolism and iconography.

In fact, Buddhapāli is a relatively well-known figure in the Mt. Wutai tradition in China.[32] According to a legend, this northern Indian (possibly Kashmiri) monk, hoping to encounter Mañjuśrī, went on pilgrimage to Mt. Wutai. When he arrived there in 677, he met an old man who asked him whether he had brought the *Sūtra of the Supreme Dharani from the Buddha's Crown* (Skt. *Uṣṇīṣa Vijaya Dhāraṇī Sūtra*; Ch. *Foding zunsheng tuoluoni jing* 佛頂尊勝陀羅尼經, *T.* 967) with him.[33] After asking this question, the old man suddenly disappeared, and Buddhapāli then realized

FIGURE 10. Monju and attendants, thirteenth c., ink and colors on silk. The Cleveland Museum of Art, Mr. and Mrs. William H. Marlatt Fund 1986.1.

that he had just encountered a manifestation of Mañjuśrī. The text circulated widely within the Mt. Wutai network and beyond, and exerted great influence on Chinese understandings of Mañjuśrī.[34] Faith in the aforementioned sutra flourished from the mid-eighth century onward in China, and was transmitted to Japan by Ennin. In Ennin's diary, we find the earliest known textual reference to an image of Buddhapāli and the mysterious old man in the above story.[35] According to Ennin, when he visited Zhulinsi 竹林寺 on Mt. Wutai in 840, he saw a painting that depicted the scene in which Buddhapāli encounters Mañjuśrī disguised as an old man.[36]

While Buddhapāli is closely associated with Shinra Myōjin in the textual tradition, Taishō Rōnin's link to Shinra Myōjin is more conspicuous on the iconographical level. Taishō Rōnin's significance within the Mañjuśri Pentad has not been fully understood thus far, though the deity's name itself offers a hint as to the figure's identity. The first two characters (Taishō 大聖) evidently derive from Mañjuśrī's full name in Chinese (Dasheng Wenshu shili 大聖文殊師利), and Rōnin is the Japanese pronunciation of the Chinese *laoren* 老人, meaning "old man."[37] In other words, Taishō Rōnin refers to Mañjuśrī when he appears as an old man. One might wonder why this figure is named after the main deity within this grouping. However, when we consider the fact that attendants are not simply secondary elements but an extension of the main deity, it is understandable that they are often intertwined, interchangeable, and even identical with him. In this way Taishō Rōnin is not simply one of Mañjuśrī's acolytes but also one of the manifestations of the bodhisattva, or even the bodhisattva himself.

The visual affinity between Shinra Myōjin and Taishō Rōnin in the Mañjuśrī Pentad can be explained in part by the Jimon's acute desire to appropriate the Mañjuśrī cult for Onjōji. As a stranger and traveler who came from afar, Taishō Rōnin, the old man who crossed the sea with Mañjuśrī (just as Shinra Myōjin did with Enchin) exhibits not only a visual similarity but also a functional affinity; both Shinra Myōjin and Taishō Rōnin serve as protectors of sea travel and appear in the form of an old man. With these observations in mind, it becomes clear that the image of Shinra Myōjin was not a completely new fabrication but was instead a product of the Jimon's strategic adaptation of elements from the Mañjuśrī cult as it existed both in China and on Mt. Hiei, and that this adaptation occurred around the eleventh and twelfth centuries.[38] It may be that the image of Shinra Myōjin was based on Taishō Rōnin as depicted in the Mañjuśrī Pentad, which would further support my contention that the Jimon attempted to appropriate the cult of Mañjuśrī in order to establish Shinra Myōjin as a more legitimate Buddhist deity.

THE NETWORK OF THE DIVINE OLD MAN DEITIES

Veneration of deities that appear as white-haired elderly men was not an isolated, local phenomenon but rather a shared tradition found throughout the East

Asian Mediterranean.[39] Although the Jimon tradition turned Shinra Myōjin into an individualized, unique deity, his appearance owes more to this network of old-man deities than to anything specific to the Jimon. The old man is something of a generic image, and thus can be difficult to categorize; however, it was precisely because of this that the image was so adaptable and able to be used in different parts of East Asia.[40]

One example appears in the *Memorabilia of the Three Kingdoms* (Kor. *Samguk yusa* 三國遺事, late-thirteenth c.), a compilation of historical records and folktales from the Korean Peninsula. Here we find a legend echoing that of Shinra Myōjin, in which a Silla prince travels to Tang China and encounters a mysterious old man in his dreams while there.

> The Queen Chinsong (r. 888–898) sent Prince Yangpae as her envoy to the Tang court in China. The voyage was a difficult one, for the sea-passage was blocked by the rebels of Later Paekche. Yangpae was therefore obliged to take fifty bowmen with him to repel any attacks on the party. When Yangpae's ship reached Kokto Island a storm began to rage at sea, and the party was unable to continue its journey for some ten days. Worried about the delay, Yangpae consulted a fortune-teller, who told him there was a dragon pool on the island and a sacrifice must be offered to the dragon. When this was done the blue water of the pool leaped ten feet into the air.
>
> That night an old man with a long beard appeared to Prince Yangpae in a dream and said, "If you leave a good bowman behind on this island you will be blessed with a favorable wind." When the prince awoke he called the men together and told them of his dream. They agreed that each man should carve his name on a piece of wood. When these were cast into the sea, the one that sank would indicate the man who would stay. When this was done only the name of the bowman Kotaji sank to the bottom.
>
> In accord with his prince's orders, the good bowman took his stand upon the shore and sadly watched the ship sail off across the calm sea toward China. As he was choking back his tears the same white-bearded old man who had appeared in the prince's dream emerged from the dragon pool and spoke to him. "I am a spirit of the Western Sea," the old man said. "Every morning at sunrise for some time now a grotesque Buddhist monk has descended from heaven and chanted a *dharani* that obliges me and my wife and children to rise to the surface of the water. He has pulled out and eaten one by one the livers of my children until now only my wife, one daughter, and I are left. Please shoot down this monster."
>
> "Shooting arrows is my pride," Kotaji answered. . . . Kotaji shot an arrow swift and true into his heart, and he changed into an aged fox and fell dead. Soon the old man reappeared. "You have saved my life," he said. "In gratitude I offer you my lovely daughter as your wife." . . . Then the old man instructed him: "I will change my daughter into a flower which you will clasp to your bosom, and I will command two dragons to carry you to the Silla ship on which the envoy is sailing; the dragons will then guide the ship to the shores of the Tang empire."[41]

This story focuses on the salvific power of the dragon king and on the Buddhist monk as exorciser, both of whom help the Silla prince successfully travel across the sea. Thinking back to the origin story of Shinra Myōjin, we see that the two narratives have much in common: not only are they both linked to Silla, but in both cases the old man is a god who guarantees safe ocean travel to Tang China and who repeatedly appears in the perilous sea between Korea and China. Furthermore, the story suggests that the old man is none other than the dragon king himself. As the archetypal symbol of water, the dragon king controls all of its forms, particularly the sea and the rain. Interestingly (but not surprisingly), Shinra Myōjin is said to be the son of the dragon king.[42]

Yanagita Kunio and several Japanese religious historians have noted that most *kami* had their origin in the form of the *okina* or old man.[43] The old man deity is often found in Daoist, Buddhist, and other local religious contexts. Evidently, Daoist immortals were typically depicted as sage old men. This is why Shinra Myōjin was thought to be a Daoist immortal (J. *shinsen* 神仙). In the *Genkō shakusho* 元亨釈書 (1322), a fourteenth-century Buddhist historical record by the Zen monk Kokan Shiren 虎関師錬 (1278–1347), Shinra Myōjin is listed under the heading "Daoist immortals."[44] The Korean mountain spirit (Kor. *sanshin* 山神) is another example of an overlap between Daoist influences and local practices: in Korean Buddhism as well as in Korean folk religions, mountain deities are typically depicted as sagely old men with white beards.[45]

In the Buddhist context, mythical figures appearing as old men often reveal that they are in fact landlord deities. Landlord deities sometimes appear to be of only minor importance, but they are the hidden authority that bequeaths auspicious land to eminent Buddhist monks or other Buddhist divinities, marking the moment of new jurisdiction. Their appearance as old men makes sense, for they have been residing in the particular place in question for eternity. Because he is thought to have been waiting, the old man was later associated with the Maitreya cult, yet another feature linking the old man to Shinra Myōjin.

Significantly, it was in Ōmi that the old-man god tradition developed and thrived. Shirahige Myōjin (White-bearded Bright Deity), a god of safe sea travel, is one example of the infiltration of Korean religious imagery into the Ōmi region, a stronghold of Korean immigrants.[46] The first Shirahige shrine was built in Ōmi and later spread throughout Japan.[47] Ōmi also played a central role in development of the cult of the future Buddha, Maitreya. The origin story of Shinra Myōjin may have arisen from this rich backdrop of local legends in Ōmi. For instance, the *Three Jewels* (*Sanbōe* 三宝絵), a tenth-century collection of Buddhist tales by Minamoto Tamenori 源為憲 (fl. tenth c.), contains one of the oldest stories of an old-man deity in Ōmi. When Emperor Shōmu 聖武 (r. 724–749) prayed to Zaō Gongen 蔵王権現, the deity of Mt. Kinpu 金峰, to let him have some of the gold of the mountain for the completion of his cherished project (i.e., the Great Buddha of Tōdaiji), the deity answered the prayer:

> Zaō responded with this revelation: "The gold in this mountain is to be saved for the future world of Maitreya. I am only its guardian; I cannot give you any. On the banks of the river in Shiga District in Ōmi Province lies a stone fished out by an old man many years ago. Make an image of the Wish-granting Kannon, place it on this rock, and worship it."[48]

In this story the image of the old man fishing on the shore of Lake Biwa echoes that of the old man in Shinra Myōjin's *engi*, which happens to be part of the origin story of the Maitreya ceremony at Onjōji. Zaō Gongen, the central divinity of Shugendō, was often believed to be a manifestation of Maitreya.[49] Mt. Kinpu, a site sacred to Shugendō, was therefore regarded as the dwelling-space of Maitreya. While this story appears to have nothing to do with Shinra Myōjin, the similarities found in it point to the intertextual nature of the old-man motif.

The imagery of the divine old man is also found in performing arts traditions (J. *geinō* 芸能). In a fragmentary work entitled the *Meishuku shū* 明宿集 by the Noh playwright Konparu Zenchiku 金春禅竹 (1405–1468), *okina*, an important old man figure in the development of performing arts, is presented as the source of all gods and buddhas, connecting all the phenomena of the universe as a primordial god.[50] The *okina* cult traces its lineage to the Hata, for the Konparu family identifies Hata no Kawakatsu 秦河勝 (var. Hata no Kōkatsu, fl. sixth to seventh c.) as its ancestor.[51] Regardless of whether or not this is historically accurate, what is important is that in Zenchiku's account *okina* arose at the beginning of the age of the gods to protect the Japanese throne and benefit the Japanese people. This mythological narrative linking the Hata to *okina* suggests that the Hata clan's prominent background as an elite immigrant group from the ancient period contributed to the discourse of the old-man deity and its special place in the performing arts.[52]

Another old-man deity, Matarajin, allows us to connect the *okina* cult back to Shinra Myōjin. Matarajin, whose origin story is almost identical to that of Shinra Myōjin, was venerated as a patron deity of the performing arts in Tendai monasteries during the medieval period. Worshipped in both Tendai and Shingon Buddhism, he is an extremely complex deity who deserves more discussion, but what is relevant to us is that the Sanmon claims that Matarajin was introduced to Japan by Ennin and enshrined in the Jōgyō zanmai-dō at Enryakuji.[53] In the Tendai tradition, he was worshipped as the protector of *nenbutsu* practice. Matarajin was also known as a protector of the dangerous northeastern direction, and accordingly was often venerated at the northeastern corner of the Jōgyō zanmai-dō, though always hidden from sight. As an extension of the same logic, in *sarugaku* 猿楽, a form of popular theater that flourished between the eleventh and fourteenth centuries, the "dangerous" backstage was dedicated to Matarajin, who naturally became the guardian deity of performers; and *sarugaku* actors performed a series of dances in front of his statue.[54] In this performance, the dancers wore masks of *okina* to invoke and impersonate Matarajin.[55]

Shinra Myōjin and Matarajin share a great deal of symbolism. Similarly to the way in which Shinra Myōjin was the guardian deity of *ennen* at Onjōji, the deification of Matarajin in the performing arts does not seem to be a coincidence, because Matarajin is also the deity of *ennen* ritual in the Sanmon tradition. In both cases, the deity's elderly appearance becomes the source of its uncanny power. The two also share strong ties to the cult of Mañjuśrī, for Matarajin's face was thought to be that of Mañjuśrī. The association goes back to Eison 叡尊 (1201–1290), the founder of the Shingon Ritsu 真言律 school at Saidaiji 西大寺 in Nara. Eison believed that Mañjuśrī practices were particularly appropriate for the time between Śākyamuni's death and the appearance of the next Buddha, Maitreya. Eison wanted to promote the worship of Mañjuśrī among outcasts (J. *hinin* 非人), for, as taught in the *Mañjuśrī Parinirvāṇa Sūtra*, Mañjuśrī was a bodhisattva who "would manifest as a poor, solitary, or afflicted sentient being in order to elicit acts of compassion."[56] With his growing popularity, Mañjuśrī came to be associated with other divinities; for example, being identified as Mañjuśrī, Matarajin was worshipped as the guardian of outcasts and the protector of their shelters. Due to its association with Matarajin, from the mid-Kamakura period onward, the *okina* mask was used as a symbol for Mañjuśrī.

This chapter has examined the image of Shinra Myōjin. Images are far more than static pictorial representations, and much more than carriers of certain ideas and traditions: they preserve both local and translocal ideas and cultural motifs. This is certainly the case with the image of Shinra Myōjin. In order to understand the significance of Shinra Myōjin's depiction as a divine old man, I have looked not simply at the local but also the larger East Asian Mediterranean context. Citing several examples from the network of the divine old-man deities, I have shown that in Japan Silla-related deities were invariably seen as, or associated with, old-man gods. Drawing attention to connections between Shinra Myōjin and Mañjuśrī, I have argued that Shinra Myōjin's image was influenced by the image of Taisho Rōnin in the Mañjuśrī Pentad, which reflects Onjōji's attempt to appropriate the Mañjuśrī cult so important to Tendai Buddhism of the time.

At the same time, this discussion has demonstrated that the old-man deity is part of a wider cultural phenomenon shared by East Asian religious traditions. At first glance, the image of an old man comes across as generic at best. Yet this seemingly bland appearance in fact reveals much more once we start connecting geographical, visual, and doctrinal nodes. Thus, the old-man deity is best understood by looking at the intersections of various cultic practices. Above all, this examination has shown that in the Jimon tradition it was in the worship of Shinra Myōjin that the idea of the old-man deity was emphasized, and that Shinra Myōjin was part of a larger network of the old-man deity that enjoyed great popularity and gained a long-standing cross-cultural currency in and beyond Japan.

Conclusion

This book has examined Shinra Myōjin, a god of Silla worshipped in medieval Japanese Buddhism. However, my narrative is neither a monolithic account limited to one particular school of Japanese Buddhism nor the tale of a linear transmission from the continent to Japan. Rather, combining a network model and a transcultural perspective, I have highlighted the transformations of Shinra Myōjin, focusing on those connections that traverse the boundaries of religion, history, mythology, literature, and visual culture. Throughout I have argued that the worship of Shinra Myōjin can be more productively understood when viewed in the context of the East Asian Mediterranean Buddhist network, in which immigrants, Buddhist monks, merchants, and a variety of gods exchanged ideas and produced new, hybrid cultures. In this way, the particular case of Shinra Myōjin can be seen as an example demonstrating that medieval Japanese religion is best understood when viewed in the context of East Asia more broadly.

The book has outlined three stages in the development of Shinra Myōjin worship. The first focused on maritime connections and examined the networks of immigrants and Silla shrines and temples during the ancient period. This period was characterized by a high degree of fluidity between immigrant groups and religious ideas; it was also a time during which Shinra Myōjin worship and worship of Silla deities was not institutionalized. With regard to the Japanese side of the East Asian Mediterranean, we have seen that Lake Biwa offered the optimal conditions for developing Silla immigrants' deities into individualized gods, a process that led to the emergence of Shinra Myōjin as a single deity. Home to both Silla immigrants and Silla deities, the lake functioned as an inland sea and was very much a part of the East Asian Mediterranean.

While mobility and fluidity were characteristic of pre–Shinra Myōjin worship of Silla deities, during the medieval period that worship was marked by sedentarization and institutionalization. Indeed, during this time the Jimon transformed the sea deity into a mountain deity. Here I have highlighted the process by which Shinra Myōjin eventually became the most prominent deity for the Tendai Jimon tradition and examined the central role this deity played in establishing Onjōji as a major esoteric Buddhist center in its own right, and thus in establishing the Jimon's institutional legitimacy and autonomy.

Interestingly, once "sedentarized," Shinra Myōjin was able to again become fluid, and thus to take on diverse roles and symbolic identities. From looking at the deity's ritual and mythological relations to Sonjōō and Susanoo, it becomes apparent that Shinra Myōjin shared major functional symbolism with Susanoo: both were deities of longevity and pestilence, suggesting a strong continental influence. The elderly appearance of Shinra Myōjin is also key to understanding his other symbolic associations. The examination of possible origins of the image of Shinra Myōjin revealed its link to the continent, as well as to the larger network of divine old-man deities in the Japanese pantheon, all of which are related to Silla or Silla immigrants in one way or another.

Four points emerge from this book's examination. First, Onjōji and its deities were far more important in the history of Japanese Buddhism than has previously been acknowledged. A common pattern can be identified by which foreign deities were integrated into the Japanese Buddhist pantheon. Shinra Myōjin is one of the earliest examples of the pairing of the eminent Japanese monk and a personal protector deity. However, in this human-centered hierarchical dyad, the roles played by gods have up to now been unjustifiably marginalized. As the case of Shinra Myōjin shows, in these relationships gods were never supplemental or incidental. Rather, they were major cultural agents who time and again entered and pervaded the medieval Japanese religious landscape.

Whereas in the study of premodern Japanese Buddhism most scholarship on Tendai has focused on Mt. Hiei, my research on Shinra Myōjin and the Jimon allows us to see another side of Tendai history. It is true that the Sanmon and Jimon sects shared in common a great deal of Buddhist doctrine and practice, as both were Tendai institutions. However, between the tenth and the sixteenth centuries, the Jimon developed its own distinct scholarly and ritual traditions and maintained its institutional identity as it claimed that its form of Tendai Buddhism was superior to that of the Sanmon. Recovering the voice of the Jimon not only provides another voice in the narrative about the institutional history of Tendai Buddhism in Japan but also helps us to more accurately understand Tendai Buddhism for the pluralistic institution that it was.

The second broad point this book makes is that, in the study of an East Asian Buddhist deity, the East Asian Mediterranean framework can facilitate critical engagement with the existing scholarship's preoccupation with dry land. In the past, most theories about the origins and development of Japanese culture have operated based on two premises. The first is that the flow of continental culture from the mainland to Japan was a strictly unidirectional affair: in other words, advanced culture traveled from China and the Korean Peninsula to northern Kyushu, whence it slowly moved east to the Yamato region and into the backwoods of Japan.[1] The second premise is that the court was at the center of every level of medieval religious culture.

These two premises arise from a land-centered way of thinking and a simplified, linear narrative. By looking at sea networks and at the sea as a contact zone, we are able to detect circular movements as well as individual nodal points along the coastlines. In other words, we are able to see connections that we fail to see if we assume that most contact and transmission occurred via land routes. In this way, my use of the East Asian Mediterranean model helps to shift the paradigm from a land-centered to a sea-centered vision, thus acknowledging that the sea should be a subject of cultural inquiry. When one moves away from a land-centric and capital-centric view, it becomes clear that seemingly peripheral areas along the coasts and the lakes were in fact real centers for new religious cults due to their constant contact with other cultures, continental technologies, immigrants, and travelers. We come to understand that these immigrants, monks, merchants, and travelers were not passive transmitters but rather active transformers, facilitating exchanges and generating new types of networks.

The third point is that the East Asian framework, when highlighting multi-directional movements among cultural agencies, provides a broader vision for a more nuanced understanding of transcultural relations. This framework helps us to overcome the more commonplace Japan-centric view of medieval Japanese religion. Many scholars of medieval Japanese religion have not looked beyond the interactions between China and Japan. Shinra Myōjin, for instance, has been seen as nothing more than a protector deity of Onjōji. However, I hope to have demonstrated that the worship of Shinra Myōjin was far more complex and significant. Furthermore, his worship extended far beyond Onjōji, particularly because he was also connected in one way or another with Silla immigrants in China and with other old-man deities related to the Korean Peninsula. This transcultural angle not only allows us to see beyond the confines of modern, national boundaries; it also helps us to arrive at a new understanding—namely, that the world of medieval Japan's religions was a far more dynamic, connected space than is usually assumed. In this way, the East Asian Mediterranean model encourages multidisciplinary and multinational approaches, which in turn can lead to a more holistic picture of East Asian religions. My book has focused mainly on Japan, Korea, and China, but future scholars could expand their study to include other players in East Asia.

Finally, the notion of the East Asian Mediterranean and the metaphor of fluidity have the potential to transform the way in which we view spaces, study East Asian religions, and think about history more generally. Considering space differently can provide a new model for studying Japanese deities as well. For instance, I have argued that Shinra Myōjin went through a three-part transformation—a period of initial fluidity, followed by sedentarization, which then led to a renewed fluidity, though bound to a particular space. Although each deity presents us with unique symbolic associations within a particular time and space, this three-part pattern, observable in the case of Shinra Myōjin, can be beneficial for the future study of other hybrid gods in the medieval Japanese pantheon.

Furthermore, as seen in the existing scholarship on the Mediterranean, which teaches us about the benefits of having both macro-level (e.g., Braudel) and micro-level (e.g., Horden and Purcell) analyses, the concept of East Asian Mediterranean can generate new questions for research. Although this study focused on the sea, viewing it as a fluid and moving space, other spaces can be studied using this perspective. Desert, for example, is another type of space that sometimes functioned like sea, complete with islands (or oases) and trade routes that connected people, goods, and ideas.[2] Possibilities for future scholarship include topics that could touch on transnationality and networks—for instance, the circulation of ideas and technology, the dissemination of religious texts and art, social networks of major religious figures and of patrons and social institutions, the spread of disease and medicine, and networks of gods and ritual knowledge in a specific country or within transcultural exchanges in the East Asian Mediterranean.

Notes

INTRODUCTION

1. I have slightly adapted the story from the *Onjōji ryūge-e engi* 園城寺龍華会縁起 (1062). The *engi* story was included in two late Heian period collections: the *Sanjūgo bunshū* 卅五文集 and *Honchō zoku monzui* 本朝續文粋. My translations are based on the text found in the *Honchō zoku monzui* (*NBT*, 24:738–741), though I also consulted the version from the *Sanjū bunshū* (*ZGR*, 12, 1:57–58). The fact that the *engi* story appears in the *Honchō zoku monzui* is significant because this text itself was seen as one of the highest literary achievements during the Heian period in terms of its specific political and literary purpose. I am indebted to David Lurie for this observation.
2. McMullin (1984, 83–106); During the eleventh and twelfth centuries, the Sanmon split into further sub-branches and eventually formed thirteen lineages (Dolce 2012, 331–332), whereas the Jimon did not create any major sub-lineages.
3. The common reading for the kingdom name 新羅 in Japanese is Shiragi (or Shiraki). But when it comes to the proper name, such as Shinra Myōjin or Shinra Saburō, "Shinra" is the more commonly used pronunciation. In the Onjōji documents, the deity's name is read as "Shinra Myōjin," and I use "Shinra" throughout the book for the deity's name, whereas I use "Silla" for the ancient Korean kingdom.
4. Schottenhammer (2005, 2).
5. Braudel 1972–1973; Braudel 1998. Braudel's idea had a big impact on later scholarship. Denys Lombard is another French scholar who developed the idea of comparing insular Southeast Asia and the Asian seas to the Mediterranean. For more on this, see Lombard and Aubin 2000. François Gipouloux uses a similar idea—the Asian Mediterranean—to describe the port cities and trading networks in China, Japan, and South Asia. See Gipouloux 2011.
6. For major scholarship on the Mediterranean, see Braudel 1972–1973; Horden and Purcell 2000; Harris 2005; Abulafia 2011; and Broodbank 2013. For its conceptual application to East Asia, see Schottenhammer 2005, 2006, and 2008.
7. Braudel (1972–1973, 1:20–21). For more on the conjunctures, see Braudel (1972–1973, 2: 892–900).

8. Here "sedentarization" means not just localization but a process by which a sea deity transforms into a mountain deity. I borrow the concept of "sedentarization" from Anne Bouchy. See Bouchy (1996, 255–298).
9. Said 1979.
10. I have slightly modified Schottenhammer's contours of the East Asian seas. Schottenhammer (2006, 6).
11. Ibid., 5.
12. Amino (2012, 31). Amino (1984, 27–31) also criticizes Marxist historians and discusses the emphasis on the lives of nonagriculturalists (J. *hinōgyōmin* 非農業民) such as merchants, artisans, and entertainers, who occupied spaces like mountains, rivers, seas, markets, and ports.
13. For a good example of the Buddhist mercantile exchanges between India and China, see Sen (2003, 102–141).
14. In his comparative work, David Abulafia has suggested this term (i.e., the "Japanese Mediterranean"). He draws attention to the common confusion between "the Mediterranean" and the "Mediterranean Sea," and makes a clear distinction between the two. Although he states that his intention is "to shift the emphasis back on the role of the relative empty space between the lands that surround the sea" (Abulafia 2006, 65), he contradicts himself by calling all the waters that surround the Japanese islands "the Japanese Mediterranean," which does not provide any geophysical connection to other parts of East Asia. Furthermore, it is based on a Japan-centered and insular vision. Abulafia (2006, 64–93).
15. There have been a handful of scholarly works that have stressed the role of Korean cultural elements in shaping Japanese Buddhist culture in English; see Best 2005; Keel 2005; Como 2008; and Como 2009. For major non-English scholarship on this issue, see Tamura 1974, 1980, 1985, and 1980; Kamata and Tamura 1989; and Nakai 1994.
16. Buswell (2005, 2).
17. Ibid.
18. In recent scholarship the French word *imaginaire* has been used to mean "what is imagined," "the contents of the imagination," or "specific imagined worlds." It is not easy to translate *imaginaire* into English, and the term has been defined differently by different scholars. This is why I choose not to translate the term; see Le Goff (1988, 1–7) and Ricoeur (1994, 118–135). On how the term has been used in Buddhist studies, see Faure (1996, 10–13, 280–282); Collins (1998, 73–74); and Lowe (2012, 207–209).
19. The conventional dates for the medieval period in Japan are 1185 to 1600. The former marks the end of the Genpei War (1180–1185) and the beginning of military rule; 1600 marks the unification of Japan under the Tokugawa shogunate and the beginning of the Edo period (1600–1868).
20. Kuroda Toshio 1963, 1975, and 1989; Amino 1984, 1986, 1990, and 2012.
21. Rambelli and Teeuwen recognize that there are moot deities who fit neither into the Japanese *kami* model nor into the Buddhist pantheon in the traditional sense. These moot deities include not only those invoked in the Daoist-like rituals or Yin-Yang ceremonies, but also Buddhist visions of the native Japanese *kami*, such as the *honji suijaku* cult of Amaterasu. Rambelli and Teeuwen (2003, 24–25).
22. We find various examples of *honji* of Shinra Myōjin: Sonjōō and Dakiniten in the Keiran *shūyōshū*; Monju, Sonjōō, Vimalakīrti, and Sekizan Myōjin in the *Jitokushū*; Monju, Fudō, Śākyamuni, Sonjōō, and Vimalakīrti in the *Jimon denki horoku*.

23. Kim Hyŏuk 2008. Edward Drott (2016, 74–117) also discusses Shinra Myōjin as an example of the *okina* god.
24. Although scholars such as Yamamoto Hiroko and Abe Yasurō use the methodology for the study of Japan's medieval period, scholars such as Saitō Hideki extend it not only to the medieval period but to all time periods from ancient to modern. Thus, Saitō uses the *chūsei shinwa* methodology when looking at the transformation of an individual god such as Susanoo; on this, see Saitō 2012. For the concept and reception of the term, see Itō 2011 and Saitō 2011.
25. Yamamoto (1998b, 4).
26. This degradation of myth/mythology might appear to be our modern bias, but as Bruce Lincoln shows, myth has undergone several phases of derogation. For instance, the Romans did not use the term, and it only reappeared in the Renaissance. For more about the historical development of myth from Greek times to its culmination in the eighteenth and nineteenth centuries, when the term was highly theorized, see Lincoln 1999.
27. The negative assessment of medieval Japanese religion started with Shinto scholars during the Edo period, who were attempting to establish an emperor-centered world order. For those Shinto ideologues, the medieval period was a time full of (and tainted by) Buddhist ideas and apocryphal texts, which were therefore unworthy of study. During the modern period, and even until recent times, people thought that mythology, by definition, should be something related to the ancient period. This bias toward both the time period and the subject has prevented scholars from studying the wide network of medieval religious literature.
28. Yamamoto 1998a and 1998b.
29. Yamamoto 1998a.
30. While some twenty articles and a handful of book chapters exist, no one has yet undertaken a book-length study of Shinra Myōjin. Tsuji Zennosuke (1931) and Miyaji Naokazu (1931) have provided two pioneering studies on Shinra Myōjin, and these continue to be the major research pieces about this deity. According to Tsuji, Shinra Myōjin was created in response to Sekizan Myōjin. Miyaji, however, argues that Shinra Myōjin was a god from Silla. The differences in their theories aside, the way in which they present Shinra Myōjin is problematic because their scholarship lacks serious textual criticism and is marked by a severe sectarian bias. The bulk of research on this deity is art-historical. Most of such scholarship focuses almost exclusively on artistic details and visual features, with Guth (1999) and Miyake (2002) being two exceptions. Faure's work on Shinra Myōjin, found in his recently published magnum opus, is by far the most comprehensive study of the deity to date (Faure 2015, 2:299–329). By shifting the previous binary Buddhist-Shinto model to the tripartitie *deva*-buddha-*kami* model as an organizing principle, Faure's work draws our attention to the medieval Japanese pantheon, especially to the relevant mythological and ritual components. He discusses Shinra Myōjin only to the extent that this deity is relevant to the evolution of Matarajin, his primary focus, leaving scholars yearning for a more complete treatment of Shinra Myōjin himself.
31. For more about theoretical approaches to Buddhist mythology, see Iyanaga (2002, 1:32–58). In two volumes of his major works, which focus on Mahākāla (J. Dakoku-ten 大黒天) and Avalokiteśvara (J. Kannon 観音) in China and Japan, Iyanaga stresses the influence of Tantrism on medieval Japanese religions.
32. For actor-network theory, see Latour 2005; Law and Hassard 1999. As to how Faure applies the theory as a complementary theory to the structuralist approach to the gods, see Faure (2015, 1:9–10).

33. Sax (2009, 94).
34. I borrow the term from Jason Neelis. Neelis (2011, 10; emphasis mine).
35. Vásquez (2008, 168).
36. Ibid.
37. For more theoretical discussion on this, see Faure (2015, 1:1–50).
38. See Faure (2015, 1:41). A rhizome is a metaphor that describes a multidimensionally complicated structure. For more on rhizomes, see Deleuze and Guattari 1987.

CHAPTER 1. BETWEEN HISTORY AND STORY

1. *Mii zokutōki* 三井続燈記, *DNBZ*, 209. An exception is a volume edited by the Jimon. On this, see *Tendai-shū Jimon-ha goonki jimukyoku* ed., 1931. In his research on the Onjōji monk Kōin 公胤 (1145–1216), Tachi provides some historical context for Onjōji during the medieval period. See Tachi (2010, 21–121).
2. *The New Selection and Record of Hereditary Titles and Family Names* (J. *Shinsen shōjiroku* 新撰姓氏録, 815) states that one of the Ōtomo branch names (Ōtomo no fubito 大友史) was from Paekche. Hoshino (1997, 168–174).
3. This immigrant Ōtomo clan is different from the Ōtomo 大友 clan that became one of the most powerful families in the Buzen Province in Kyushu between the Kamakura and Senkoku periods. The Ōtomo in Kyushu, however, had a feudal tie with the Minamoto clan. Ōtomo Yoshinao 大友能直 (1172–1223), the progenitor of the Ōtomo, who was born in the Sagami 相模 Province, was a retainer of Minamoto no Yoritomo 源頼朝 (1147–1199). Ōtomo Yoshinao may have been an illegitimate son of Yoritomo. Mass (1989, 65n26). For more about the Ōtomo clan and the rich immigrant culture in the area, see Miyaji (1931, 343–347).
4. Hoshino (1997, 168–174).
5. *Sōgō bunin shōshutsu*, 120.
6. Tachi (2010, 21–24).
7. Ibid., 22.
8. Contrary to what the *Onjōji engi* claims, however, other historical sources suggest that Sūfukuji continued to exist independently, or at least was rebuilt, in the tenth and eleventh centuries. Nakanishi (2008, 49).
9. Hoshimiya (1990, 138).
10. This continued affiliation can be seen in a document titled "The Request of Ōtomo" (J. *Ōtomoshi kusshō* 大友氏屈請) written in 871, which records the clan's offering to the temple. *Onjōji monjo* 園城寺文書, 1:384.
11. *Onjōji denki*, 56.
12. On Maitreya, see Goodwin 1977; Sponberg and Hardacre 1998. For Japanese scholarship, see Hayami 1971; Hiraoka 1977.
13. Maitreya became popular in Japan during the mid-seventh century. Nakai Shinkō (1994, 37–39) points out that in ancient Japan it was unusual that an imperial temple such as Sūfukuji would enshrine Maitreya as its *honzon*, and that Sūfukuji is therefore a representative example of Maitreya worship in this area during the seventh period.
14. *Onjōji denki*, 56.
15. Aston (1972, 1:101). The Soga clan was a powerful clan who revered the Buddhist tradition, largely due to influence from Paekche. The Japanese elite was polarized when the Buddhist statue arrived from there. After the military dispute between the pro-Buddhist Soga clan and the Mononobe clan, the Soga eventually won in 587 CE. Interestingly,

the *Nihon shoki* editor gives more credit for the victory to Shōtoku than to the Soga in order to portray Shōtoku as the protector and patriarch of the Japanese Buddhist tradition. See Como (2008, 19).

16. This Maitreya statue is not the first Buddhist statue from Paekche, but it is one of the earliest images that Japan received during the sixth century. According to the *Nihon shoki*, King Sŏng 聖 of Paekche sent a gilt-bronze image of Śākyamuni to Japan in 552. Most scholars, however, consider a 538 date to be more accurate, based on other Japanese records (McCallum 2001, 149–188). The *Nihon shoki* further states that, in 577, King Widŏk 威德 (r. 554–598) of Paekche sent another Buddhist image, and, in 584, a stone statue of Maitreya and yet another image (simply identified as a buddha) were sent as part of a diplomatic exchange.
17. For more about the details of the image, see Izumi (2010, 189–191). One more painting of the Maitreya triad (Maitreya, Enchin, and Shinra Myōjin) from the thirteenth century is currently stored at the Museum of Fine Arts, Boston.
18. When conflict arose between Onjōji and Enryakuji over the establishment of an independent ordination platform, the Maitreya connection strengthened the alliance between Onjōji and Nara temples. From the tenth century onward, Onjōji monks continued to go to Tōdaiji 東大寺 in Nara to receive the full precepts despite Enryakuji's objection. See Tachi (2010, 100–101).
19. Hazama (1995, 69–98).
20. The Jimon claims that Shinra Myōjin was already being worshipped during the reign of Emperor Seiwa 清和 (r. 858–876). *Onjōji denki* says that the size of the Shinra Myōjin statue is based on the size of the emperor Seiwa. "During the reign of Jōkan 貞観 (859–877), Enchin made a statue of the deity according to the height of the present emperor, Emperor Seiwa" (*Onjōji denki*, 59). Alternatively, it is also possible that the Seiwa connection became crucial around the time the Jimon's chronicle was compiled because of Onjōji's political ties to the Seiwa Genji or the Minamoto clan, who claimed descent from the emperor.
21. After Saichō's death, there was a succession dispute between Enchō (Saichō's disciple) and Enshū (Gishin's disciple), which marked the beginning of the Sanmon-Jimon schism. In 868, Enchin (Gishin's line) was appointed the fifth *zasu*. By the middle of the tenth century the Saichō-Ennin line had come to be less powerful than the Gishin-Enchin line both in the number of monks and in the number and condition of the buildings that it owned. The large size of Enryakuji led to departmentalized groups of monks, and those subgroups had ties to their personal patrons at court. For more on this, see McMullin (1984, 83–105); Groner (2002, 233–236).
22. During the tenth and eleventh centuries, there were often quarrels and fights between bands of armed monks during communal ceremonies and rituals. Groner notes that the warrior monks emerged in the late-tenth century at Enryakuji but the actual use of them developed after Ryōgen's death; Groner (2002, 293).
23. For the lineage of the Tendai zasu from the Tendai patriarch Saichō (the first *zasu* is Gishin) to the one hundred sixty-fourth *zasu*, appointed in 1927, see Shibuya 1935.
24. For a comprehensive study on the Tendai factionalism during the tenth century in the Tendai tradition, see Adolphson (2000, 63–65; 2007, 29–35); and Groner (2002, 15–44, 218–236).
25. For a detailed discussion on terms for armed monks and the fluid nature of the group, see Adolphson (2000, 62–63).
26. Adolphson (2000, 89–91).

27. For *hōshinnō*, see Ruppert (2011, 795).
28. Adolphson (2000, 137–138).
29. Okubo (2005, 738–798).
30. The aristocratization of the high offices occurred on the Mt. Hiei side as well. At Enryakuji, every *zasu* after Myōku 明求 (fl. eleventh c.) was either a son of the ruling family or from the branches of the Fujiwara clan. Bowring (2008, 160).
31. Kageyama (1975, 398).
32. The *Gukanshō* 愚管抄, compiled by the Tendai Sanmon monk Jien 慈円 (1155–1225) in 1220, sheds light on Onjōji's involvement in the war and portrays Shinra Myōjin as the protector of Onjōji, in particular when it addresses Onjōji's provision of asylum to Prince Mochihito 以仁王 (1151–1180), the second son of Emperor Goshirakawa 後白河 (r. 1155–1158). Brown and Ishida (1979, 398).
33. While the Kamakura regents, Hōjō Tokuyori 北条時頼 (r. 1246–1256) and Hōjō Tokimune 北条時宗 (r. 1268–1284), were less interested in Onjōji's esoteric rituals, Onjōji monks were still active in Kamakura.
34. Uozumi (1931, 425). While some records state it was 1336, several reports after repairs of the shrine suggest that it was rebuilt in 1347. See Fuke (1998, 139n5); Sakata (1987, 96, 98n30).
35. Taira (2009, 111–206).
36. Both the *Onjōji denki* and the *Jimon denki horoku* can be found in *DNBZ* (vol. 86). On the date of *Jimon denki horoku*, it has been suggested that it was compiled 1394–1427. See *DNBZ kaitai* (99:191–194); Tachi (2010, 155); Shindō (2005, 20). But Nagai thinks it was compiled between 1716 and 1730. Nagai (2006, 487). *Miidera zokutōki* is edited by the Onjōji monk Sontsū 尊通. See the text in *DNBZ* (67:161–230).
37. Asano (1931, 579–595).
38. *Onjōji koki* in the *Onjōji kiroku* 園城寺記録, 10, 11, 17, and 22. The ninth month was the fête month for Shinra Myōjin.
39. This Enshin is different from another Onjōji monk, Enshin 圓親, who lived during the thirteenth century.
40. I am indebted to Fuke Toshihiko, the chief administrative official of Onjōji for this information. Mr. Fuke informed me about the text and also kindly provided me with a copy of it when I visited the temple on March 13, 2018. According to the text, the Buddhist service for Shinra Myōjin starts with a recitation of the *Heart Sutra* as an offering to the deity. The liturgy includes: the deity's connection with Enchin; reciting the title of the *Lotus Sutra*; a vow to attain enlightenment; Shinra Myōjin's acolytes; and ending with praying for the various kinds of blessings from the deity.
41. For the image of the barracks, see *Shiga-ken shin fudoki*, 32–33. Also, this is the time when the famous art critic Ernest Francisco Fenollosa (1853–1908) came to be associated with Onjōji. In 1885, he studied Buddhism and eventually took the tonsure from the Onjōji monk, Sakurai Keitoku 桜井敬徳 (1834–1885) at Hōmyōin 法明院 of Onjōji. Fenollosa's ashes were enshrined at Hōmyōin after his sudden death in 1908. For more about Fenollosa and his relationship with Sakurai, see Yamaguchi (1982, 1:437–451). See also Fenollosa (2007 [1912], xi–xxviii).
42. For a detailed explanation of the modern military history of Ōtsu, see Nakajima 2000.
43. In recent years Onjōji has published a collection of remaining Onjōji documents, the *Onjōji monjo* (1999–2004). The *Onjōji monjo* consists of seven volumes (vol. 1–2, medieval period; vol. 3–7, early modern period). The *Onjōji kiroku* (2007) is another

complementary volume to the *Onjōji monjo*. There are a handful of newly discovered Onjōji documents from the medieval period stored at Keio University. See Nakajima (2012, 273–281); Nakajima (2015, 574–581).

44. For the major English scholarship on the topic of buddha–*kami* interactions in the medieval period, see Rambelli and Teeuwen 2003; Faure 2006–2007; Dolce and Mitsuhashi 2013; Faure 2015, vols. 1, 2.
45. The *Nakatomi harae kunge* 中臣祓訓解 (Reading and Explanation of the Nakatomi Purification Formula) is another example of such, marking an important step during the twelfth century in the amalgamation of Shintō thought and practice with Tendai esoteric Buddhism. On the authorship of the text, recent scholarship suggests that Onjōji monks might have produced it. See Matsumoto (2008, 83). For its English translation, see Teeuwen and Veere 1998.
46. In this paradigm, *kami* receive more importance and they become the *honji*. Although the idea has been understood as a reactionary movement from the Shinto side, it has to be noted that the idea was developed and promoted by Buddhist intellectuals. See Teeuwen and Rambelli (2003, 35–36).
47. Besides *Onjōji denki* and *Jimon denki horoku*, *Mii ōjōden* 三井往生伝 (1217), *Mii zokutōki*, and *Jimon kosōki* 寺門高僧記 (after 1506), there are other major textual sources for the medieval history of the Jimon.
48. The text was not discovered until the 1950s, and it was only in 1958 that the *Onjōji engi* was made known to the public through its appearance in an exhibition held by the Archives and Mausolea Department of the Imperial Household Agency (J. Kunaichō shoryōbu 宮内庁書陵部). It had been stored in the archives of the Kujō 九条 family, a branch of the Fujiwara 藤原 clan that had many of its family members appointed to the Tendai abbotship (both the Jimon and the Sanmon) from the eleventh to the thirteenth century (Tachi 2010, 26). The Kujō family was closely associated with Onjōji. For instance, Enjō 圓静 (ca. thirteenth c.), the *chōri* of Onjōji, was from the Kujō family. Also, the *Hōhiki* 宝秘記 (ca. 1217), which contains various rituals and legends about the Jimon, was compiled by the Kujō family. See Matsumoto (2009, 82).
49. Kunaichō shoryōbu (1970, 129–135); Drott (2016, 93).
50. For more on this discussion, see Oyamada (1990, 138–158); Akamatsu (1996, 482–495); and Nakamae (2003, 18–37).
51. For a study and English translation of the *Tengu zōshi*, see Wakabayashi 2012.
52. While Akamatsu thinks that it was composed in the eleventh century, Oyamada suggests that, given the content in which territorial disputes are addressed, it was probably created much later.
53. Kuroda Satoshi (2001, 75).
54. Shindō (2005, 21). There are strong textual affinities between the *Shinra Myōjin ki* and the *Shinra ryakki*.
55. Shindō (2005, 20).
56. Ibid.
57. Shindō (2005, 20–27; 2009, 28–29).
58. The term "*engi*" is an abbreviation of the Buddhist term "*innen shōki*" 因縁生起 (codependent origination; Skt. *pratītyasamutpāda*). By extension, it refers to narratives regarding the historical origins and miraculous tales of temples and shrines. The oldest *engi* in Japan is known as the *Garan engi narabi ni ruki shizai chō* 伽藍縁起幷流記資財帳 from Hōryūji 法隆寺, Daianji 大安寺, and Gangōji 元興寺, dated to 747. In the mid-late

Heian period, *engi* collections came to be widely produced; Nakano Takeshi and others theorize that the new movement was connected to the Heian trend of Buddhist pilgrimage. The contents of the *engi* covered a wide range of records, from a temple's founding story to daily monastic life. It also typically includes the origin story of Buddhist statues, stories of eminent monks of the temple, records of the temple's rituals, information about the site where the temple is situated, miraculous tales associated with the temple, and ritual and prayer texts. The compilers of those texts were monks from the temple and shrine, but aristocrats also often participated in their production at the request of a temple; see Nakano Takeshi (1995, 245–247). For a reevaluation of *engi* literature, see Blair and Tsuyoshi (2015, 1–26); Blair (2015, 246–269).

59. The term *jisha engi* is a scholarly neologism, which refers to a wide range of textual and visual narratives that focus on the histories of temple-shrine complexes. Blair and Kawasaki (2015, 1–2).
60. The term *jisha* is often translated as "temples and shrines," but I join Allan Grapard's criticism of the vagueness of the translated word, which does not capture the interconnected units. See Grapard (2016, 261n2).
61. Gorai (2008, 4).
62. Ibid., 3.
63. Nakano (1995, 246). Historians of early Japan use the concept of *kokka Bukkyō* (governmental Buddhism) to characterize early Japanese Buddhism, and the *ritsuryō* system was understood as one of the institutional frameworks of this model. However, Kamikawa Micho criticizes this *kokka Bukkyō* model for its ambiguity and calls upon scholars to understand Japanese Buddhist history within the broader context of East Asian history.
64. McNeil 1986. According to Joseph Mali, "Mythistory is concerned with collective experiences and impressions of historical events, and not with the events themselves, it does not—and cannot—answer the main historical question of what actually happened." See Mali (1991, 88).
65. Examples of the pairing include Kūkai's Seiryū Gongen 清滝權現 (the first mention is found in 1089), Ennin's Sekizan Myōjin, and Dōgen's Inari Myōjin.
66. Oyamada (1990, 126–137); Drott (2016, 81).
67. *Honchō zoku monzui*, 738.
68. Dykstra (1998, 72–73). For more about Enchin's Yellow Fudō Myōō, see Bogel (2009, 71, 198).
69. *Taiheiki* (1976, 1:413).
70. See Aston (1972, 2:99ff.); Heldt (2004, 166ff.) His name is written differently in different texts. Shiotsuchi no kami 塩椎神 is the name in the *Kojiki*, while Shiotsuchi oji 塩土老翁/塩筒老翁 is used in the *Nihon shoki*. I am grateful to David Lurie for this source.
71. *Onjōji denki*, 58.
72. Watson (2013, 25–26).
73. *Onjōji denki*, 59.
74. *Honchō zoku monzui*, 738–739; *Sanjū bunshū* in *ZGR* (12, 1:57–58).
75. *Honchō zoku monzui*, 739–740. After this, the *engi* explains Onjōji's association with the Maitreya cult and it ends with the extolment of the merit of Maitreya worship in the voice of Sanenori.
76. Kyōtai's story circulated widely beyond Onjōji and came to be featured in several *setsuwa* collections. See Drott (2016, 81–82).

77. Tsuji sees him as a mythological figure, whereas Saeki argues that he was a head monk of Onjōji. See Tsuji (1931, 214); Saeki (1989a, 208–209).
78. Drott (2016, 82–95).

CHAPTER 2. THE NETWORK OF SILLA IMMIGRANTS AND THE EMERGENCE OF SHINRA MYŌJIN

1. Latour (2005, 39).
2. Ibid., 46–59.
3. Batten (2006, 91); Como (2008, 9).
4. Como (2008, 9).
5. Katō argues that the term *toraijin* has a more neutral meaning, and should be used to refer to immigrants from China and Korea in premodern Japan. See Katō (1998, 5–8).
6. Arai (2015, 19–35).
7. For a study of this text, see Saeki (1965, 3–72); Kiley (1969, 177–189). The text is found in *ST* (*koten hen*), vol. 6.
8. Kiley (1969, 184–185).
9. At the same time, however, the *Shinsen shōjiroku* helped to establish "native" cultural and political identities on the Japan side. See Como (2008, 16).
10. For more discussion on this process from the seventh century to eighth century, see Ooms (2008, 101–104).
11. Katō (1998, 8).
12. Batten (2006, 82–86).
13. Ōhashi and Amino (2005, ix).
14. For more on the Korean-style tumuli found in Ōmi, see Ishihara (1984, 54–82).
15. Kyushu was another place with a concentration of Chinese and Korean immigrants. Here continental religious cultures thrived from early on. Buddhism was brought by immigrants to Kyushu and was known there even before it received attention from the Yamato court. Grapard argues that the establishment of Mirokuji 弥勒寺 in Usa 宇佐 supports this view. Grapard (1992, 20, 261n2).
16. Mizuno (1969, 77–92).
17. For Paekche settlers in Ōmi, Aston (1972, 1:282).
18. For details of the transportational systems of Lake Biwa in the medieval period, see Kimura (2003, 129–149); Sakurai (1995, 240–279); Harada and Watanabe (1975, 113–114).
19. Adolphson (2000, 88–89); Murai (2003, 18).
20. Ancient Japanese often called Koguryŏ 高句麗 "Koryŏ 高麗," as we find in the *Nihon shoki*. On Koraiji and Hyakusaiji, see Ishihara (1984, 153–158).
21. Dewa (2004, 4). Although the majority of Shinra shrines belong to the first category, there are many examples of the second. Most shrines in the former category claim that their main deity is associated with Jingū, consort to the emperor of Chūai. This legendary ruler is said to have conquered the southern part of the Korean Peninsula during the third century, and the legend played an instrumental role in shrines and temples in Japan that have some connection to Silla. Ame no Hiboko is another figure often identified with the main deity of the shrines and temples with the name Silla in their names. However, it is above all Susanoo who appears most commonly as the main deity in these shrines and temples, which very likely happened after the separation of Shinto and Buddhist divinities in Meiji. A common pattern that we can observe is that all these deities have a

mythological connection with Silla in their origin narratives. For the local transmission on the Shinra related deities in Japan, see Dewa 2014.

22. The Silla immigrant communities appear in neither Chinese nor Korean sources; Ennin's diary thus provides valuable historical information for understanding Silla immigrants in ninth-century China. For a Japanese translation and detailed study of the text, see Ono 1964 (4 vols.). Also see Saitō (2006, 61–224). For an English translation and discussion of Ennin's diary, see Reischauer 1955a and 1955b.
23. Curtin (1984, 11); Abramson (2014, 139).
24. Ono (1964, 4:408).
25. Yi Yujin (2009, 1–20). These Silla communities in China were mostly created after the Silla-Tang alliance defeated the Korean kingdoms of Koguryŏ and Paekche and unified the peninsula in 668. But within the peninsula Silla served as an important traffic hub due to its geographically advantageous position; it linked together Tang China, Silla, Parhae, Japan, and even Southeast Asian kingdoms and Muslim merchants both in and outside of official tributary channels. From the time of Silla's unification of the peninsula in 668 onward, diplomatic relations between Silla and Japan slowly deteriorated, until finally, in 779, Silla ceased sending diplomatic envoys to Japan.
26. Although Silla was an enemy of Japan from the time of Japan's failed aid to Paekche in 663, they maintained official, diplomatic relations for the next century. For details of diplomatic relations between Silla and Japan, see Batten (2006, 52–77).
27. This was not easy, however. As can be seen from an incident in which an eighth-century Koguryŏ monk named Yŏhae 如海 was forced to return to Korea from China, there were tensions among Chinese, Japanese, and Koreans due to Koreans' dominance of the East China trade routes. Abramson (2014, 140). See *Tang da heshang Dongzheng zhuan* 唐大和尚東徵傳, 249.
28. Yi Songsi (1997, 160).
29. Ibid., 161.
30. The practice of sending *kentōshi* ceased in 838. *Kentōshi* had a commercial role in accelerating a maritime trade network in East Asia. For more about *kentōshi*, see Fuqua 2004.
31. This was largely due to the fact that in the ninth century Japan had not yet fully developed the means or knowledge necessary to build ships capable of long-distance travel. For instance, the Japanese sailors who manned the *kentōshi* vessels did not completely understand how to use seasonal winds and how to avoid typhoons. Thus, it was common practice for Japanese student-monks to travel on the vessels of Korean or Chinese merchants. See Iida (1980, 14); Mozai (1984, 89).
32. Ono (1964, 4:404); Saeki (1989b, 108–109).
33. His name crops up several times in histories of China, Japan, and Korea. In China, his name is written 張保皐 and 弓福 (or 弓巴) in Silla. In Japanese sources his name is written 張寶高. For more about Chang Pogo, see Reischauer (1955a, 100–101); Okada (1933, 303–330); Ono (1964, 4:413–419); and Saeki (1989b, 107–121).
34. Reischauer (1955a, 168).
35. Because of his economic and military power, Chang Pogo exercised great political power in Silla. He was deeply involved with the succession to the throne there, which eventually led to his untimely death. For more about Chang Pogo, see *Samguk sagi* 177, 183–185.
36. Tanaka Fumio (2007, 141).
37. Ibid., 141–142.
38. *Samguk sagi*, 184–185.

39. It was the same for Enchin. According to the *Chishō daishi ryakubu* 智証大師略譜, Enchin also traveled with Silla merchants on his outbound voyage from Japan to China. For more on Enchin's connections with Silla merchants, see Kagamiyama (1972, 806–807).
40. According to Ennin, the Lotus Flower Monastery of Mt. Chi was thriving and had several hundred lay followers, as well as monks and nuns dispatched from Silla. The temple also provided lodging to Silla monks and other travelers. Ennin notes that for their rituals and ceremonies they followed the customs of Silla; see Reischauer (1955a, 131). For the Silla communities in China, see Kwŏn Deuk'yŏng (2006, 143–165). There are a handful of articles in Korean on the relationship between Ennin and Chang Pogo; see Kim Munkyŏng 1987 (in Japanese, Kim Munkyŏng 2001); Lee Byŏngro (2006, 319–341).
41. Reischauer (1955a, 161–162). Chang Yŏng later offered his ship for Ennin's return journey, but Ennin was not able to take that boat. See Mori (1964, 44).
42. Mori Katsumi (1964, 41–42).
43. For the whole letter, see Reischauer (1955a, 166–167).
44. This episode does not appear in Ennin's personal diary.
45. Saitō (1992, 34). The biography reads: "当処山神."
46. Saitō (1992, 43).
47. Ibid.
48. Japanese scholars provided different theories about the origin of Sekizan Myōjin. Tsuji (1931, 217) suggests that Sekizan Myōjin is not a Silla deity but a deity (Taizan Fukun 泰山府君) worshipped by Silla immigrants in China. Ono (1964, 2:52), however, argues that Sekizan Myōjin is Ennin's own deity. Saitō (2010, 166–170) maintains that Sekizan Myōjin is not a Silla deity but a Chinese deity worshiped in the Mt. Chi area.
49. The colophon states that the text was compiled in 948, but Shiozawa Hirohito (2008, 29) suggests it was written sometime between 949 and 957.
50. *Sekizan Daimyōjin engi, ST* (*ronsetsu hen* 4): 624.
51. Lee Byŏngro (2006, 328).
52. Different sources give different dates. According to the *Sekizan Daimyōjin engi*, Annen built the temple in 868 in accordance with Ennin's will, whereas the *Jikaku daishiden* states that it was in 888. Shiozawa Hirohito argues that the altar for Sekizan Myōjin was completed in 868 and that the entire temple was finished in 888. See Shiozawa (2008, 32). Here I follow the record from the *Jikaku daishiden*, which is regarded as the official version of Ennin's life.
53. Kageyama (1973, 243).
54. Inviting a foreign god and transforming him into a local deity was in no way perceived as an odd practice; instead, it was thought to increase the power of the native gods by means of creating a kind of resonance between the two. Takatori (1979, 369).

CHAPTER 3. THE MEDIEVAL TRANSFORMATIONS OF SHINRA MYŌJIN

1. Miyaji 1931; Ogino 1964; Kameda 1973; Kageyama 1975; Miyayi 1992; Itō Shirō 1996; Kuroda Satoshi 1998; Guth 1999; Miyake 2002; and Hakamada 2012.
2. For the primary sources, see the *Chishō daishi den* 智証大師伝, *Gyōrekishō* 行歴抄, *Enchin keizu* 円珍系図, and other documents gathered in *Onjōji monjo* (vol.1). For major scholarship on Enchin and his life, see Saeki 1989, 1990; Oyamada 1990; and Okano 2016.

Okano's work uses Onjōji documents that were not available to Saeki and Oyamada. Also, for the genealogy of Enchin in *Enchin keizu*, see Masanobu Suzuki (2017, 16–18).

3. Bogel (2009, 218).
4. Tohyŏn's name frequently appears in Ennin's diary. But his name disappears once Ennin arrives in the Chishan area. The last entry about Tohyŏn is on the twenty-ninth day of June in the year of 839. Ono (1964, 2:63).
5. Upon Enchin's arrival in Dazaifu in 858, several of his travel companions composed farewell poems at Kōrokan. In the collected documents of Enchin's poetry and letters, called "the Tōjinsōbetsushi narabini sekitoku 唐人送別詩并尺牘," we find a letter written by Tohyŏn (Kim Munkyŏng 2001, 146n356). For the letters, see *Kokuhō Miidera-den* (2008, 57).
6. *Onjōji denki*, 72. The text also claims that the deity already manifested himself at Onjōji around 858, the year that Enchin returned from China. *Onjōji denki*, 72.
7. For more about these deities, see Faure 2015 (vols. 1, 2).
8. I follow this division—mountain gods and sea gods—for heuristic purposes. However, the realm of each deity cannot always be delimited with certainty because there are many gray areas. Fields can be seen as extensions (or sometimes divisions) of the mountain, and the river as an extension of the sea. Furthermore, the mountain deity is closely associated with the field god (mountain gods transform into field gods during spring and summer), and the sea deity is associated with the river deity. See Ōmori Tarō (1990, 151–152).
9. Ibid., 148–149.
10. From the seventh to the ninth century, Buddhist masters went to Tang China with *kentōshi*, official Japanese diplomatic and trade missions. For the historical background and the biographical information of those Japanese student-monks of the seventh and early eighth centuries, see Bingenheimer 2001.
11. *Shoku Nihon kōki* in *KT* 3:70; Kagamiyama (1972, 772–773); Nakano Hatayoshi (1983, 101); and Ōwa (1993, 168–186).
12. Kagamiyama (1972, 780).
13. Reischauer (1955a, 407–408).
14. The text can be found in the *Dazaifu shiryō* 太宰府資料. For the full text, see Kagamiyama (1972, 780–781).
15. Several similar stories of *jinushigami* can be found in the Onjōji area, all of which share mythological elements with the legend of Shinra Myōjin. For instance, including the narrative in *Tōdaiji yōroku* (twelfth c.), there are several legends of an old fisherman known as Hira Myōjin, a *junishigami* around Lake Biwa. See Drott (2016, 84–85). In the *Fusō kogo ryōishū* 扶桑古語靈異集 (late Kamakura period), a man meets an old man next to Lake Biwa, and the old man tells him that he is a *jinushigami* named Shirahige Myōjin. Another story in the *Tale of the Soga Brothers* (*Soga Monogatari* 曽我物語, ca. fourteenth c.) also features Shirahige Myōjin as a *jinushigami* of Shiga 滋賀 who reluctantly relinquishes his land to Śākyamuni (Cogan 1987, 168–170). These stories show that the old-man image was used to assert the primordial status of a number of deities in the Ōmi region, thus further corroborating my own interpretation of the Shinra Myōjin *engi* story. By applying the Daoist theme to the Japanese setting, the old man can be identified as or likened to a Daoist immortal. This fits with the nature of *jinushigami* and their foreign character.
16. It is not uncommon to see local deities conceding their rights to territory by handing over land to a foreign Buddhist deity. The common story line is that a *jinushigami* appears in front of an eminent monk and gives his or her land to a foreign deity who

has been invited to Japan by the eminent monk. Okada (1966, 19–20). Okada gives two examples: the *Katsuragawa engi* 葛川縁起 (Kamakura period) and the *Daigoji engi* 醍醐寺縁起 (late Heian period). According to the *Katsuragawa engi*, the Tendai monk Sōō 相応 (831–919), the founder of *kaihōgyō* 回峰行 practice, encountered an old man during his ascetic practices. This old man, who was actually the god Shikobuchi Myōjin 志古淵明神, gave his land to Sōō, who built Myōōin on that site. The deity was incorporated into the temple as a *jinushigami*. In the *Daigoji engi*, an old man named Yokoo Myōjin 横尾明神 (the mountain god of Mt. Daigo) reveals himself to Shōbō 聖宝 (832–909) and transfers the land to him.

17. Because Hie Shrine 日枝神社 is located to the northeast of Kyoto, Sannō came to be regarded as a guardian against the evil spirits entering the capital from the demon gate (J. *kimon* 鬼門), i.e., the northeast. As David Bialock has noted, Mt. Hiei was not only a sacred site that guarded the demon gate but was also a demon-gate itself and developed the capacity to "provoke dangerous demonic obstructions." See Bialock (2007, 401).
18. Saeki (1989a, 205).
19. Take (2008, 216).
20. Oyamada (1978, 33–48).
21. For the different images of Sekizan Myōjin, see Faure (2015, 2:313–314).
22. Hurst (1976, 3).
23. The mutual dependence of the imperial law and the Buddhist law emerged during the latter part of the eleventh century in connection with the development of the estate system of land tenure. Kuroda Toshio (1983, 9–13).
24. There are other disagreements as well, such as disputes over doctrinal education. For instance, *Tendai Hokkeshū gishū* 天台法華宗義集 (Collected doctrines of the Tendai Lotus school), a summary of Tendai teachings written by Gishin shortly after Saichō's death, played a significant role in doctrinal training at Onjōji. The text became significant because Gishin was Enchin's teacher. While Gishin's text became important at Onjōji, monks at Enryakuji ignored it. Enchin's *Juketsushū* 授決集 (*T.* 2367, 2 fascicles), a collection of Enchin's questions about Tendai doctrine and his Chinese master Liangqing's 良請 answers, was also a key source of Tendai doctrine in the Jimon. For more about the doctrinal differences between the two, see Hazama (1995, 71–84). During the Edo period, the study of logic and the *Abhidharmkośa* received a certain degree of significance in the Jimon, which was not true of the Sanmon. Notomo (2000, 149–150).
25. Ishikawa (2018, 196).
26. Tachi (2010, 101).
27. The ordination platform issue was not only a question of securing institutional autonomy, but also was part of a wider issue at the time—namely, how to interpret precepts in Tendai Buddhism. The dispute over the independent ordination platform seems to suggest that Buddhist precepts still played a significant role in upholding religious authority in Tendai. For more on the Tendai views of the precepts and ordination, see Groner 1987, 2007, and 2014.
28. Adolphson (2000, 140).
29. The most direct expression of Goshirakawa's favor was his becoming a devotee of the Onjōji in 1169, ten years after his abdication.
30. *Jimon denki horoku*, 142. Originally the *sanmaya* precepts were performed as the initial precepts prior to *kanjō* 灌頂 (Skt. *abhiṣeka*) or the consecration ritual for the Shingon monks. The esoteric precepts were introduced to the Tendai Jimon by Myōson. The Sanmon and the Jimon disagreed on the position of the *kanjō*. According to the Enryakuji

monk, Zengen 全玄 (1113–1193), the *sanmaya* precepts were additional, supplementing more major ones such as the ten major precepts (J. *jūjū kai* 十重戒) and forty-eight minor precepts (J. *yonjūhachikyō kai* 四十八輕戒) of the apocryphal *Brahma's Net Sutra* (J. *Bonmokyō* 梵網經). In other words, the *sanmaya* precepts were a minor step. But the Jimon monks elevated the *sanmaya* precepts above all others, claiming that anyone, even without *kanjō*, could receive them. Compared to the precepts observed in Nara Buddhism and the Sanmon's precepts, Onjōji's *sanmaya* precepts interpreted monastic responsibility somewhat more liberally; see Tachi (2010, 107–112). For studies on Onjōji's *sanmaya* precepts, see Ishida (1980, 47–74); Hiraoka (1981, 167–227).

31. This seems to refer to an esoteric ritual based on the *Sanshu shitchi hajigoku ten gosshō shutsu sangai himitsu darani hō* 三種悉地破地獄轉業障出三界祕密陀羅尼法 (*Secret Dhārṇī Method of Three Attainments Which Destroy Hell and Reverse Karmic Hindrances in the Three Worlds*, *T.* 905), a text falsely attributed to Śubhakarasiṃha. It includes passages drawing a correlation between the five syllables (J. *goji* 五字) and the five families (J. *gobu* 五部) of Buddhist esotericism and the theory of Five Agents (J. *gogyō setsu* 五行說). It has been widely cited as an example of Sino-Indian syncretic thought. However, Chen Jinhua suggests that this text was fabricated within the inner circles of Japanese Tendai, perhaps by Annen 安然 (841–?), to bolster the esoteric credentials of Saichō. See Jinhua Chen (1998, 21–76).
32. *Onjōji denki*, 58–59.
33. On Daoxuan, see Huaiyu Chen 2007.
34. *Enkyōbon Heike monogatari*, 3:61–65. Raigō's story is also found in the *Genpei jōsuiki* 源平盛衰記 (vol. 10), the *Hie Sannō rishōki* 日吉山王利生記 (vol. 3), and the *Gukanshō* (vol. 4). For the English translation of the *Gukanshō*, see Brown and Ishida (1979, 83–88).
35. Prince Atsufumi died in 1077, while Raigō died in 1084. Thus, the claim that Raigō died right after the birth of the prince is anachronistic. For more on this, see Sakaguchi 1998.
36. *Enkyōbon Heike monogatari*, 3:61–65.
37. See also the *Raigō ajari emaki* 頼豪阿闍梨絵巻. For this document, see Kisaka (2016, 111–124). Raigō became popular in ghost stories in the Edo period as well. In the *Gazu hyakki yagyō* 画図百鬼夜行 (1776), for instance, he came to be known as Iron Rat (J. Tesso 鉄鼠) (Yoda 2016, 42). For more about the *Gazu hyakki yagyō* and Toriyama Sekien 鳥山石燕 (1712–1788), the artist of the painting, see Foster (2009, 30–76).
38. *Genpei jōsuiki*, 123. For the *Hie Sannō rishōki*, see *Myōhōin shiryō*, 5:45. On the discussion of the date of *Hie Sannō rishōki*, see Simosaka (1988, 53–78).
39. Nanami (1984, 84); Yamamoto (1996, 47); and Sakaguchi (1998, 64). Note that the Sekizan Myōjin story is a later variation inspired by Shinra Myōjin's *tatari* story.
40. Brown and Ishida (1979, 83–84). For a study of angry spirts, see Shibata 1984; McMullin (1988, 270–293). Groner also discusses how the individualized *goryō* becomes both a new threat for the nobles and an opportunity for the monks to create new esoteric rituals in the Tendai context. See Groner (2002, 78–81).
41. Yamamoto (1998a, 30–34).
42. Teeuwen and Rambelli (2003, 115). The *tatarigami* aspect was not always appreciated. Satō Hiroo notes that Amaterasu's perceived *tatarigami* character in the ancient period was one of the major obstacles to her promotion to the status of divine ancestor, and, accordingly, it had to be erased during her transformations in the medieval period. Satō 2000.
43. *Jimon denki horoku*, 120; *Fusō ryakki*, 315. Another account is found in the *Gukanshō*. Brown and Ishida (1979, 87).

44. *Jimon denki horoku*, 120.
45. Ibid. Mt. Nyoi was the gate that connected Kyoto and Onjōji in Ōtsu. The route thus means the direction to Onjōji; Sakaguchi (1998, 62).
46. *Jimon denki horoku*, 120.
47. *Myōkaikishō* 妙槐記抄 (Senji-an 宣旨案), in *Shiryō taisei* (1981, 204–205).
48. *Onjōji denki*, 95.
49. On the lineage of the Shinra Myōjin Shrine priesthood, see Kuroda Satoshi (2001:80–81).
50. Ibid., 75.
51. The progenitor of Seiwa Genji was Prince Tsunemoto 經基 (?–961?). The Kawachi Genji 河内源氏 were members of a family line within the Seiwa Genji, which in turn was one of several branches of the Minamoto clan. Tachi (2010, 122–141).
52. The Hōjō family was another clan that sponsored the Jimon. Henben 顕弁, a member of the Hōjō clan, for instance, was appointed as Onjōji's *chōri* in 1327. The Hōjō clan was one of the main supporters from this point until the end of the Kamkura *bakufu*. Nagai (2006, 285).
53. *Onjōji denki*, 67; *Jimon denki horoku*, 123.
54. Dewa (2004, 59).
55. For a detailed study of this text see Shindō 2005; Shindō 2009.
56. Some scholars have questioned its reliability as a historical record. Shindō (2009, 9).
57. Shindō (2005, 19–28); Shindō (2009, 4–6).
58. For more on Hachiman, see Bender 1982; Nakano Hatayoshi 1983; Guth (Kanda) 1985; and Grapard 2016.
59. *Onjōji denki*, 67. Like his brother Shinra Saburō, Hachiman Tarō came to be a devotee of the Jimon as well. For example, when his first daughter was suffering from an eye disease, Yoshiie prayed for her recovery at Onjōji. Ōmori Keiko (2010, 62).
60. Grapard (2016, 78).
61. Nakamura (1931, 385–416).
62. Ooms (2009, 205).
63. On the Hachiman cult at the Tsurugaoka Shrine, see Guth (Kanda) (1985, 44).
64. *Azuma kagami* 吾妻鏡 (1939, 1:106). A part of the *Azuma kagami* (covering the period between 1180 and 1185) is translated into English. See Shinoda (1960, 149–364).
65. Nagai (2006, 440).
66. However, the role of *gojisō* was not reserved for the Jimon. Together with monks from Enryakuji and Tōji, three esoteric Buddhist lineages served in this role. Ryūben also reinstalled the *ryūge-e* ritual at Onjōji as a way to promote the Jimon ritual. For more about Ryūben's association with the Minamoto, see Nagai (2006, 439–490).
67. Nagai (2006, 443).
68. For a more detailed treatment of Iwashimizu Hachiman, see Grapard (2016, 38–48); Hardacre (2017, 121–122).
69. Latour (2005, 59).
70. Due to Gorai Shigeru's and Miyake Hitoshi's presentation of Shugendō as a unique, ancient Japanese religion, scholars used to think that Shugendō must have begun around the end of the Heian period. However, a newer generation of scholars has suggested that Shugendō as an independent religion was established sometime after the fourteenth century; see Hasegawa (1989, 56–75); Tokunaga (2002, 74–75); and Tokunaga (2015, 77–92). Heather Blair and Caleb Carter join this revised view and state that, as an independent "way," Shugendō dates to the late Kamakura period. Blair (2015, 270–272); Carter (2014, 6–9).

71. Kumano's fame as a sacred site began to be documented in the tenth century. According to the *Nihon shoki* and *Kojiki*, for instance, Kumano is the burial site of Izanami. The Buddhist belief that the pilgrimage can ensure rebirth in the Pure Land made this extended journey even more appealing to the retired sovereigns and the aristocracy. Bowring (2008, 224–226).
72. Tokunaga (2002, 79–81).
73. Miyake (2001, 19); Moerman (2005, 18–19). The three Kumano shrines consist of Hongū 本宮, Shingū 新宮, and Nachi 那智.
74. Moerman (2005, 49).
75. Shirakawa made the Kumano pilgrimage nine times, Toba twenty-one times, Goshirakawa thirty-four times, and Gotoba twenty-eight times. Mikaye (1996, 125).
76. Miyake (1996, 126).
77. *Kōfukuji sōjō*, 105. Jōkei 貞慶 (1155–1213) wrote the text to criticize Hōnen 法然 (1133–1212). For more about the text, see Kamata and Tanaka (1975, 509–510).
78. The full name of the temple is Shōtaigojiin, "Temple for the protection of the sacred body," which symbolizes both the body of the imperium and the body of the emperor; see Grapard (2016, 76, 273n176). Shōgoin was an important *monzeki*, a temple whose abbacy was reserved for imperial princes and court nobles.
79. Miyake (1996, 133); Blair (2015, 281–282).
80. For the images of Shinra Myōjin stored at Shōgoin, see the catalog, *En no Gyōja to Shugendō no sekai* 1999.
81. For more about the Kumano honji mandara, see Zitterbart 2008.
82. For more on Zaō, see Blair 2015.
83. Miyake (2002, 1–33).
84. *En no Gyōja to Shugendō no sekai* (1999, 104ff.).

CHAPTER 4. SHINRA MYŌJIN, THE MULTIFACETED DEITY

1. On the issue of dating this work, see Childs (1980, 129). There are several examples of *chigo emakimono* 絵巻物: the *Hōnen shōnin eden* 法然上人絵伝 (Narrative Painting of the Life of Saint Hōnen, thirteenth c.); *Chigo Kannon engi* 稚児観音縁起 (Narrative Painting of the Origin of Chigo Kannon, early fourteenth c.); and *Ashibiki-e* 芦引絵 (Narrative Painting of a Love Story of Chigo, ca. Muromachi period).
2. Sawada (1976, 24–25). Paul Atkins also agrees that the story deploys actual practices and historical incidents. Atkins (2008, 953–954).
3. The text is found in Ichiko Teiji, ed., *Otogi Zōshi* 御伽草子, *NKBT*, 38:460–485. The detailed description of the Sanmon-Jimon battle is found in sections 13, 14, and 15. For an English translation of the text, see Childs (1980, 132–151).
4. While *chigo* have often been presented in previous scholarship as boys between the ages of seven and fourteen who reside in temples for educational purposes but who are often involved in homosexual relationships with priests (Childs 1980, 127), Or Porath argues that *chigo* is not a simplistic category that can be biologically determined, but more a social and cultural one. Or (2017, 19–20).
5. For more on the different editions and versions of the *emaki*, see Kim Yujin (2015, 107n3).
6. Tendai monks developed elaborate initiation rituals for *chigo* in which the boys were depicted as avatars of Avalokiteśvara. The medieval popularity of *chigo* is attested to in the popular saying: "[Worship] the *chigo* first, then Sannō (J. *ichi ji ni sannō* 一兒二山王)";

see Abe (1984, 50–52). The same motif of a *chigo* being depicted as a reincarnation of Avalokiteśvara is also found in the *Chigo Kannon engi*, a story set at Kōfukuji.

7. *Aki no yo no nagamonogatari*, 482–483.
8. In the *Kojidan* 古事談, an early thirteenth-century *setsuwa* collection, we find a similar story. *Kojidan*, 111.
9. The *Shasekishū* took its motif from an earlier text, the *Hosshin shū* 発心集 by Kamo no Chōmei 鴨長明 (1155–1216); Watanabe (1981, 270). Variations on the same story can be found in several *setsuwa* collections, such as the *Ruijū kigen shō* 類聚既験抄 (ca. thirteenth c.) and the *Shōzai shū* 聖財集 (ca. fourteenth c.) another collection compiled by Mujū.
10. Morrell (1985, 87–88, 153–154).
11. *Onjōji denki*, 72–73.
12. For more on *waka-dhāraṇī* theory, see Kimbrough (2005, 4–11).
13. After the lectures on the *Nihon shoki* (J. *Nihongi kōen* 日本紀講筵) at court, poems related to the *Nihon shoki* were composed about topics such as *kami*, emperors, and aristocrats, and these poems are known collectively as the *Nihongi kyōen waka* 日本紀竟宴和歌. They were compiled into a collection in 943.
14. *Dhāraṇī* were widely in use in Japan at least as early as the early eighth century. See Abé (1999, 161–162). *Dhāraṇī* consist of indecipherable phonic fragments and are usually transliterated from the Sanskrit into Chinese. Their incomprehensibility allowed *dhāraṇī* to transform into superlative signs that express the spiritual power contained within words. They also operate according to the idea that spiritual power can be created and/or wielded through the intonation of words.
15. Saichō is the first one to use the term *sangoku* in the context of Buddhist theories about degeneration; Blum (2006, 34–35). On the text, see Ichikawa 1999; Yokouchi 2004.
16. For more about *sangoku Bukkyō shikan*, see Sasaki 1987; Sueki 1993; Tamura 1994; and Blum 2006. Interestingly, while Gyōnen was aware of the historical transmission of Buddhism from Korea to Japan, he accepted the idea of the three-kingdoms framework for Buddhist histories. Even though contemporary Japanese Buddhist intellectuals, including Gyōnen, were aware of the significance of Silla in Buddhism's transmission, Silla was no longer recognized as being a major Buddhist country in this three-kingdoms model. It was either regarded as part of China or was simply neglected.
17. Iyanaga (1998, 105:36).
18. *NKBT*, 85:222–223. For the English translation, see Morrell (1985, 163–164).
19. Klein 2002. On the question how the Tendai monk Chōken 澄憲 (1126–1203) and Jien 慈円 (1155–1225) theorized *waka* as a means of praising the Buddha and how *waka* was incorporated into esoteric Buddhist rites and liturgies in this context, see Bushelle (2015, 141–278). Also, for a discussion of poems as valued and prestigious items of writing in early Japan, see Lurie (2011, 254–311).
20. *Onjōji denki*, 95.
21. On the *waka* competition at the Shinra Shrine and the body of *waka* presented at the competition, see *Jimon denki horoku*, 126–132; *Shinra ryakki*, 337–339.
22. *Jimon denki horoku*, 125–132.
23. *Onjōji denki*, 92.
24. *Jimon denki horoku*, 119.
25. The deity also appears in the *Genpei jōsuiki*, again as an old man dressed in a red robe. In the *Akoneura kuden* 阿古根浦口伝, Sumiyoshi appears as an eighty-year-old man

in a red robe. In another work, the *Sangoki* 三五記, the deity appears wearing a red silk hat. His acolyte is often described as wearing a red robe. The color red symbolizes an exorcistic effect against evil spirits or contamination. See Kim Hyŏnuk (2008, 51–52).

26. Christine Guth speculates that Shinra Myōjin's portrayal as a Chinese literatus in the typical visual representation of the deity is related to his role as the *waka* deity of Onjōji. Guth further thinks that Shinra Myōjin's personification of a Chinese literatus was parallel to or was even influenced by other deities, such as Kitano Tenjin 北野天神, the deified form of Fujiwara no Michizane, who also came to be identified as a patron of poetry. He is often depicted as a Chinese scholar. How the association was made is not known, but his image as both a Chinese literatus and an immortal must have helped shape his new role as a *waka* deity at Onjōji. Guth (1999, 116–118).
27. Matsuo (1997, 35–36).
28. *Mii zokutōki*, 215–218.
29. *Jimon denki horoku*, 209.
30. For the name of leading masters of each month of the year's ceremony, see *Mii zokutōki*, 215.
31. *Jimon denki horoku*, 121.
32. This could have been similar to the recitation of the name of the Buddha Amitābha as practiced at the Jōgyō zanmai-dō at Enryakuji. There was also a Jōgyō zanmai-dō at Onjōji. This *Shinra nenbutsu* is possibly related to the *himitsu nenbutsu* 秘密念仏, given the contemporaneous popularity of the latter practice in the Shingon tradition.
33. *Shinra Myōjin ki*, in Kuroda Satoshi (2001, 94–95).
34. For *ennen*, see Matsuo 1997.
35. Matsuo (1989, 9).
36. On *Yuima-e*, see Bauer (2011, 161–179).
37. Matsuo (1997, 395).
38. Ibid., 393.
39. Ibid, 168–169.
40. In 1052, 1125, 1154, and 1210. For the full description of the 1210 *matsuri*, see *Jimon denki horoku*, 117–118. There is no record of *matsuri* after 1210. However, from the late-thirteenth century onward, a ritual for Hachiman was carried out. Matsuo (1997, 396–397).
41. *Onjōji denki*, 95; *Jimon denki horoku*, 117.
42. An everyday male dress worn by lower-class nobles during the Heian period. An example of a child wearing a *suikan* is found in the sixth section of volume 13 of the *Hōnen jōnin eden*.
43. *Jimon denki horoku*, 118.
44. In the *Shinra ryakki* there are numerous miracle stories related to Shinra Myōjin's sword as well. For instance, one story tells of a Fujiwara woman who became pregnant when she dreamed that she received a sword from Shinra Myōjin's two *dōji* (*Shinra ryakki*, 347). Another story tells of a woman of the Ōtomo family. One day she dreamed of Shinra Myōjin, who put a sword into her mouth. The woman subsequently gave birth to a boy, who later became the priest of the Shinra Myōjin Shrine (*Shinra ryakki*, 348).
45. *Jimon denki horoku*, 117.
46. *Onjōji denki*, 95.
47. *Jimon denki horoku*, 117.
48. The use of youths in religious ceremonies is also found in Buddhist and Daoist ceremonies in China. Strickmann (2002, 227).

49. Tanaka (1995, 205). There were several subcategories of child or *dō* 童 in medieval society, differentiated by role; Niunoya (1997, 463–464). For more on *dōji*, see Niunoya (1997, 481–482).
50. *Onjōji denki*, 95.
51. Matsuo (1997, 396).
52. *Onjōji denki*, 59, 70.
53. *Shinra ryakki*, 324.
54. Ibid., 325.
55. *Onjōji denki*, 72; *Shinra Myōjin ryakki*, 325.
56. For more about *kushōjin*, see Faure (2015, 1:93–108).

CHAPTER 5. TREK FOR THE STAR DEITY

1. Orzech, Payne, and Sørensen (2011, 13–18).
2. On this issue, see Lopez (1996, 86–91); Payne (2006, 1–31); Wedemeyer (2012, 1–67); and Proffitt (2015, 84–98). For more specific discussions of Tendai esoteric Buddhism, see Dolce 2006a, 2011, and 2012.
3. The Jimon esoteric Buddhist tradition is an example of this. Jimon esotericism constructed a specific ritual and textual system beginning with Enchin's transmission of esoteric Buddhism from China.
4. On the question of how the term "esoteric" is grounded in the notion of "secrecy," see Dolce 2006a.
5. Kyushu has a strong tradition of star worship and divination that can be traced back to the Korean Peninsula. The Myōken cult in Kyushu is one such example. Myōken worship in Kyushu arguably began at a shrine in modern-day Yatsushiro 八代 in Kumamoto Prefecture. It is not clear when the cult began, but the Yatsushiro Shrine claims that its Myōken deity was brought by a Paekche prince named Imsŏng 琳聖 (fl. six to seven centuries), who is also recognized as the ancestral founder of the Ōuchi 大内 family. The written record is found only in the documents of the Ōuchi, a powerful military clan active during the reign of the Ashikaga shogunate (fourteenth to sixteenth centuries). The Ōuchi clan played a major role in supporting the Ashikaga in the Nanbokuchō wars against the imperial court. A Korean historical source confirms the clan's claim that they are descendants of a Paekche prince. In 1453, Ōuchi clan members visited the Chosŏn court in search of their roots and asked the court if there were any written records of the prince's departure to Japan. See *Tanjong sillok* 端宗實錄, in *Chosŏn wangjo sillok* 朝鮮王朝實錄, 6:601.
6. Tusda (2006, 149–151).
7. For an in-depth study of Myōken, see Faure (2015, 1:51–114). For a comprehensive treatment of the different aspects of Japanese star worship, see Dolce 2006b.
8. On the Big Dipper cult in Buddhism and Daoism, see Franke (1990, 75–111); Mollier (2008, 134–173); and Huang (2012, 38–52).
9. *Onjōji denki*, 64.
10. Dolce (2012, 356–358).
11. *Asabashō*, *T. zuzō*, 9:462b; Misaki (1992, 226–227).
12. *Myōken zasshū* 妙見雜集, *T. zuzō*, 10:1160b. The *Myōken zasshū* is part of the *Commentaries of White Treasures* (J. *Byakuhōshō* 白實抄) compiled in 1284 by Chōen 澄円 (1290–1371) at Kongōbuji 金剛峯寺.
13. For the ritual offerings and arrangements, see *Kakuzensho*, *T. zuzō*, 5:399.

14. The Sanmon criticized the Jimon's worship of Sonjōō, saying that the deity is not in line with the standard esoteric Buddhist practice, but rather belongs to the practice of yin-yang masters. *Asabashō*, *T. zuzō*, 9:462b–462c.
15. *Keiran shūyōshū*, *T. zuzō*, 76:853a. In other Jimon sources, Sonjōō is the original ground of the Sannō deity of Mt. Hiei, which possibly reflects the sectarian consciousness.
16. Misaki (1992, 226–261); Tsuda (2006, 145–193); and Dolce (2012, 356–358).
17. Tsuda (2006, 145–193).
18. Groner (2002, 90–92).
19. The Sanmon incorporated other divinities into its star ritual: Ichiji Kinrin 一字金輪, the Cosmic Buddha of the Golden Wheel, and Sannō are three such examples. For more on this, see Dolce (2011, 766); Faure (2015, 1:51–114); and Hirase (2014, 32–34).
20. During the tenure of Eien 永圓, in the eleventh century, the ritual was performed almost everyday. *Mii zokutōki*, 210.
21. *Zōho shiryō taisei* (1975, 53, 98).
22. Hayami (1975, 96–97).
23. *T. zuzō*, 9:462b. Two Sonjōō halls were established in the Onjōji complex: one at Byōdōin in the Middle Quarter, in which Emperors Gotoba and Goshirakawa prayed to Sonjōō, and another in the Northern Quarter, in which Shirakawa prayed. The two Sonjōō halls do not exist any more, although the Sonjōō ritual is still carried out at Onjōji's Hōmyōin.
24. Matsumoto (2009, 84).
25. Keihan was originally from the Taira 平 clan and was the first monk to establish an institutional tie between Onjōji and Nyoiji 如意寺. During the Kempō era (1213–1219), when Enryakuji monks burned Onjōji down, Keihan performed a *kanjō* ceremony at Nyoji because Onjōji was under construction. Tachi (2010, 520–521).
26. For the original text of the *Hōhiki*, see the *Onjōji monjo*, 7:94–282. For a discussion of the text, see Shimozaka (2004, 444–451).
27. *Myōken zasshū*, *T. zuzō*, 10:1160.
28. *Mii zokutōki*, 210.
29. Matsumoto (2009, 87).
30. *Hōhiki*, 160.
31. Matsumoto (2009, 82–83).
32. Taira (2009, 127–128). Shinra Myōjin's association with young children continues even now. According to the Mr. Fuke, the chief administrative official of Onjōji, local people worship the deity as a child-protecting deity.
33. *Hōhiki*, 165–166.
34. Ibid., 166, 171.
35. *T. zuzō*, 10:1160. What we can tell from the passage is that the ritual for Sonjōō was pervaded by a deer theme, a crucial link between the Jimon and the Fujiwara clan.
36. The equation is found in the *Myōken zakki*. On this see, Misaki (1992, 238). Myōken is usually depicted as a male, but on rare occasions we find him as a female. For Myōken depicted as a female deity, see the catalog *Bushōga sugatta shinbutsu tachi* (2013, 45).
37. *Hōhiki*, 171.
38. Among the multiple forms of Kannon, the Jimon developed an emphasis on Nyoirin Kannon 如意輪観音. For more on Nyoirin Kannon, see Fremerman 2008; Faure (2015, 1:271–328).
39. The earliest extant mention of the Saikoku pilgrimage is found in an account of a pilgrimage made between 1093 and 1094 by an Onjōji monk. We find another record of a

monk (whose name is Kakuchū) who made the pilgrimage. He visited thirty-three Kannon temples as part of his pilgrimage, each of which had close links to Onjōji (Reader 2014, 65–66). Onjōji's association with the Kannon cult continues into the modern age, and the temple is popularly known as the fourteenth temple in the pilgrimage of the thirty-three temples devoted to Kannon in the Kansai area.

40. Sekimori (2006, 237).
41. Fukūkensaku Kannon was enshrined in the Nan'endō 南円堂 of Kōfukuji as well. For an in-depth study on the Kasuga deity, see Grapard 1992.
42. Tyler (1990, 91).
43. Note that most extant images of Sonjōō depict the deer but that sometimes a boar appears instead.
44. *Jimon denki horoku*, 233–234. Modern scholarship does not believe that this is the case. However, Enchin indeed did bring various unique esoteric images from China to Japan. What he transmitted to the Japanese Buddhist audience, including the *Gobushinkan* 五部心観, provided newer forms of images that differed from what Kūkai had introduced a half-century before. Bogel (2009, 218).
45. Tsuda (1998b, 75).
46. Tsuda Tetsuei suggests that the one who created the Sonjōō image in the ritual may have been Yokei. Tsuda (2002, 17–37).
47. Izumi (1990, 3); Tsuda (2006, 154).
48. *Kakuzenshō*, *DNBZ*, 50:5a. There are numerous interpretations of the relationship between Sonjōō and the seven stars. Some see it as one between husband and wife, or between a ruler and his ministers.
49. Sometimes these three are identified as three luminous celestial deities (J. Sankō Tenshi 三光天子). Sometimes Venus replaces the Big Dipper.
50. For instance, robes that the emperors wore during the *abhiṣeka* ceremony were decorated with the sun, the moon, and the Big Dipper. See Dolce (2006c, 10).
51. *Onjōji denki*, 79.
52. Izumi (1990, 1–4). Because of their functional similarity, it seems that Chintaku reifujin and Sonjōō were merged at Onjōji, although Chintaku reifujin was also worshipped independently at the temple. Several images of the deity, such as paintings and on talismans, are stored at Onjōji. A transcription of a ritual manual for the Chintaku reifujin ritual (1697) was transmitted to Onjōji's Hōmyōin. See Izumi (2010, 22).
53. Sekimori (2006, 238).
54. On Fugen, see Fabricand-Person 2001.
55. Sekimori (2006, 238–239).
56. Schipper (1993, 174). The marvelous fungus is closely associated with the deer, both physically and symbolically. Its shape resembles deer antlers, and this association probably led to their shared symbolism of longevity. The deer became almost identical with the practitioner, as it was believed that it alone could find the object of the practitioner's desire, namely the marvelous fungus.
57. Sekimori (2006, 237). Marui has suggested that the deer is a symbol of metallurgic technology that was brought to ancient Japan by immigrants from the Korean Peninsula. He argues that deerskin was used to increase temperature in the process of refining metals. Many of these technicians were also ritual specialists of the Myōken cult. See Marui (2013, 77).
58. Mollier (2008, 135).

59. Ibid.
60. A similar idea is found in another Chinese text that was composed a century earlier. For instance, according to the *Yunji qiqian* 雲笈七籤 (Seven Tablets in a Cloudy Satchel, 1029), if one sees one of these invisible stars, one may live three hundred years longer; if one sees both, this number could be doubled; *Yunji qiqian*, 2:547–548 and 563, and 3:256. The *Kakuzenshō* also states: "If one can see the Auxiliary Star, it is possible to know when the person dies." *T. zuzō*, 9:463.
61. Andersen (1989–1990, 15–53). For more on the ritual, see Huang (2012, 40–85).
62. Huang (2012, 42).
63. Lewis (2006, 104). Lewis has shown that the glyph that represented his name was derived from the character for a type of dragon.
64. Lewis (2006, 102–106).
65. Lewis (2006, 141–143); Schipper (1993, 173–174); and Granet (1953, 245–249).
66. Hirase (2014, 33).
67. Later, Shingon also adopted the ritual steps in the iconography and the ritual of the Rokuji Myōō 六字明王 (Enlightened King of the Six Words). Worship of Rokuji Myōō was established in the late eleventh century by Hanjun 範俊 (1038–1112), the founder of the Ono 小野 branch of Shingon. For Rokuji Myōō and the six-syllable ritual, see Tsuda 1998a; Tsuda 1998b; and Lomi (2011, 110–168). According to Tsuda, it is possible that Sonjōō's image influenced the creation of Rokuji Myōō. See Tsuda (1998a, 27–54).
68. *Asabashō*, *T. zuzō*, 9:462.
69. Harper (1998, 367n2).
70. Pu (1998, 136).
71. Ibid., 139.
72. *Onjōji denki*, 58c–59a.
73. Teeuwen (2006, 173–174).
74. Urban (2001, 12).
75. Teeuwen (2006, 172–203). Transmission is another concept intimately related to secrecy. Yet both secrecy and transmission are ambiguous terms. Fabio Rambelli has noted that the conventional emphasis on transmission in esoteric Buddhism is overstated. See Rambelli (2006, 107–129).
76. Teeuwen (2006, 197).
77. Ibid., 173–175.
78. Taimitsu theoreticians such as Ennin, Enchin, and Annen were interested in combining the continental interpretation of the *Lotus Sutra* as the perfect teaching and the esoteric interpretation of the sutra, and by doing so they were able to transform esotericism into a more sophisticated and complex concept. For more on Taimtsu, see Sueki (1994, 69–86); Stone (1999, 21–33); and Dolce (2011, 744–767). For issues in the definition and legitimation of Taimitsu as a distinct Tantric tradition by focusing on the medieval ritual world, see Dolce 2012.

CHAPTER 6. SHINRA MYŌJIN AS A PESTILENCE DEITY

1. The Silla kingdom had disappeared by the tenth century, but even after its demise Japanese records continued to use the name, just as "Tang" meant "China" to the Japanese long after the end of the Tang dynasty. For instance, in the earliest Japanese world map (from the fourteenth century), the Korean Peninsula is called "Silla." See Murai (2010, 26–27).

2. Ricoeur (2000, 541).
3. Le Goff 1982, 1988.
4. Faure (1996, 3).
5. Maurice Halbwachs's notion of "collective memory" is intended to explain how memory can be translated into myth and rituals in religious traditions. The initiator of the sociological study of memory, he explored the principal locations of memory from the religious to the domestic spheres, from memory in the area of stratification to various other group memories (Halbwachs 1992). Inspired by Halbwachs, Jan Assmann reinvigorated the study of collective memory and developed the notion of cultural memory. He distinguished various types of social memory. According to him, collective memory refers to shared memories whose task is to transmit a collective identity, and this is particularly susceptible to political interference. "Cultural memory" is a step beyond collective memory and refers to shared memories that become part of a tradition beyond the three-generation cycle of communicative memory. Cultural memory, emphasizing the social and cultural dimensions of memory, explains how memory is inscribed and continued through practices repeated regularly in a communal form. See Assmann (2006, 3–8). On cultural imagination, see Huhndorf 2001; Smyth 2001.
6. *Onjōji denki*, 65.
7. Susanoo's association with Gozu Tennō has been well researched. See Kwŏn Dongwoo (2013, 241–271). For a fuller treatment of Susanoo, see Weiss 2016.
8. Blum (2006, 32–34).
9. Ibid., 32.
10. Souyri (2001, 140).
11. Interestingly, this complex was not limited to Japan. The same logic can be found in the worldview of Chinese monks with regard to attitudes toward India. Tansen Sen describes the Chinese anxiety over India's perfection as a "borderland complex"; Sen (2003, 11). Whereas most Chinese assumed that China, the "Middle Kingdom" (Ch. Zhongguo 中國), was the center of the world, Chinese monks often reserved the term for India. See Mair (2014, xiii).
12. Blum (2006, 34–38).
13. Even before the adoption of the three-kingdoms model, it was said of most Buddhist divinities in the *honji suijaku* paradigm that they appeared in all three kingdoms in question (i.e., India, China, and Japan). See Teeuwen and Rambelli (2003, 2).
14. *Onjōji denki*, 65.
15. *Jimon denki horoku*, 109.
16. The term *hankoku* or "vassal country" clearly connotes an inferior status, and it is highly possible that the text comes from a Chinese source.
17. *Onjōji denki*, 59.
18. *Jimon denki horoku*, 113. Among those five names, the name Shitenfujin does not fit into the clustering of mountain-god names. This name provides a potential mythic link between Shinra Myōjin and the goddess Mago 痲姑 of Korean mythology. Although there are several different transmissions and stories concerning Mago, she is identified as the goddess of Mt. Ch'ŏnt'ae 天台 in Korean folk literature. In Korean mythology Mago seems to come from the Chinese cult of Magu 麻姑, the Hemp Lady. In legends about her, it is said that she was the child of Emperor Ming of the Han (r. 57–55 CE). See Despeux and Kohn (2003, 94–98).
19. *Onjōji denki*, 49, 78.

20. On the history of this period, see Farris (2009, 27–52). When Silla and Tang allied to defeat Paekche in 660, most of the Paekche royal house fell into the hands of the alliance, but some escaped to Japan.
21. For more about the war, see Batten (1986, 208–216); Batten (2006, 18–23).
22. Yamasaki (2000, 1–13).
23. Verschuer 2006.
24. For more about the Mongol invasions, see Conlan's introduction to and translation of Takezaki Suenaga's 竹崎季長 (1246–1314) scroll of the Mongol invasions (J. *Mōko shūrai ekotoba* 蒙古襲来絵詞; Conlan 2001).
25. The term *shinkoku* begins to appear as an attribute of the word "Nippon" from the Insei period. Rambelli (1996, 393).
26. Emperor Seiwa's reign was the time period when Enchin came back from Tang China and supposedly initiated worship of Shinra Myōjin in the Jimon tradition.
27. Inoue Nobutaka (1998, 113–114). According to Kuroda Toshio, the *shinkoku* discourse developed within the exo-esoteric system as a way to protect the ruling power of the ruling elites. See Rambelli (1996, 393).
28. *Onjōji denki*, 65.
29. Jingū's successful invasion of Silla epitomized the aversion to Silla. According to the conventional Japanese mythology, Jingū was a consort of a male ruler named Chūai 仲哀. She served as regent from the time of her husband's death in 201 until her son Ōjin 応神 acceded to the throne. Hachiman is regarded as the spirit of Ōjin, although the origin of the Hachiman cult remains something of a mystery. Nakano believes that the Hachiman cult did not originate exclusively at Usa 宇佐 but was the result of a process of amalgamation of the *ujigami* beliefs of various clans, which found its center at Usa. For more on Hachiman in Usa, see Nakano Hatayoshi 1983; Grapard 2016.
30. Inoue Mai (2009, 65).
31. Douglas 1966; Valentine (1990, 38).
32. For the role of epidemics in Japan throughout the eighth and ninth centuries, see Farris (1985, 50–73).
33. Hong (2012, 10).
34. For more on the inside-outside dichotomy in relation to the notion of the pure and the impure, see Aho 2002.
35. For Koreans, for instance, China, and particularly the Jiangnan 江南 area of China (south of the Yangzi River), was seen as being the directional source of epidemics. This reflected the actual climate and epidemiology; as Chinese historical records confirm, the southern part of China is a subtropical zone in which epidemic outbreaks frequently did occur. Katz (1995, 41); Goldschmidt (2007, 56).
36. Fujikawa (1969 [1904], 290–291).
37. Smallpox is an endemic disease (restricted to a particular region over an extended period of time), but it could become an epidemic (afflicting many individuals within a community during a brief time span). A pandemic is the combination of the two, which occurs over a wide area and afflicts a high proportion of the populace. Katz (1995, 40).
38. Farris (2009, 35).
39. Farris (1985, 53–54).
40. Ibid., 54. Whether the smallpox epidemic in the eighth century really stemmed from contact with the Silla people or not, the port city of Dazaifu in Kyushu was its first victim. The great smallpox epidemic wreaked broad devastation. At first it was just people in Dazaifu who suffered from the outbreak. Then it spread north and east, finally

reaching the capital in 737. The epidemic killed an estimated one-third to one-fourth of the population and caused great terror among aristocrats of the time. Farris (1985, 54–59); Farris (2009, 66).

41. The *Engi shiki* 延喜式 (Regulations and Laws of the Engi Era, 927) informs us that the offerings (such as skins of cow, bear, deer, and wild boar) made during rites for warding off the pestilence deity were the same as the offerings that were made during rites for deities of Silla origin. However, the offerings used in the ritual seem not to have been inspired by Buddhist ideas, which might suggest the continuation of ancient, local practices. Inoue (2009, 68).
42. Como (2007, 405–407).
43. *Jimon denki horoku*, 119–120.
44. Mt. Song is known as the Central Peak of China's Five Sacred Peaks and is often identified as the home of Shinra Myōjin (*Onjōji denki*, 71; *Jimon denki horoku*, 109). Claiming that Shinra Myōjin's shrine is located in a cave on Mt. Song and that his other name is "King of Mt. Song" suggests the Jimon's attempt to emphasize the divinity's superiority over other deities.
45. *Onjōji denki*, 78.
46. *Jimon denki horoku*, 109.
47. Faure (2004, 524–525); Faure (2011, 59).
48. As Saitō Hideki has shown, in the medieval period Susanoo rose to be the most prominent deity, becoming the father of the sun goddess Amaterasu and ultimately the ruler of Japan; see Saitō (2012, 101). For the medieval transformations of Susanoo, see Saitō 2012; Kwŏn Dongwoo 2013.
49. Susanoo in the form of a powerful pestilence god may have been transmitted to Izumo through the Tendai Buddhist network. In Izumo, there is Gakuenji 鰐淵寺, a Shugendō center, which became a branch temple (J. *matsuji* 末寺) of Enryakuji during the eleventh century.
50. Aston (1972, 1:57).
51. *Jimondenki horoku*, 108.
52. *Shaku nihongi*, 173.
53. As part of the ideological expansion of Shinto theories and interests in the reinterpretation of Japanese mythology during the Sengoku period (1467–1568), there were several Yoshida Shinto texts that address the identification of Shinra Myōjin with Susanoo; Yamamoto (1998a, 151). In Yoshida Kanetomo's commentary on the *Nihon shoki*, titled the *Nihon shoki jindai no maki shō* 日本書紀神代券抄 (ca. fifteenth c.), we find a passage in which he explains why Shinra Myōjin is identical to Susanoo. See *Nihon shoki jindai no maki*, 209. On Yoshida Kanetomo, see Grapard 1992.
54. Yoshida Shinto is a prominent branch of Shinto that arose during the Sengoku period through the teachings and works of Yoshida Kanetomo. As part of Yoshida Shinto's attempt to position Shinto as the highest and the most autochthonous system, he affirmed the so-called reverse *honji suijaku*, a theory promoted at the Outer Shrine of Ise. Here, the claim was that buddhas and bodhisattvas are manifestations of the Shinto *kami*, not the other way around, as had been previously thought. As Kuroda Toshio and others have argued, in the beginning the reverse *honji suijaku* theory did not necessarily indicate a nascent consciousness of a metahistorical Japanese "nation" or "Shinto" as an indigenous tradition, because it was mostly used by the older sects as a means of criticizing the new *nenbutsu* and other single-practice sects' refusal to show respect to and worship native *kami* as Buddhist avatars. Yoshida Shinto used the theory as a polemical tool, asserting

that Shinto was the primal religion of the world, and that it, in turn, gave rise to Buddhism, Daoism, and Confucianism. For a concise definition and an explanation of the complicated layers of evolution pertaining to the term "Shinto," see Grapard (1988, 247).

55. Anderson 1991.

CHAPTER 7. SHINRA MYŌJIN AS PART OF THE NETWORK OF THE DIVINE OLD MAN

1. Onjōji is publishing the collected Buddhist images of the temple, chronologically organized. See *Onjōji no butsuzō*, 5 vols. (2016–).
2. A good counterexample is Basu sennin 婆藪仙人 (Skt. Vasu), an immortal who accompanies Thousand-armed Avalokiteśvara (J. Senju Kannon 千手観音). Iconographically similar to Shinra Myōjin, he also holds a staff and carries a scroll, which is often identified as the *Prajñāpāramitā Sūtra*. One of the most famous examples of Basu sennin can be found at Sanjūsangendō 三十三間堂 hall in Kyoto, where he is included among the Nijūhachibushū 二十八部衆, the twenty-eight attendants of Kannon.
3. *San Tendai Godaisan ki*, 59.
4. It is beyond the scope of this book to explain how Mañjuśrī came to be depicted as an old man at Mt. Wutai, but it is possible that the Buddhist cult of Piṇḍola at Mt. Wutai provides a significant mythological link between Mañjuśrī and a cult of the divine old man. As for the worship of Piṇḍola on Mt. Wutai, it was the Chinese monk Daoan 道安 (314–385) who tried to institute the cult of Piṇḍola as the god of the refectory. But by the eighth century Mañjuśrī's fame superseded that of Piṇḍola at Mt. Wutai due to the effort of the Indian Tantric master Amoghavajra (704–774), who was largely responsible for the development of the Mañjuśrī cult on Mt. Wutai (Strong 1979, 56; Cartelli 2013, 34–35). During the ninth century, when Ennin traveled to China, Piṇḍola's role as a guardian deity of the refectory was significantly diminished, as is recorded in Ennin's diary; see Reischauer (1955a, 226–227).
5. On scholarship that deals with Mt. Wutai's development as the center of Mañjuśrī worship, see Andrews (2013, 5–13).
6. Groner (2002, 180).
7. The tower was closely related to Ennin and his lineage. Ennin constructed it in 861, and after a fire in 966, it was rebuilt with help from the nobility. Groner (2000, 180).
8. Wu, however, contends that the Pentad was introduced to Japan by either Ennin or Chōnen 奝然 (938–1016), or both. Wu (2002, 81).
9. The cult of Mañjuśrī was favored by Shingon as well. Eison was particularly well known for popularizing the Mañjuśrī cult during the medieval period. For more about Eison and his Mañjuśrī worship, see Quinter 2015.
10. Among the new rituals that Ennin brought back from Tang China were the Eight-syllable Rite for Mañjuśrī (J. *Monju hachiji hō* 文殊八字法), first used in Japan when Ninmyō Tennō fell ill in 850; it became the central Tendai rite for protection of the ruler and the state. Quinter (2015, 82).
11. *Onjoji denki*, 58.
12. Ibid., 72. Having Mañjuśrī as *honji* of *kami* was not a common practice. Kannon, Yakushi, Amida, and Śākyamuni were more often identified as *kami* originals, although Miroku and Jizō were often used as well. Fabio Rambelli and Mark Teeuwen (2003, 17).
13. For a discussion on the formation of *kami* icons in medieval Japan, see Kadoya (2006–2007, 151–182).

14. There are about fourteen images (paintings and statues) of Shinra Myōjin (seven of them are stored at Onjōji) in which the deity is prominently featured. Also, thirty-five images of the deity appear as part of the Mii mandara and the Kumano honji mandara or with other divinities, such as Maitreya and Benzaiten. On the most recent discussion and for a comprehensive list of images of this deity, see Ishikawa (2018, 190–205). Several art historians have attempted to decode the statue's unique features, though most research has been restricted to visual similarities between Shinra Myōjin and other deity images, such as Fujiwara no Kamatari (Kuroda 1998, 15–33), Fudō Myōō (Itō 1996, 7–18), and En no Gyōja (Miyake 2000, 1–33).
15. For more on the *hibutsu*, see Rambelli (2002b, 271–307).
16. *Onjōji denki*, 59.
17. Ishikawa (2018, 195). Several scholars, including Guth, have argued that it was made around the twelfth century; Guth (1999, 112).
18. Grapard (1987, 291). This different mode of reading reminds us of the *kanjin* 観心, or "contemplation of the mind," a hermeneutic device found in medieval oral transmission texts (J. *kuden*) used to retrieve hidden meanings. Stone (1999, 153–189).
19. Grapard (1987, 291) argues that there was a recognizable pattern: less emphasis was given to the phonetic resemblance and more to "graphic and visual deconstruction" in this linguistic game.
20. *Onjōji denki*, 59.
21. Ibid., 58.
22. Ibid., 59.
23. Davidson (1950, 242). For a more detailed discussion of the *ruyi* 如意, see Kieschnick (2003, 138–156).
24. For the textual sources on Mañjuśrī and his origin, see Hirakawa (1983, 12–33); Lamotte (1960, 1–96).
25. For other tales of Shinra Myōjin and Mañjuśrī, see *Jimon denki horoku*, 115; For the visual association, see Ishikawa 2018.
26. *Jitokushū*, 18.
27. *Mii zokutōki*, 218. This doctrinal interpretation may have been the idea behind the painting of the Miroku accompanied by Enchin and Shinra Myōjin.
28. *Onjōji denki*, 59; *Jimon denki horoku*, 112.
29. Wu (2002, 131).
30. Ibid., 76–81, 118–130. For further research on the Monju Pentad, see Kojima (1995, 43–49); Asanuma (2008, 30–44). For the Monju Pentad at Chūsonji 中尊寺, see Yiengpruksawan 1998.
31. The Mañjuśrī Triad—Mañjuśrī riding on a lion, Mañjuśrī as a child, and Mañjuśrī as a groom with a central Asian appearance—predates the Mañjuśrī Pentad. More on this can be found in Wu (2002, 88–89). During the Heian period, a popular custom developed whereby an icon of Mañjuśrī in the guise of a monk (or in a Chinese robe in the Tang fashion) was enshrined in kitchens in order to symbolize wisdom and discipline. Frédéric (1995, 193).
32. For more on Budhapāli on Mt. Wutai, see Kroll (2001, 41–44).
33. *T.* 967.19.349c–352a.
34. The belief in *dhāraṇī* texts flourished from the mid-eighth century onward. On this, see Copp (2014, 158–165).
35. Reischauer (1955a, 217).

36. Ennin also briefly relates the entire legend in his diary. There is an illustration of this legend in the late-Tang Dunhuang sketch in the Paris National Library, the Musée Guimet Mañjuśrī painting, and a mural from Dunhuang Cave 61. See Wu (2002, 104).
37. Wu (2002, 105).
38. There is also an intriguing wooden statue of a lion originally from the Shinra Myōjin Shrine, which dates to the eleventh or twelfth century. It is not clear whether the lion was part of the Monju Pentad or a single Monju statue riding on a lion, but this example suggests that at some point the Shinra Myōjin Shrine may have held a ritual for Monju. The piece is currently stored at the Nara National Museum.
39. As Walther Heissig's research suggests, the old-man deity is widely known in central Asia as well. There this type of deity is often thought of as a "white old man" who determines "the duration of men's lives." Heissig (1980, 76–79).
40. This idea that old age began at forty was common in premodern East Asia. For example, the *Huangdi neijing su wen* 皇帝內經素問 (ca. 400 BCE–260 CE), a classic of Chinese medicine, stated that the vital energies begin to decline beginning at the age of forty; see Formanek (1988, 11–13). On the study of the text and especially on the compilation date, see Unschuld (2003, 1–3).
41. *Samguk yusa* (1972, 110–112; translation slightly modified).
42. *Onjōji denki*, 58.
43. Blacker (1992, 37). On this question, see Yanagita 1970; Yamaori 1991; and Origuchi 2004.
44. *Genkō shakusho*, 1:417. See also Yamaori (1991, 216n75). Guth argues that the deity's appearance "may have been inspired by a figure of Taoist origins." Guth (1985, 70).
45. Mason 1999.
46. It may be that Shinra Myōjin was homophonous with *shira* 白, meaning "white," and that the god was therefore related to a network of "white" deities, including deities that appeared as old men, such as Shirahige Myōjin and Sumiyoshi. Yanagita Kunio suggests that Shinrahige Myōjin could be a god from Silla. Kim Hyŏnuk also discusses this matter. For more on this, see Yanagita (1990b, 154); Kim Hyŏnuk (2008, iii–iv).
47. Although officially this shrine is dedicated to Sarutahiko, the famous god who greeted Ninigi-no-Mikoto 瓊瓊杵尊 on his descent to earth as described in the *Kojiki*, the association seems to have been established later on in the medieval period.
48. Kamens (1998, 328).
49. Fremerman (2008, 88–89). On the cult of Mt. Kinpu, see Blair 2015.
50. On this question, see Takahashi 2014.
51. Kim Hyŏnuk 2008.
52. Pinnington (1998, 508–510).
53. For more on Matarajin, see Faure (2015, 2:299–329); Kawamura 2008.
54. Hattori Yukio 2009.
55. Marra (1993, 58).
56. Quinter (2015, 58).

CONCLUSION

1. Amino (2012, 40).
2. Abulafia (2005, 65).

Bibliography

PRIMARY SOURCES AND COLLECTIONS

Ainōshō 壒嚢鈔. In *Jinten ainōshō, Ainōshō* 塵添壒嚢鈔, 壒嚢鈔. Edited by Hamada Atsushi 濱田敦, Satake Akihiro 佐竹昭広, and Sasakawa Sachio 笹川祥生. Kyoto: Rinsen Shoten, 1968.

Aki no yo no naga monogatari 秋夜長物語. *NKBT*, vol. 38.

Asabashō 阿娑縛抄. *T, zuzō*. 8–9, no. 3190.

Daianji engi 大安寺縁起. In *Shugendō shiryōshū* 修験道史料集. Edited by Gorai Shigeru 五来重. Tokyo: Meicho Shuppan, 1983–1984.

Dai Nihon Bukkyō zensho (*DNBZ*) 大日本佛教全書. Tokyo: Kōdansha hatsubai, 1970–1973.

Engishiki 延喜式. *KT*, vol. 8.

Enkei-bon Heike monogatari 延慶本平家物語. Tokyo: Benseisha, 1996–1999.

Fudoki 風土記. *KBT*, vol. 2.

Fusō ryakki 扶桑略紀. *KT*, vol. 12.

Genpei josuiki 源平盛衰記. Edited by Ichiko Teiji 市古貞次. Tokyo: Miyai Shoten, 1993.

Gonki 権記. In *Zōho shiryō taisei* 増補史料大成, vol. 1. Kyoto: Rinsen Shoten, 1975.

Gyōrekishō 行歴抄. *DNBZ*, vol. 28.

Hachiman gudōkun 八幡愚童訓. In *Nihon sisō taikei* 日本思想大系, vol. 23. Tokyo: Iwanami Shoten, 1974.

Hiyoshi Sannō riseiki 日吉山王利生記. In *Myōhōin shiryō* 妙法院史料, vol. 5. Tokyo: Yoshikawa Kōbunkan, 1980.

Hōhiki 宝秘記. In *Onjōji monjo* 園城寺文書, 7 vols. Tokyo: Kōdansha, 1999–2004.

Honchō seiki 本朝世紀. *KT*, vol. 9.

Honchō zoku monzui: Kōchū Nihon bungaku taikei 本朝續文粹: 校註日本文学大系, vol. 24. Tokyo: Kokumintosho, 1925–1928.

Jimon denki horoku 寺門伝記補録. *DNBZ*, vol. 86.

Jitokushū 寺徳集. In *Zoku gunsho ruijū* 續群書類從, vol. 28. Tokyo: Zoku Gunsho Ruijū Kanseikai, 1957–1959.

Keiran shūyōshū 渓嵐拾葉集. *T*, vol. 76, no. 2410.

Kōfukujisōjō 興福寺奏状. *DNBZ*, vol. 124.

Kojidan 古事談. In *Kojidan・Zoku Kojidan* 古事談・続古事談. *SNKBT*, vol. 41. Tokyo: Iwanami Shoten, 2005.

Kojiki 古事記. *NKBT*, vol. 1. Edited by Kurano Kenji 倉野憲司. Tokyo: Iwanami Shoten, 1963.

Kōtei Enkyō-bon Heike monogatari 校訂延慶本平家物語. Edited by Tochigi Yoshitada 栃木孝惟 and Taniguchi Kōichi 谷口耕一. Tokyo: Kyūko Shoin, 2000–2009.

Kundoku Genkō shakusho 訓読元亨釈書. Edited by Kokan Shiren 虎関師錬 and Fujita Takui 藤田琢司. Kyoto: Zen Bunka Kenkyūjo, 2011.

Miidera zokutōki 三井寺続燈記. *DNBZ*, vol. 67.

Mochizuki bukkyō daijiten 望月佛教大辭典. Edited by Mochizuki Shinkō 望月信亨. 3rd ed. 10 vols. Kyoto: Seikai Seiten Kankō Kyokai, 1954–1971.

Nihon ryōiki 日本靈異記. *Nihon koten bungaku zenshū*, vol. 6.

Nihon sandai jitsuroku 日本三代實錄. *KT*, vol. 4.

Nihon shoki 日本書紀. *NKBT*, vols. 67–68.

Nihon shoki jindai no maki 日本書紀神代券抄. *ST*, vol. 4.

Nihon shomin seikatsu shiryō shūsei 日本庶民生活資料集成. Edited by Miyamoto Tsuneichi 宮本常一, Haraguchi Torao 原口虎雄, and Higa Shunchō 比嘉春潮. 31 vols. Tokyo: San'ichi Shobō, 1968–1984.

Onjōji denki 園城寺伝記. *DNBZ*, vol. 86.

Onjōji engi 薗城寺縁起. In *Fushimi no Miyake Kujōke kyūzō shoji engishū* 伏見宮家九条蔵諸寺縁起集. Edited by Kunaichō Shoryōbu 宮内庁書陵部. Tokyo: Kunaichō Shoryōbu, 1970.

Onjōji monjo 園城寺文書. 7 vols. Tokyo: Kōdansha, 1999–2004.

Onjōji ryūge-e engi 園城寺龍華會縁起. In *Honchō zoku monzui: Kōchū Nihon bungaku taikei* 本朝續文粹: 校註日本文学大系, vol. 24. Tokyo: Kokumintosho, 1925–1928.

Onmyōdō kiso shiryō shūsei 陰陽道基礎史料集成. Edited by Murayama Shūichi 村山修一. Tokyo: Tōkyō Bijutsu, 1987.

Ryūkyū shintō ki: Benrensha taichū shū 琉球神道記: 弁蓮社袋中集. Edited by Yokoyama Shigeru 横山重. Tokyo: Kadokawa Shoten, 1970.

Samguk yusa 三國遺事. *T*, 49, no. 2039.

Sanjūgo bunshū 卅五文集. *Zoku gunsho ruijū* 続群書類従, vol. 12 (1).

San Tendai Godaisan ki 參天台五臺山記. Edited by Hirabayashi Fumio 平林文雄. Tokyo: Kazama Shobō, 1978.

Sekizan Daimyōjin engi 赤山大明神縁起. In *ST* (ronsetsu hen 4: Tendai Shintō), vol. 2. Tokyo: Shintō Taikei Hensankai, 1992.

Settsu meijozue 摂津名所図会. Edited by Akisato Ritō 秋里籬島. Tokyo: Shintensha, 1984.

Shaku Nihongi 釋日本紀. *ST* (koten chūshaku hen), vol. 5.

Shasekishū 沙石集. *NKBT*, vol. 85.

Shinkō gunsho ruijū 新校群書類従. Edited by Ueda Mannen 上田蔓年 et al., vol. 19. Tokyo: Naigai Shoseki, 1932.

Shinra ryakki 新羅略記. *ST* (ronsetsu hen), vol. 17.

Shinsen shōjiroku 新撰姓氏錄. *ST* (koten hen), vol. 6.

Shiojiri 塩尻. In *Nihon zuihitsu taisei* 日本随筆大成. 3, vols. 13–16. Tokyo: Yoshikawa Kōbunkan, 1995–1996.

Shirahige myōjin engi 白鬚明神縁起. *ST* (jinja hen: Ōmi no kuni), vol. 23.

Shoku Nihongi 続日本紀. *SNBTK*, vols. 12–16.

Shoku Nihon kōki 続日本後記. In *Nihon kōki, Shoku Nihon kōki, Nihon Montoku Tennō jitsuroku* 日本後紀, 續日本後紀, 日本文德天皇實錄. *KT*, vol. 3.

Sinchū Ōmi yochi shiriyaku 新註近江輿地志略. Edited by Samukawa Tokikyo 寒川辰清. Otsu: Kōbundō Shoten, 1976.
Sōgō bunin shōshutsu 僧綱補任抄出. *DNBZ*, vol. 64.
Taiheiki 太平記. Edited by Takahashi Sadaichi 高橋貞一. 2 vols. Kyoto: Shibunkaku, 1976.
Taishō shinshū daizōkyō 大正新修大藏經. Edited by Takakusu Junjirō and Watanabe Kaigyoku. 88 vols. Tokyo: Taishō Issaikyō Kankōkai, 1924–1932.
Taishō shinshū daizō kyō zuzō 大正新脩大蔵経図像. 12 vols. Taishō Issaikyō Kankōkai, 1933–1935.
Tanjong sillok 端宗實錄. In *the Chŏson wangjo sillok* 朝鮮王朝實錄 (The veritable records of the Chŏson dynasty). Edited by Kuksa p'yŏnch'an wiwŏnhoe. 48 vols. Seoul: Kuksa P'yŏnch'an Wiwŏnhoe, 1955–1958.
Tendaishū Enryakuji zasu Enchin den 天台宗延暦寺座主圓珍傳. *DNBZ*, vol. 72.
Yunji qiqian 雲笈七籤. Edited by Zhang Junfang 張君房. Beijing: Zhonghua shu ju, 2003.
Zoku Tendaishū zensho 續天台宗全書. Edited by Tendai Shūten Hensanjo 天台宗典編纂所. Tokyo: Shunjūsha, 1987–.

SECONDARY SOURCES

Abé, Ryūichi. *The Weaving of Mantra: Kūkai and the Construction of Esoteric Buddhist Discourse.* New York: Columbia University Press, 1999.
Abe Yasurō 阿部泰郎. "Jidō setsuwa no keisei: Tendai sokuihō no seiritsu wo megurite–jō・ge" 慈童説話の形成: 天台即位法の成立をめぐりて-上・下. *Kokugo Kukobun* 国語国文 53, no. 8 (1984): 1–29; 53, no. 9 (1984): 30–56.
Abulafia, David. *The Mediterranean in History.* Los Angeles, CA: J. Paul Getty Museum, 2003.
———. "Mediterraneans." In *Rethinking the Mediterranean*, edited by Harris William, 64–93. Oxford: Oxford University Press, 2005.
———. *The Great Sea: A Human History of the Mediterranean.* New York: Oxford University Press, 2011.
Adolphson, Mikael S. *The Gates of Power: Monks, Courtiers, and Warriors in Premodern Japan.* Honolulu: University of Hawai'i Press, 2000.
———. *The Teeth and Claws of the Buddha: Monastic Warriors and Sōhei in Japanese History.* Honolulu: University of Hawai'i Press, 2007.
Aho, James. *The Orifice as Sacrificial Site: Culture, Organization and the Body.* New York: A. de Gruyter, 2002.
Akamatsu Toshihide 赤松俊秀. *Zoku Kamakura bukkyō no kenkyū* 続鎌倉仏教の研究. Kyoto: Heirakuji Shoten, 1966.
Allen, Chizuko T. "Early Migrations, Conquests, and Common Ancestry: Theorizing Japanese Origins in Relation with Korea." *Sungkyun Journal of East Asian Studies* 8, no. 1 (2008): 105–130.
Amino Yoshihiko 網野善彦. *Igyō no ōken* 異形の王権. Tokyo: Heibonsha, 1986.
———. *Nihon ron no shiza: rettō no shakai to kokka* 日本論の視座: 列島の社会と国家. Tokyo: Shōgakkan, 1990.
———. *Rethinking Japanese History.* Translated by Alan S. Christy. Ann Arbor: Center for Japanese Studies, University of Michigan, 2012.
Anderson, Benedict. *Imagined Communities: Reflections on the Origin and Spread of Nationalism.* Rev. ed. London: Verso, 1991.
Andersen, Poul. "The Practice of Bugang." *Cahiers d'Extrême-Asie* 5 (1989–1990): 15–53.

Andrews, Susan. "Representing Mount Wutai's 五臺山 Past: A Study of Chinese and Japanese Miracle Tales about the Five Terrace Mountain." PhD diss., Columbia University, 2013.

Arikiyo Saeki 佐伯有清. *Chishō daishi den no kenkyū* 智証大師伝の研究. Tokyo: Yoshikawa Kōbunkan, 1989.

Asano Nagatake 浅野長武. "Keichō nenkan ni okeru Onjōji no saikō" 慶長年間に於ける園城寺の再興. In *Onjōji no kenkyū* 園城寺之研究, edited by Tendaishū Jimonha go'onki jimukyoku 天台宗寺門派御遠忌事務局, 323–384. Otsu: Onjōji, 1931.

Asanuma Takeshi 浅湫毅. "Konkaikomyoji no Monjubosatsukishizō oyobi kenzoku ni tsuite" 金戒光明寺の文殊菩薩騎獅像および眷属像について. *Kairitsu bunka* 戒律文化 6 (2008): 30–44.

Assmann, Jan. *Religion and Cultural Memory: Ten Studies*. Stanford, CA: Stanford University Press, 2006.

Aston, W. G., trans. *Nihongi: Chronicles of Japan from the Earliest Times to A.D. 697*. 2 vols. Rutland, VT: Charles E. Tuttle, 1972.

Atkins, Paul S. "Chigo in the Medieval Japanese Imagination." *The Journal of Asian Studies* 67, no. 3 (2008): 947–970.

Batten, Bruce Loyd. "Foreign Threat and Domestic Reform: The Emergence of the Ritsuryō State." *Monumenta Nipponica* 41, no. 2 (1986): 199–219.

———. *To the Ends of Japan: Premodern Frontiers, Boundaries, and Interactions*. Honolulu: University of Hawai'i Press, 2003.

———. *Gateway to Japan: Hakata in War and Peace, 500–1300*. Honolulu: University of Hawai'i Press, 2006.

Bauer, Mikaël. "The Yuima-e as Theater of the State." *Japanese Journal of Religious Studies* 38, no. 1 (2011): 161–179.

Bender, Ross L. "The Political Meaning of the Hachiman Cult in Ancient and Early Medieval Japan." PhD diss., Columbia University, 1982.

Best, Jonathan W. "Paekche and the Incipiency of Buddhism in Japan." In *Currents and Countercurrents: Korean Influences on the East Asian Buddhist Traditions*, edited by Robert E. Buswell Jr., 15–42. Honolulu: University of Hawai'i Press, 2005.

Bialock, David T. *Eccentric Spaces, Hidden Histories: Narrative, Ritual, and Royal Authority from The Chronicles of Japan to The Tale of the Heike*. Stanford, CA: Stanford University Press, 2007.

Bingenheimer, Marcus. *A Biographical Dictionary of the Japanese Student-Monks of the Seventh and Early Eighth Centuries: Their Travels to China and Their Role in the Transmission of Buddhism*. Munich: Iudicium, 2001.

Birnbaum, Raoul. *Studies on the Mysteries of Mañjuśrī: A Group of East Asian Maṇḍalas and Their Traditional Symbolism*. Boulder, CO: Society for the Study of Chinese Religions, 1983.

Blacker, Carmen. *The Catalpa Bow: A Study of Shamanistic Practices in Japan*. London: Mandala, 1992.

Blair, Heather Elizabeth. *Real and Imagined: The Peak of Gold in Heian Japan*. Cambridge, MA: Harvard University Asia Center, 2015.

Blair, Heather, and Kawasaki Tsuyoshi. "*Engi*: Forging Accounts of Sacred Origins." *Japanese Journal of Religious Studies* 42, no. 1 (2015): 1–26.

Blum, Mark L. "The *Sangoku-Mappō* Construct: Buddhism, Nationalism, and History in Medieval Japan." In *Discourse and Ideology in Medieval Japanese Buddhism*, edited by Richard K. Payne and Taigen D. Leighton, 31–51. London: Routledge, 2006.

Bodiford, William. "Matara: A Dream King between Insight and Imagination." *Cahiers d'Extrême-Asie* 16 (2006–2007): 233–262.

———. "The Monastic Institution in Medieval Japan: The Insider's View," In *Buddhist Monasticism in East Asia: Places of Practice*, edited by James A. Benn, Lori Meeks, and James Robson, 125–147. New York: Routledge, 2010.

Bouchy, Anne. "Le littoral, espace de médiations-Cultes des monts Sengen, Asama, Aomine et systèmes de représentations chez les gens de mer de la côte orientale de la péninsule de Kii." *Cahiers d'Extrême-Asie* 9 (1993): 255–298.

Bowring, Richard John. *The Religious Traditions of Japan, 500–1600*. Cambridge; New York: Cambridge University Press, 2008.

Braudel, Fernard. *The Mediterranean and the Mediterranean World in the Age of Philip II*. 2 vols. New York: Harper & Row, 1972–1973.

———. *Afterthoughts on Material Civilization and Capitalism*. Baltimore: Johns Hopkins University Press, 1977.

Braudel, Fernand, Ayala Roselyne, Paule Braudel, Jean Guilaine, and Pierre Rouillard. *Les mémoires de la Méditerranée: Préhistoire et antiquité*. Paris: Editions de Fallois, 1998.

Breen, John, and Teeuwen Mark. *A New History of Shinto*. Chichester; Malden, MA: Wiley-Blackwell, 2010.

Broodbank, Cyprian. *The Making of the Middle Sea: A History of the Mediterranean from the Beginning to the Emergence of the Classical World*. London: Thames & Hudson, 2013.

Brown, Delmer M., and Ichirō Ishida, trans. *The Future and the Past: A Translation and Study of the Gukanshō, an Interpretative History of Japan Written in 1219*. Berkeley: University of California Press, 1979.

Bushelle, Ethan David. "The Joy of the Dharma: Esoteric Buddhism and the Early Medieval Transformation of Japanese Literature." PhD diss., Harvard University, 2015.

Bushōga sugatta shinbutsu tachi 武将が縋った神仏たち. Ōmi Hachiman: Shiga Kenritsu Azichijō Kōko Hakubutsukan, 2013.

Buswell, Robert E. Jr., ed. *Currents and Countercurrents: Korean Influences on the East Asian Buddhist Traditions*. Honolulu: University of Hawai'i Press, 2005.

Butsuzō hanto: Boso no utsukushiki hotoketachi 仏像半島: 房総の美しき仏たち. Chiba: Chibashi Bijutsukan, 2013.

Campany, Robert. *Signs from the Unseen Realm: Buddhist Miracle Tales from Early Medieval China*. Honolulu: University of Hawai'i Press, 2012.

Cartelli, Mary A. *The Five-Colored Clouds of Mount Wutai: Poems from Dunhuang*. Leiden: Brill, 2013.

Carter, Caleb. "Producing Place, Tradition and the Gods: Mt. Togakushi, Thirteenth through Mid-Nineteenth Centuries." PhD diss., University of California at Los Angeles, 2014.

Chavannes, Édouard. *Le T'ai chan: Essai de monographie d'un culte chinois*. Paris: Librairie Ernest Leroux, 1910.

Chen, Huaiyu. *The Revival of Buddhist Monasticism in Medieval China*. Bern: Peter Lang, 2007.

Chen, Jinhua. "The Construction of Early Tendai Esoteric Buddhism: The Japanese Provenance of Saichō's Transmission Documents and Three Esoteric Buddhist Apocrypha Attributed to Subhakarasimha." *Journal of the International Association of Buddhist Studies* 21, no. 1 (1998): 21–76.

———. *Legend and Legitimation: The Formation of Tendai Esoteric Buddhism in Japan*. Brussels: Institut Belge des Hautes Études Chinoises, 2009.

Childs, Margaret H. "Chigo Monogatari. Love Stories or Buddhist Sermons?" *Monumenta Nipponica* 35, no. 2 (1980): 127–151.

Choi Kwan 최관. "Samhan ui wang un ilbon ui gaeda" 삼한의 왕은 일본의 개다 (The kings of the Three Kingdoms are dogs of the Japanese). *Ilbon'ŏ munhak* 日本語文学 8 (1999): 177–189.

Cobbing, Andrew. *Kyushu, Gateway to Japan: A Concise History*. Folkestone, Kent, UK: Global Oriental, 2009.

Cogan, Thomas, trans. *The Tale of the Soga Brothers*. Tokyo: University of Tokyo Press, 1987.

Collins, Steven. *Nirvana and Other Buddhist Felicities: Utopias of the Pali Imaginaire*. Cambridge: Cambridge University Press, 1998.

Como, Michael. "Horses, Dragons, and Disease in Nara Japan." *Japanese Journal of Religious Studies* 34, no. 2 (2007): 393–415.

———. *Shōtoku: Ethnicity, Ritual, and Violence in the Japanese Buddhist Tradition*. New York: Oxford University Press, 2008.

———. *Weaving and Binding: Immigrant Gods and Female Immortals in Ancient Japan*. Honolulu: University of Hawai'i Press, 2009.

Conlan, Thomas. *In Little Need of Divine Intervention: Takezaki Suenaga's Scrolls of the Mongol Invasions of Japan*. Translation with an interpretive essay. Ithaca, NY: East Asia Program, Cornell University, 2001.

Copp, Paul. *Body Incantatory: Spells and Ritual Imagination in Medieval Chinese Buddhism*. New York: Columbia University Press, 2014.

Dai Izumo den 大出雲殿 (The Grand Izumo Exhibition: On the occasion of the renovation of Izumo Taisha Shrine and 1,300 years of the *Kojiki* chronicle). Kyoto: Kyoto National Museum, 2012.

Davidson, J. Leroy. "The Origin and Early Use of the Ju-i." *Artibus Asiae* 13, no. 4 (1950): 242–257.

Deleuze, Gilles, and Félix Guattari. *A Thousand Plateaus: Capitalism and Schizophrenia*. Minneapolis: University of Minnesota Press, 1987.

Despeux, Catherine, and Livia Kohn. *Women in Daoism*. Dunedin, FL: Three Pines Press, 2003.

Dewa Hiroaki 出羽弘明. *Shiragi no kamigami to kodai Nihon: Shinra jinja no kataru sekai* 新羅の神々と古代日本: 新羅神社の語る世界. Tokyo: Dōseisha, 2004.

Dolce, Lucia. "Duality and the Kami: The Ritual Iconography and Visual Constructions of Medieval Shintō." *Cahiers d'Extrême-Asie* 16 (2006–2007): 119–150.

———. "Reconsidering the Taxonomy of Esoteric." In *The Culture of Secrecy in Japanese Religion*, edited by Bernhard Scheid and Mark Teeuwen, 130–171. London: Routledge, 2006a.

———, ed. *The Worship of Stars in Japanese Religious Practice*. Special double issue of *Culture and Cosmos: A Journal of the History of Astrology and Cultural Astronomy* 10, nos. 1–2. Bristol: Culture and Cosmos, 2006b.

———. "The Worship of Celestial Bodies in Japan: Politics, Rituals and Icons." *Culture and Cosmos* 10, nos. 1–2 (2006c): 3–43.

———. "The Esoteric Buddhism of the Tendai School." In *Esoteric Buddhism and the Tantras in East Asia*, edited by Charles D. Orzech, Henrik H. Sørensen, and Richard Karl Payne, 744–767. Leiden; Boston: Brill, 2011.

———. "Taimistu Rituals in Medieval Japan: Sectarian Competition and the Dynamics of Tantric Performance." In *Transformations and Transfer of Tantra in Asia and Beyond*, edited by Istvan Keul, 329–363. Berlin: Walter de Gruyter. 2012.

Dolce, Lucia, and Mitsuhashi Tadashi, eds. *Shinbutsu shūgō saikō* 「神仏習合」を再考. Tokyo: Bensei shuppansham, 2013.
Douglas, Mary. *Purity and Danger: An Analysis of the Concepts of Pollution and Taboo.* London: Routledge, 1966.
Drott, Edward R. *Buddhism and the Transformation of Old Age in Medieval Japan.* Honolulu: University of Hawai'i Press, 2016.
Dykstra, Yoshiko Kurata, trans. *The Konjaku Tales: Japanese Section*. Vol. 1. Osaka: Gaidai University, 1998.
Ebersole, Gary L. "The Buddhist Ritual Use of Linked Poetry in Medieval Japan." *The Eastern Buddhist* 16, no. 2 (1983): 50–71.
———. *Ritual Poetry and the Politics of Death in Early Japan*. Princeton, NJ: Princeton University Press, 1989.
En no Gyōja shinpen daibosatsu 1300-nen onki kinen, En no Gyōja to Shugendō no sekai: sangaku shinkō no hihō 役行者神變大菩薩 1300 年遠忌記念, 役行者と修験道の世界: 山岳信仰の秘宝. Tokyo: Mainichi Shinbunsha, 1999.
Enshin, Saitō 圓真齊藤, trans. *Jikaku daishi den: The Biography of Jikaku Daishi* 慈覺大師傳. Tokyo: Sankibō Busshorin, 1992.
Fabricand-Person, Nicole Diane. "Filling the Void: The Fugen *jūrasetsunyo* Iconography in Japanese Buddhist Art." PhD diss., Princeton University, 2001.
Fairbank, John K., and Denis C. Twitchett. *The Cambridge History of China*. Taipei: Caves Books, 1979.
Farris, William W. *Population, Disease, and Land in Early Japan, 645–900*. Cambridge, MA: Harvard University Press, 1985.
———. *Japan to 1600: A Social and Economic History*. Honolulu: University of Hawai'i Press, 2009.
Faure, Bernard. *Visions of Power: Imagining Medieval Japanese Buddhism*. Princeton, NJ: Princeton University Press, 1996.
———. "The Buddhist Icon and the Modern Gaze." *Critical Inquiry* 24, no. 3 (1998): 768–813.
———. *The Power of Denial: Buddhism, Purity, and Gender*. Princeton, NJ: Princeton University Press, 2003.
———. "La double vie du patriache." In *Eloge des sources: Reflets du Japon ancien et modern*, edited by Josef A. Kyburz et al., 509–538. Arles: Picquier, 2004.
———. "Kegon and Dragons: A Mythological Approach to Huayan Doctrine." In *Reflecting Mirrors: Perspectives on Huayan Buddhism*, edited by Imre Hamar, 297–308. Wiesbaden: Harrassowitz Verlag, 2007.
———. "From Bodhidharma to Daruma: The Hidden Life of a Zen Patriarch." *Japan Review*, no. 23 (2011): 45–71.
———. "The Cultic World of the Blind Monks: Benzaiten, Jūzenji, and Shukujin." *Journal of Religion in Japan* 2, nos. 2–3 (2013): 171–194.
———. "Indic Influences on Chinese Mythology: King Yama and His Acolytes as Gods of Destiny." In *India in the Chinese Imagination: Myth, Religion, and Thought*, edited by John Kieschnick and Meir Shahar, 46–60. Philadelphia: University of Pennsylvania Press, 2014.
———. *The Fluid Pantheon: Gods of Medieval Japan*. Vol. 1. Honolulu: University of Hawai'i Press, 2015.
———. *Protectors and Predators: Gods of Medieval Japan*. Vol. 2. Honolulu: University of Hawai'i Press, 2015.

Faure, Bernard, and Michael Como, eds. *Medieval Shinto*, special issue of *Cahiers d'Extrême–Asie* 16 (2006–2007 [2009]).

Fong, Wen. "The Lohans and a Bridge to Heaven." *Freer Gallery of Art Occasional Papers* 3, no. 1 (1958): 23–43.

Ford, James L. *Jōkei and Buddhist Devotion in Early Medieval Japan*. Oxford: Oxford University Press, 2006.

Formanek, Susanne. "Old Age in Pre-Nara and Nara Periods." *Nachrichten der Gesellschaft für Natur und Völkerkunde Ostasiens* 144 (1988): 11–27.

Franke, Herbert. "The Taoist Elements in the Buddhist Great Bear Sūtra (Pei-tou ching)." *Asia Major* 3, no. 1 (1990): 75–111.

Frédéric, Louis. *Buddhism: Flammarion Iconographic Guides*. Paris, NY: Flammarion, 1995.

Fremerman, Sarah Alizah. "Divine Impersonations: Nyoirin Kanon in Medieval Japan." PhD diss., Stanford University, 2008.

Fujikawa Yū 富士川游. *Nihon shippei shi* 日本疾病史. Tokyo: Heibonsha, 1969.

Fukuda Akira 福田晃. *Shinwa no chūsei* 神話の中世. Tokyo: Miyai Shoten, 1997.

Fuqua, Douglas Sherwin. "The Japanese Missions to Tang China and Maritime Exchange in East Asia, 7th–9th centuries." PhD diss., University of Hawai'i, Manoa, 2004.

Geertz, Clifford. *The Interpretation of Cultures: Selected Essays*. New York: Basic Books, 1973.

Gipouloux, François. *The Asian Mediterranean: Port Cities and Trading Networks in China, Japan and South Asia, 13th–21st Century*. Cheltenham, UK: Edward Elgar, 2011.

Glassman, Hank. "The Religious Construction of Motherhood in Medieval Japan." PhD diss., Stanford University, 2001.

Goldschmidt, Asaf. "Epidemics and Medicine during the Northern Song Dynasty: The Revival of Cold Damage Disorder." *T'oung pao* (2nd ser.) 93, nos. 1–3 (2007): 53–109.

Goodwin, Janet. "The Worship of Miroku in Japan." PhD diss., University of California, Berkeley, 1977.

Gorai Shigeru 五来重. *Jisha engi to denshō bunka* 寺社縁起と伝承文化. Vol. 4 of *Gorai Shigeru chosakushū* 五来重著作集. Kyoto: Hōzōkan, 2008.

Granet, Marcel. *Études sociologiques sur la Chine*. Paris: Presses universitaires de France, 1953.

Grapard, Allan G. "Flying Mountains and Walkers of Emptiness: Toward a Definition of Sacred Space in Japanese Religions." *History of Religions* 20, no. 3 (1982): 195–221.

———. "Linguistic Cubism: A Singularity of Pluralism in the Sannō Cult." *Japanese Journal of Religious Studies* 14, nos. 2–3 (1987): 211–234.

———. "Institution, Ritual, and Ideology: The Twenty-Two Shrine-Temple Multiplexes of Heian Japan." *History of Religions* 27, no. 3 (1988): 246–269.

———. *The Protocol of the Gods: A Study of the Kasuga Cult in Japanese History*. Berkeley: University of California Press, 1992.

———. *Mountain Mandala: Shugendō in Kyushu*. London; New York: Bloomsbury Academic, 2016.

Gregory, Derek. *The Colonial Present: Afghanistan, Palestine, and Iraq*. Malden, MA: Blackwell, 2004.

Groner, Paul. "Annen, Tankei, Henjō, and Monastic Discipline in the Tendai School: The Background of the Futsū jubosatsukai kōshaku." *Japanese Journal of Religious Studies* 14, nos. 2–3 (1987): 129–159.

———. *Saichō: The Establishment of the Japanese Tendai School*. Honolulu: University of Hawai'i Press, 2000.

———. "Icon and Relics in Eison's Religious Activities." In *Living Images: Japanese Buddhist Icons in Context*, edited by Robert H. Sharf and Elizabeth H. Sharf, 114–150. Stanford, CA: Stanford University Press, 2001.

———. *Ryōgen and Mount Hiei: Japanese Tendai in the Tenth Century*. Honolulu: University of Hawai'i Press, 2002.

———. "Can the Precepts Be Lost? Can the Precepts Be Violated? The Role of the Pusajie Yiji 菩薩戒義記 in Medieval Tendai Discussions of the Precepts." *Tendai gakuhō* 天台学報 (*tokubetsu gō*) 2007: 165–200.

———. "The *Lotus Sutra* and the Perfect-Sudden Precepts." *Japanese Journal of Religious Studies* 41, no. 1 (2014): 103–131.

Guth (Kanda), Christine M. E. *Shinzō: Hachiman Imagery and Its Development*. Cambridge, MA: Harvard University Press, 1985.

Guth, Christine M. E. "Mapping Sectarian Identity: Onjōji's Statue of Shinra Myōjin." *RES* 35 (1999): 111–124.

Ha, TaeHung, and Grafton Mintz, trans. *Samguk yusa*. Seoul: Yonsei University Press, 1972.

Hakamada Mitsuyasu 袴田光康. "Heian bukkyō ni okeru Gairaijin: Ennin to shinrajin nettowāku" 平安佛教における外来神: 円仁と新羅人ネットワーク. *Yeonmin hakji* 淵民學志 15 (2011): 173–238.

———. "Heian bukkyō ni okeru Shinra Myōjin: Onjōji no yūrai denshō to Shinra no Miroku shinkō" 平安佛教における新羅明神: 園城寺の由来伝承と新羅の弥勒信仰. *Yeonmin hakji* 淵民學志 17 (2012): 87–128.

Halbwachs, Maurice. *On Collective Memory*. Edited and translated by Lewis A. Coser. Chicago: University of Chicago Press, 1992.

Hall, John W., and Delmer M. Brown. *The Cambridge History of Japan*. New York: Cambridge University Press, 1993.

Han Yŏng'gu 한영구. "Koryŏ togyŏng e nat'anan Sŏ Kŭng ŭi Han'guksa ch'egye" 고려도경에 나타난 서긍의 한국사 체계 (The system of Korean history as reflected in Xu Jin'g *Gaoli tujing*). *Kyujanggak* 7 (1983): 15–29.

Hansen, Wilburn. *When Tengu Talk: Hirata Atsutane's Ethnography of the Other World*. Honolulu: University of Hawai'i Press, 2008.

Hara Katsuaki 原克昭 *Chūsei Nihongi ronkō: Chūshaku no shisōshi* 中世日本紀論考: 註釈の思想史. Kyoto: Hōzōkan, 2012.

Harper, Donald John. *Early Chinese Medical Literature: The Mawangdui Medical Manuscripts*. London: Kegan Paul International, 1998.

Harris, William V. *Rethinking the Mediterranean*. Oxford: Oxford University Press, 2005.

Hasegawa Kenji 長谷川賢二. "Chūse kōki ni okeru kenmitsu jisha soshiki no saihen: Shugendō honzanha no seritsu wo megutte" 中世後期における顕密寺社組織の再編: 修験道本山派の成立をめぐって. *Historia* ヒストリア 125 (1989): 56–75.

Hashimoto Tetsuo 橋本鉄男. "Mio jinja" 水尾神社. In *Nihon no kamigami: jinja to seichi* 日本の神々: 神社と聖地, edited by Tanigawa Ken'ichi 谷川健一, 5:353–355. Tokyo: Hakusuisha, 1984–1987.

Hattori Toshirō 服部敏良. *Muromachi azuchi Momoyama jidai igakushi no kenkyū* 室町安土桃山時代医学史の研究. Tokyo: Yoshikawa Kōbunkan, 1971.

Hattori Yukio 服部幸雄. *Shukujin ron: Nihon geinōmin shinkō no kenkyū* 宿神論: 日本芸能民信仰の研究. Tokyo: Iwanami Shoten, 2009.

Hayami Tasuku 速水侑. *Miroku shinkō: Mō hitotsu no jōdo shinkō* 弥勒信仰: もう一つの浄土信仰. Tokyo: Hyōronsha, 1971.

———. *Heian kizoku shakai to bukkyō* 平安貴族社会と仏教. Tokyo: Yoshikawa Kōbunkan, 1975.

Heissig, Walther. *The Religions of Mongolia*. Berkeley: University of California Press, 1980.

Heldt, Gustav, trans. *The Kojiki: An Account of Ancient Matters*. NY: Columbia University Press, 2014.

Hirakawa, Akira 平川彰. "Mañjuśrī and the Rise of Mahayana Buddhism." *Journal of Asian Studies* 1, no. 1 (1983): 12–33.

Hiraoka Jōkai 平岡定海. *Nihon miroku jōdo shisō tenkaishi no kenkyū*. 日本彌勒淨土思想展開史の研究. Tokyo: Daizō Shuppan, 1977.

———. *Nihon ji'in no kenkyū* 日本寺院史の研究. Tokyo: Yoshikawa Kōbunkan, 1981.

Hirase Naoki 平瀬直樹. "Nihon chūsei no Myōken shinkō to Chintaku reifu shinkō" 日本中世の妙見信仰と鎮宅靈符信仰. *Bukkyō shigaku kenkyū* 佛教史學研究 56, no. 1 (2014): 21–37.

Hong Sŏnghwa, Wanbŏm Song, Pohan Kim, Tonggyu Sin, and Sŏnghwa Hong. *Chŏn'gŭndae Ilbon ŭi yŏngt'o insik* 전근대 일본의 영토인식 (Conceptualization of national territory in premodern Japan). Seoul: Tongbuga Yŏksa Chaedan, 2012.

Hongō Masatsugu 本郷真紹. *Ritsuryō kokka bukkyō no kenkyū* 律令国家仏教の研究. Kyoto: Hōzōkan, 2005.

Horden, Peregrine, and Nicholas Purcell. *The Corrupting Sea: A Study of Mediterranean History*. Oxford: Blackwell, 2000.

Hoshimiya Chikō 星宮智光. "Miidera no Rekishi" 三井寺の歴史. In *Miidera hihōten: Chishō daishi senhyakunen gōnki kinen* 三井寺秘宝展: 智証大師一一年御遠忌記念, 138–153. Tokyo: Nihon Keizai Shinbunsha, 1990.

Hoshino Ryōsaku 星野良作. *Jinshin no ran kenkyū no tenkai* 壬申の乱研究の展開. Tokyo: Yoshikawa Kōbunkan, 1997.

Huang, Shih-shan S. *Picturing the True Form: Daoist Visual Culture in Traditional China*. Cambridge, MA: Harvard University Asia Center, 2012.

Huhndorf, Shari M. *Going Native: Indians in the American Cultural Imagination*. Ithaca, NY: Cornell University Press, 2001.

Hurst, Carmeron C. *Insei: Abdicated Sovereigns in the Politics of Late Heian Japan, 1086–1185*. New York: Columbia University Press, 1976.

Hwang Chongdae, Dongjin Chu, and Donggyu Kim. "Han'guk Hapgido ŭi t'aedong gwa paljŏn sa: Taedongryu Hapgi yusul ŭl chungsim ŭro" 한국 합기도의 태동과 발전사: 대동류합기유술을 중심으로 (The origins and historical development of Korean Hapkido: A case of Taedongryu Hapkiyusul). *The Journal of Korean Alliance of Martial Arts* 14, no. 1 (2012): 1–55.

Ichikawa Hiroshi 市川浩史. *Nihon chūsei no hikari to kage: 'Uchinaru sangoku' no shisō* 日本中世の光と影–「内なる三国」の思想. Tokyo: Perikansha, 1999.

Iida Yoshirō 飯田嘉郎. *Nihon Kōkaijutsushi: Kodai kara bakumatsu made* 日本航海術史: 古代から幕末まで. Tokyo: Hara Shobō, 1980.

Ikawa Kazuko 猪川和子. "Miidera Shinra Myōjin zazō" 三井寺新羅明神座像. In *Nihon kochōkoku shiron* 日本古彫刻史論, 287–288. Tokyo: Kodansha, 1975.

Im Namsu 林南壽. *Kōryūji shi no kenkyū* 廣隆寺史の研究. Tokyo: Chūō Kōron Bijutsu Shuppan, 2003.

Imahori Taitsu 今堀太逸. "Ekibyō to jingi shinkō no tenkai: Gozu tennō to Somin shōrai no shison" 疫病と神祇信仰: 牛頭天王と蘇民将来の子孫. *Bukkyō shigaku kenkyū* 佛教史学研究 35, no. 1 (1993): 1–44.

———. "Gozu tennō engi no keisei" 牛頭天王縁起の形成. *Kokubungaku kaishaku to kanjō* 國文學解釋と鑑賞 60, no. 775 (1995): 140–145.
Imai Keiichi 今井啓一. *Kikajin no kenkyū* 帰化人の研究. Kyoto: Sōgeisha, 1972.
Imanishi Ryū 今西龍. *Shiragi shi kenkyū* 新羅史研究. Keijō: Chikazawa Shoten, 1933.
Inoue Kazutoshi 井上一稔. "Heian jidai no Gozu tennō" 平安時代の牛頭天王. *Nihon shūkyō bunka shi gakkai* 日本宗教文化史学会 15, no. 1 (2011): 27–52.
Inoue Mai 井上舞. "Jūyon seiki Harima no jisha enki ni miru 'Shinra'" 14 世紀播磨の寺社縁起にみる '新羅.' *Kaikō toshi kenkyū* 海港都市研究 4 (2009): 65–76.
Inoue Nobutaka 井上順孝, ed. *Shintō: Nihon umare no shūkyō shisutemu* 神道: 日本生まれの宗教システム. Tokyo: Shin'yōsha, 1998.
Ishida Mizumaro 石田瑞麿. "Onjōji kaidan" 園城寺戒壇. *Musashino jyoshi daigaku kiyō* 武蔵野女子大学紀要 15 (1980): 47–74.
Ishihara Michihiro 石原道博. *Yakuchū Chūgoku seishi Nihon den* 訳注中国正史日本. Tokyo: Kokusho Kankōkai, 1975.
Ishihara Susumu 石原進. *Kodai Ōmi no Chōsen* 古代近江の朝鮮. Tokyo: Shin Jinbutsu Ōraisha, 1984.
Itō Masayoshi 伊藤正義. "Chūsei nihongi no rinkaku: Taiheiki ni okeru Urabe Kanekazu setsu wo megutte" 中世日本紀の輪郭: 太平記における卜部兼員説をめぐって. *Bungaku* 文学 40 (1972): 28–48.
Itō Satoshi 伊藤聡. *Chūsei shinwa to jingi: Shintō sekai* 中世神話と神祇: 神道世界. Tokyo: Chikurinsha, 2011.
Itō Shirō 伊東史郎. "Dōjūin Fudō Myōōzō to Onjōji Shinra Myōjin zō: Jōchōyo seiritsu ni itaru zuzō to gihō" 同聚院不動明王像と園城寺新羅明神像: 定朝様成立に至る図像と技法. *Kokka* 國華 1203 (1996): 7–18.
Iwasa Kanzō 岩佐貫三. "Shina Simei sisō no Nihon teki juyō: Taizan fukun to Syakusan Myōjin o rei toshite" シナ司命思想の日本的受容: 泰山府君と赤山(しゃくさん)明神を例として. *Tōyōgaku kenkyū* 東洋学研究 1 (1965): 85–93.
Iyanaga Nobumi 彌永信美. "Dairoku Tenmaō to chūsei Nihon no sōzō shinwa–jō・chū・ge" 第六天魔王と中世日本の創造神話–上・中・下. *Hirosaki daigaku kokushi kenkyū* 弘前大学國史研究 104 (1998): 44–68; 105 (1998): 23–39; 106 (1999): 17–41.
———. *Daikokuten hensō: Bukkyō shinwagaku* 大黒天変相: 仏教神話学. Vol. 1. Kyoto: Hōzōkan, 2002.
———. *Kannon hen'yōtan: bukkyō shinwagaku* 観音変容譚: 仏教神話学. Vol. 2. Kyoto: Hōzōkan, 2002.
Izumi Takeo 泉武夫. "Sonjōō to Chintaku reifushin" 尊星王と鎮宅霊符神. In *Miidera no Bukkyō bijutsu: kenkyū happyō to zadankai* 三井寺の仏教美術: 研究発表と座談会. 1–4. Kyoto: Bukkyō Bijutsu Kenkyū Ueno Kinen Zaidan Josei Kenkyū kai, 1990.
Joo, Bongseok. "The Arhat Cult in China from the Seventh through Thirteenth Centuries: Narrative, Art, Space and Ritual." PhD diss., Princeton University, 2007.
Kagamiyama Takeshi 鏡山猛. *Kyūshū kōkogaku ronkō* 九州考古學論攷. Tokyo: Yoshikawa Kobunkan, 1972.
Kageyama Haruki 景山春樹. *Shintaizan* 神体山. Tokyo: Gakuseisha, 1971.
———. *Shintō bijutsu* 神道美術. Tokyo: Yūzankaku, 1973.
———. "Onjōji no chinshusha to sono ihō" 園城寺の鎮守社とその遺宝. In *Hieizan to Tendai Bukkyō no kenkyū.* 比叡山と天台仏教の研究, edited by Murayama shūichi 村山修一. Sangaku shūkyōshi kenkyū sōsho, 2:392–404. Tokyo: Meicho shuppan, 1975.

Kajiwara Yoshimitsu 梶原義実. "Saikō no kanei sanji・Sūfukuji (Shiga ken): So no zōei to iji" 最古の官営山寺・崇福寺 (滋賀県): その造営と維持. *Ars Buddhica* 佛教芸術 265 (2002): 96–113.

Kameda Tsutomu 亀田孜. "Bosuton bijutsukan zō Shinra Myōjin o kyōji to suru Miroku nyorai zō" ボストン美術館蔵新羅明神を脇侍とする弥勒如来像. *Ars Buddhica* 90 (1973): 94–104.

Kamens, Edward, trans. *The Three Jewels: A Study and Translation of Minamoto Tamenori's Sanbōe*. Ann Arbor: Center for Japanese Studies, University of Michigan, 1988.

Kamikawa Michio 上川通夫. *Nihon chūsei Bukkyō keiseishi ron* 日本中世仏教形成史論. Tokyo: Azekura Shobō, 2007.

Karube Tadashi 苅部直, Kurozumi Makoto 黒住真, Satō Hirō 佐藤弘夫, Sueki Fumihiko 末木文美士, and Tajiri Yūichirō 田尻祐一郎. *Nihon shisōshi kōza: Chūsei* 日本思想史講座: 中世. Vol. 2. Tokyo: Perikansha, 2012.

Katō Kenkichi 加藤謙吉. *Hata shi to so no tami: Torai shizoku no jitsuzō* 秦氏とその民: 渡来氏族の実像. Tokyo: Hakusuisha, 1998.

Katz, Paul R. *Demon Hordes and Burning Boats: The Cult of Marshal Wen in Late Imperial Chekiang*. Albany: State University of New York Press, 1995.

Kawaguchi Hisao 川口久雄, ed. *Kohon setswa shū* 古本説話集. Tokyo: Asahi Shinbunsha, 1967.

Kawamura Minato 川村湊. *Gozu tennō to Somin shōrai densetsu: Shōsareta ijin tachi* 牛頭天王と蘇民将来伝説: 消された異神たち. Tokyo: Sakuinsha, 2007.

———. *Yami no Matarajin: Hengen suru ishin no nazo o ou* 闇の摩多羅神: 変幻する異神の謎を追う. Tokyo: Kawade Shobō Shinsha, 2008.

Keel, Hee-Sung. "Kyŏnghŭng in Shinran's Pure Land Thought." In *Currents and Countercurrents: Korean Influences on the East Asian Buddhist Traditions*, edited by Robert E. Buswell Jr., 43–72. Honolulu: University of Hawai'i Press, 2005.

Kida Teikichi 喜田貞吉 and Yamada Norio 山田野理, eds. *Fukujin* 福神. Tokyo: Hōbunkan, 1976.

Kieschnick, John. *The Impact of Buddhism on Chinese Material Culture*. Princeton, NJ: Princeton University Press, 2003.

Kiley, Cornelius. "A Note on the Surnames of Immigrant Officials in Nara Japan." *Harvard Journal of Asiatic Studies* 29 (1969): 177–189.

Kim Ensook 金恩淑. "Ilbon ch'oihu ŭi kyŏndangsa p'agyŏn gwa Chang Pogo seryŏk" 일본 최후의 견당사 파견과 장보고 세력 (The last Japanese envoy to Tang China and Chang, Pogo). *Han'guk kodaesa yŏn'gu* 한국고대사연구 42 (2006): 273–312.

Kim Hyŏnuk 金賢旭. *Okina no seisei: torai bunka to chūsei no kamigami*. 翁の生成: 渡来文化と中世の神々. Kyoto: Shibunkaku Shuppan, 2008.

Kim, Hyunkoo 김현구. "A Study of Korea-Japan Relations in Ancient Times: Centering on the Taika Reforms and the Formation of Cooperation among Silla, Japan, and Tang China." *Korea Journal* 29, no. 10 (1989): 18–27.

Kim Imjung 金任仲. "Nihon no naka no Chōsen torai bunka: Saitama ken Korai jinjya o megutte" 日本の中の朝鮮渡来文化: 埼玉県高麗神社をめぐって. *Nihongo bungaku* 日本語文学 30 (2006): 201–219.

Kim Moonkyŏng 金文經. "TangIl Munhwa kyoryu wa Silla shin'ang: Ilbon ch'ŏnt'aesŭng Ch'oizŭng・Wŏnin・Wŭnchin ŭl chŭngshim ŭro" 唐日文化交流와新羅神信仰: 日本天台僧 最澄・圓仁・圓珍을 中心으로 (Cultural exchanges between Tang and Japan and the Silla deity worship: Focusing on Japanese Tendai monks, Saichō, Ennin, Enchin). *Tongbang hakji* 동방학지 54 (1987): 141–165.

———. "Zaitō shiragijin shakai to bukkyō: *Nittō guhō junrei kōki* o chushin ni shite" 在唐新羅人社会と仏教–入唐求法巡礼行記を中心にして–. *Asia yugaku* アジア遊学, 26 (2011): 6–22.

Kim, Sujung. "Frogs Looking beyond a Pond: Shinra Myōjin in the East Asian Mediterranean Network." In *The Sea and the Sacred in Japan: Aspects of Maritime Religion*, edited by Fabio Rambelli, 79–87. New York: Bloomsbury Academic, 2018.

Kim Taedo 김태도. "Silla Myŏngshin go" 新羅明神考. *Ilbon munhwa hakbo* 일본문화학보 9 (2000): 165–184.

Kim Yŏngt'ae 김영태. "Paekche Imsŏng T'aeja wa Myŭgyŭn shin'ang ui ilbon chŏnsu" 백제 임성태자와 묘견 신앙의 일본 전수 (The Paekche Prince Imsŏng and his transmission of Myōken worship to Japan). *Pulgyo hakbo* 불교학보 20 (1983): 45–83.

Kim Yujin. "'Aki no yono nagamonogatari' emaki to nara e hon ni tsuite: Tokyō daigaku bungakubu kokubungaku kenkyūshitsu zō no emaki wo chūshin ni"『秋夜長物語』の絵巻と奈良絵本について: 東京大学文学部国文学研究室蔵の絵巻を中心に. *Kokusai Nihon bungaku kenkyū shūkai kaigiroku* 国際日本文学研究集会会議 38 (2015): 85–108.

Kimbrough, Keller R. "Reading the Miraculous Powers of Japanese Poetry: Spells, Truth Acts, and a Medieval Buddhist Poetics of the Supernatural." *Japanese Journal of Religious Studies* 32, no. 1 (2005): 1–33.

Kimura Hirokazu 木村博. "Yōsan goshin to shite no Kokūzō bosatsu" 養蚕護神としての虚空蔵菩薩. In *Kokūzō shinkō* 虚空蔵信仰, edited by Sano Kenji 佐野賢治, 85–91. Tokyo: Yūzankaku Shuppan, 1991.

Klein, Susan Blakeley. *Allegories of Desire: Esoteric Literacy Commentaries of Medieval Japan*. Cambridge, MA: Harvard University Press, 2002.

Kobayashi Michinori 小林道憲. *Kodai Nihonkai bunmei kōryūken: Yūrashia no bunmei hendō no naka de* 古代日本海文明交流圏: ユーラシアの文明変動の中で. Kyoto: Sekai Shisōsha, 2006.

Kōhei Shigeki 字野茂樹. "Onjōji Shinra Myōjin zō" 園城寺新羅明神像. *Shiseki to bijutsu* 史迹と美術 38, no. 4 (1968): 133–143.

Kohn, Livia, ed. *Taoist Meditation and Longevity Techniques*. Ann Arbor: Center for Chinese Studies, University of Michigan, 1989.

Kohn, Livia, and Harold D. Roth, eds. *Daoist Identity: History, Lineage, and Ritual*. Honolulu: University of Hawai'i Press, 2002.

Kojima Aya 小島彩. "Kizō Fugen to kishi Monju no zuzō" 騎象普賢と騎獅文殊の図像. *Bijutsushi* 美術史 44, no. 1 (1995): 43–59.

Kokuhō Miidera ten: Chishō daishi kichō 1150 nen tokubetsu ten 国宝三井寺展: 智証大師帰朝 1150 年特別展. Osaka: NHK Ōsaka Hōsōkyoku, 2008.

Komine Kazuaki 小峯和明. *Chūsei hōe bunkei ron* 中世法会文芸論. Tokyo: Kasama Shoin, 2009.

Kondo Yasuke 近藤祐介. "Shugendō Honzanha ni okeru senkokuki teki kōzō no shutsugen" 修験道本山派における戦国期的構造の出現. *Shigaku zasshi* 史学雑誌 119, no. 4 (2010): 445–448.

Kroll, Paul W. *Dharma Bell and Dhāranī Pillar: Li Po's Buddhist Descriptions*. Kyoto: Scuola Italiana di Studi sull'Asia Orientale, 2001.

Kumoi Shozen 雲井昭善. "Miroku shinkō ni miru Kan'nichi no hikaku: Kan'nichi bunka no sōgo rikai o megutte" 弥勒信仰にみる韓日の比較: 韓日文化の相互理解をめぐって. *Hikaku shisō to hikaku bunka* 比較思想と比較文化 22 (1995): 85–90.

Kunaichō shoryōbu 宮内庁書陵部, ed. *Fushimi no Miyake Kujōke shoji engishū* 伏見宮家九条家旧蔵諸寺縁起集. Tokyo: Kunaichō Shoryōbu, 1970.

Kurata Bunsaku 倉田文作. "Onjōji Shinra Myōjin zō" 園城寺新羅明神像. *Kobijutsu* 古美術 3 (1963): 44–46.

Kuroda Hideo 黒田日出男. *Ryū no sumu Nihon* 龍の棲む日本. Tokyo: Iwanami Shoten, 2003.

Kuroda Satoshi 黒田智. "Shinra Myōjin to Fujiwara no Kamatari" 新羅明神と藤原鎌足. *Bukkyō geijutsu* 仏教芸術 238 (1998): 15–33.

———. "Shinra myōjin ki" 新羅明神記. *Tokyo daigaku shiryō hensanjo kiyō* 東京大学史料編纂所研究紀要 11 (2001): 75–98.

Kuroda Toshio 黒田俊雄. "Chūsei kokka to tennō" 中世国家と天皇. In *Iwanami kōza Nihon rekishi* 岩波講座日本歴史, edited by Ienaga Saburō et al., vol. 6 (chūsei 2), 261–301. Tokyo: Iwanami Shoten, 1963.

———. *Nihon chūsei no kokka to shūkyō* 日本中世の国家と宗教. Tokyo: Iwanami Shoten, 1975.

———. *Ōhō to buppō: Chūsei shi no kōzu* 王法と仏法: 中世史の構図. Kyoto: Hōzōkan, 1983.

———. "Historical Consciousness and Hon-jaku Philosophy in the Medieval Period on Mount Hiei." Translated by Allan Grapard. In *The Lotus Sūtra in Japanese Culture*, edited by George Tanabe and Willa Tanabe, 143–158. Honolulu: University of Hawai'i Press, 1989.

———. *Shinkoku shisō to senju nenbutsu* 神国思想と専修念仏. Kyoto: Hōzōkan, 1995.

———. "The Development of the Kenmitsu System as Japan's Medieval Orthodoxy." Translated by James C. Dobbins. *Japanese Journal of Religious Studies* 23, nos. 3–4 (1996a): 233–269.

———. "The Discourse on the 'Land of Kami' (*Shinkoku*) in Medieval Japan: National Consciousness and International Awareness." Translated by Fabio Rambelli. *Japanese Journal of Religious Studies* 23, nos. 3–4 (1996b): 353–385.

Kwŏn Deukyŏng 권덕영. "Chungguk Sandongsŏng Muyŏmwŏn (ji) e gwanhan mŏk gaji munje" 中國 山東省 無染院(址)에 관한 몇 가지 問題. *Silla Munhwa* 신라문화 28, no. 8 (2006): 143–165.

Kwŏn Dongwoo 權東祐. *Susanoo no henbō: Kodai kara chūsei e* スサノオの変貌: 古代から中世へ. Kyoto: Bukkyō Daigaku, 2013.

Kwŏn Ugŭn 權又根. *Kodai Nihon bunka to Chōsen toraijin* 古代日本文化と朝鮮渡来人. Tokyo: Yūzankaku, 1988.

LaFleur, William R. *Karma of Words: Buddhism and the Literary Arts in Medieval Japan*. Berkeley and Los Angeles: University of California Press, 1986.

Lamotte, Étienne. "Mañjuśrī." *T'oung Pao* 48 (1960): 1–96.

Latour, Bruno. *Reassembling the Social: An Introduction to Actor-Network Theory*. Oxford; New York: Oxford University Press, 2005.

Law, John, and John Hassard, eds. *Actor Network Theory and After*. Oxford and Keele: Blackwell and the Sociological Review, 1999.

Lee Byŏngro 이병로. "Ilbon esŏ ŭi Silla shin gwa Chang Pogo: Chŏksan Myŏngshin gwa Silla Myŏngshin ŭl chŭngshim ŭro" 일본에서의 신라신과 장보고: 적산명신과 신라명신을 중심으로 (Silla deities in Japan and Chang Pogo: Sekizan Myōjin and Shinra Myōjin). *Tongbuk'a Munhwa Yŏn'gu* 동북문화연구 10 (2006): 319–341.

———. "Heian shoki ni okeru hokutō ajia sekai no kōshō to genkyō: Chō Hōkō to Ennin o chūshin toshite" 平安初期における北東アジア世界の交渉と現況: 張保皐と円仁を中心として. *Hokutō Ajia Kenkyū* 北東アジア研究 22 (2012): 67–79.

Lee, Richard E. *The Longue Duree and World-Systems Analysis* (Fernand Braudel Center Studies in Historical Social Science). New York: State University of New York Press, 2013.
Le Goff, Jacques. *Time, Work, and Culture in the Middle Ages.* Translated by Arthur Goldhammer. Chicago: University of Chicago Press, 1980.
———. *The Medieval Imagination.* Translated by Arthur Goldhammer, Chicago: University of Chicago Press, 1988.
Lévi, Sylvain, and Édouard Chavannes. "Les seize arhat protecteurs." *Journal Asiatique* 8 (1916): 205–275.
Lévi-Strauss, Claude. "Overture to Le Cru et le cuit." Translated by Joseph H. McMahon. *Yale French Studies*, nos. 36–37 (1966): 41–67.
Lewis, Mark Edward. *The Flood Myths of Early China.* New York: SUNY Press, 2006.
Lincoln, Bruce. *Theorizing Myth: Narrative, Ideology, and Scholarship.* Chicago: University of Chicago Press, 1999.
———. *Gods and Demons, Priests and Scholars: Critical Explorations in the History of Religions.* Chicago: University of Chicago Press, 2012.
———. *Between History and Myth: Stories of Harald Fairhair and the Founding of the State.* Chicago: University of Chicago Press, 2014.
Link, Arthur E. "The Biography of Shih Tao-an." *T'oung pao* 46 (1958): 1–48.
Lombard, Denys, and Jean Aubin. *Asian Merchants and Businessmen in the Indian Ocean and the China Sea.* New Delhi: Oxford University Press, 2000.
Lomi, Benedetta. "The Precious Steed of the Buddhist Pantheon: Ritual, Faith and Images of Batō Kannon in Japan." PhD diss., SOAS, University of London, 2011.
Lopez, Donald S. Jr. *Elaborations on Emptiness: Uses of the Heart Sūtra.* Princeton, NJ: Princeton University Press, 1996.
Lowe, Bryan D. "Rewriting Nara Buddhism: Sutra Transcription in Early Japan." PhD diss., Princeton University, 2012.
———. *Ritualized Writing: Buddhist Practice and Scriptural Cultures in Ancient Japan.* Honolulu: University of Hawai'i Press, 2017.
Lurie, David B. *Realms of Literacy: Early Japan and the History of Writing.* Cambridge, MA: Harvard University Asia Center, 2011.
Mair, Victor, ed. *Contact and Exchange in the Ancient World.* Honolulu: University of Hawai'i Press, 2006.
———. "Introduction." In *India in the Chinese Imagination: Myth, Religion, and Thought,* edited by John Kieschnick and Meir Shahar, ix–xvii. Philadelphia: University of Pennsylvania Press, 2014.
Mali, Jacob Burckhardt. "Myth, History and Mythistory." *History and Memory* 3, no. 1 (1991): 88–118.
Marra, Michele. *Representations of Power: The Literary Politics of Medieval Japan.* Honolulu: University of Hawai'i Press, 1993.
Marui Keiji 丸井敬司. *Chibashi to Myoken shinkō* 千葉氏と妙見信仰. Tokyo: Iwata Shoin, 2013.
Mason, David A. *Spirit of the Mountains: Korea's San-shin and Traditions of Mountain Worship.* Elizabeth, NJ; Seoul: Hollym, 1999.
Mass, Jeffrey P. *Lordship and Inheritance in Early Medieval Japan: A Study of the Kamakura Soryō System.* Stanford, CA: Stanford University Press, 1989.
Matsumoto Ikuyo 松本郁代. "Chūgū gosan to mikkyō: 'Hōhiki' Sonjōō hō mishūhō o megutte" 中宮御産と密教:『宝秘記』尊星王法御修法をめぐって. In *Nihon ni okeru*

shūkyō tekusuto no shoisō to tōjihō 日本における宗教テクストの諸位相と統辞法, edited by Abe Yasurō, 1–88. Nagoya: Nagoya Daigaku Daigakuin Bungaku Kenkyūka, 2009.

Matsuo Kōichi 松尾恒一. "Onjōji en'nen kaisai no keiki" 園城寺延年開催の契機. *Geinō shi kenkyū* 芸能史研究 106 (1989): 9–29.

———. *Ennen no geinōshi teki kenkyū* 延年の芸能史的研究. Tokyo: Iwada Shoin, 1997.

Matsuoka Shinpei 松岡心平. "Shinbutsu shūgō to okina: junka・konton・konkō" 神仏習合と翁: 純化・混沌・混淆. *Kokubungaku: kaishaku to kanshō* 国文学: 解釈と教材の研究 44, no. 8 (1999): 38–44.

Mayumi Tsunetada 真弓常忠, ed. *Gion shinkō jiten* 祇園信仰事典. Tokyo: Ebisu Kōshō Shuppan, 2002.

McCallum, Donald F. "The Earliest Buddhist Statues in Japan." *Artibus Asiae* 61, no. 2 (2001): 149–188.

McMullin, Neil. "The Sanmon-Jimon Schism in the Tendai School of Buddhism: A Preliminary Analysis." *Journal of the International Association of Buddhist Studies* 7 (1984): 83–105.

———. "The Enryakuji and the Gion Shrine-Temple Complex in the Mid-Heian Period." *Japanese Journal of Religious Studies* 14, nos. 2–3 (1987): 161–184.

McNeill, William H. *Plagues and Peoples*. Garden City, NY: Anchor Press, 1976.

———. "Mythistory or Truth, Myth, History and Historians." *The American Historical Review* 91, no. 1 (1986): 1–10.

Meeks, Lori R. *Hokkeji and the Reemergence of Female Monastic Orders in Premodern Japan*. Honolulu: University of Hawai'i Press, 2010.

Michinori Kobayashi 小林道憲. *Kodai Nihonkai bunmei kōryūken: Yū rashia no bunmei hendō no naka de* 古代日本海文明交流圏: ユーラシアの文明変動の中で. Kyoto: Sekai Shisōsha, 2006.

Misaki Ryōshū 三崎良周. *Mikkyō to jingi shishō* 密教と神祇思想. Tokyo: Sōbunsha, 1992.

Mitsuhashi Tadashi 三橋正. *Heian jidai no shinkō to shūkyō girei* 平安時代の信仰と宗教儀礼. Tokyo: Zoku Gunsho Ruijū Kanseikai, 2000.

Miwa Masatane 三輪正胤. "Kagaku denju to Shintō" 歌学伝授と神道. *Kokubungaku: Kaishaku to kanshō* 国文学: 解釈と鑑賞 60 (1995): 92–98.

Miyahara Kengo 宮原健吾, Uno Takao 宇野隆夫, and Usui Tadashi 臼井正. "Hōi kara mita Ōtsu no miya to Sūfukuji" 方位からみた大津宮と崇福寺. *Ars Buddhica* 285 (2006): 73–95.

Miyai Yoshio 宮井義雄. "Susanoo no mikoto to Shinra Myōjin" 素戔嗚尊と新羅明神. In *Nihon shōki kenkyū* 日本書紀研究, edited by Mishina Shoei 三品彰英, 8: 335–350. Tokyo: Hanawa Shobō, 1992.

Miyaji Naokazu 宮地直一. "Heianchō ni okeru Shinra Myōjin" 平安朝における新羅明神. In *Onjōji no kenkyū* 園城寺之研究, edited by Tendaishū Jimon-ha go'onki jimukyoku 天台宗寺門派御遠忌事務局, 323–384. Otsu: Onjōji, 1931.

Miyake, Hitoshi 宮家準. *Shugendō: Essays on the Structure of Japanese Folk Religion*. Edited by H. Byron Earhart. Ann Arbor: Center for Japanese Studies, University of Michigan, 2001.

———. "Shinra Myōjin shinkō to En no gyōja zō" 新羅明神信仰と役行者像. *Shintō shūkyō* 神道宗教 188 (2002): 1–33.

Mizuno Masayoshi 水野正好. "Shiga gun shojū no kanjinkei kika shizoku to so no bosei" 滋賀郡所住の漢人系帰化氏族とその墓制. *Shiga ken bunkasai chōsa hōkokusho* 滋賀県文化財調査報告書, 4: 77–92. Otsu: Shigaken Kyōiku Iinkai, 1969.

Moerman, D. Max. *Localizing Paradise: Kumano Pilgrimage and the Religious Landscape of Premodern Japan*. Cambridge, MA: Harvard University Asia Center, 2005.

———. "Demonology and Eroticism." *Japanese Journal of Religious Studies* 36, no. 2 (2009): 351–380.

Mollier, Christine. *Buddhism and Taoism Face to Face: Scripture, Ritual, and Iconographic Exchange in Medieval China*. Honolulu: University of Hawai'i Press, 2008.

Mori Katsumi 森克己. "Jikaku Daishi to Shinrajin" 慈覚大師と新羅人. In *Jikaku daishi kenkyū* 慈覚大師研究, edited by Fukui Kōjun 福井康順, 33–48. Tokyo: Tendai Gakkai, 1964.

Mori Yukie 森由紀恵. "Sonjōō o meguru sho mondai: inkenryoku・Heishi seiken no shūkyō seisaku sairon ni mukete" 尊星王をめぐる諸問題: 院権力・平氏政権の宗教政策再論にむけて. *Ningen bunka kenkyūka nenpō* 人間文化研究科年報 15 (1999): 271–280.

Morrell, Robert E., trans. *Sand and Pebbles: The Tales of Mujū Ichien, a Voice for Pluralism in Kamakura Buddhism*. Albany: State University of New York, 1985.

Morse, Samuel C. "The Healing Buddha as Kami: Shinto-Buddhist Syncretism in the Early Heian Period and the Unified Silla-Period Standing Buddha at Watasumi Shrine, Tsushima." Conference presentation, "The Cult of the Healing Buddha in East Asia," Daegu, Korea, May 30, 2013.

Mozai Torao 茂在寅男. *Rekishi wo hakonda fune: Shinwa densetsu no jisshō* 歴史を運んだ船: 神話伝説の実証. Tokyo: Tōkai Daigaku Shuppankai, 1984.

Murai Shōsuke 村井章介. "Kyōkai to chiiki" 境界と地域. In *Higashi ajia sekai no seiritsu* 東アジア世界の成立, edited by Arano Yasunori 荒野泰典, Ishii Masatoshi 石井正敏, and Murai Shōsuke 村井章介. Tokyo: Yoshikawa Kōbunkan, 2010.

Murayama Shūichi 村山修一, ed. *Hieizan to Tendai bukkyō no kenkyū* 比叡山と天台仏教の研究. Tokyo: Meicho Shuppan, 1975.

———. *Shinbutsu shūgō no seichi* 神仏習合の聖地. Kyoto: Hōzōkan. 2006.

Nagai Susumu 永井晋. *Kanazawa hōjōshi no kenkyū* 金沢北条氏の研究. Tokyo: Yagi Shoten, 2006.

Nakai Shinkō 中井真孝. *Chōsen to Nihon no kodai bukkyō* 朝鮮と日本の古代仏教. Osaka: Tōhō Shuppan, 1994.

Nakajima Keiichi 中島圭一. "Komonjoshitsu shozō no Onjōji monjo to Todaiji monjo" 古文書室所蔵の園城寺文書と東大寺文書. *Shigaku* 史學 81, nos. 1–2 (2012): 273–281.

———. "Keio gijuku daigaku bungakubu komonjoshitsu shozō 'Onjōji monjo'" 慶應義塾大学文学部古文書室所蔵「園城寺文書」. *Shigaku* 史學 85, nos. 1–3 (2015): 574–581.

Nakamae Masashi 中前正志. "Onjōji engi no kyōju" 薗城寺縁起の享受. *Ōtani gakuhō* 大谷覚報 82, no. 1 (2003): 18–37.

Nakamura Naokatsu 中村直勝. "Onjōji to Genji" 園城寺と源氏. In *Onjōji no kenkyū* 園城寺之研究, edited by Tendaishū Jimon ha go'onki jimukyoku 天台宗寺門派御遠忌事務局, 385–416. Otsu: Onjōji, 1931.

Nakanishi Tsuneo 中西常雄. "Sūfukuji ni kansuru saikentō" 崇福寺に関する再検討. *Ars Buddhica* 299 (2008): 31–52.

Nakano Hatayoshi 中野幡能. *Hachiman Shinkō* 八幡信仰. Tokyo: Yūzankaku Shuppan, 1983.

Nakano Takeshi 中野猛. *Setsuwa to engi* 説話と縁起. Tokyo: Shintensha, 1995.

Nakano Teruo 中野照男. *Sangaku shinkō no bijutsu: Kumano* 山岳信仰の美術: 熊野. Tokyo: Shibundō, 2005.

Nanami Hiroaki 名波弘彰. "'Taikei monogatari' ni arawareru Hiyoshi jinjya kankei setsuwa no kōsatsu" 『平家物語』に現れる日吉神社関係説話の考察. *Bungei gengo kenkyū: bungei hen* 文藝言語研究: 文藝篇 9 (1984): 69–113.

Naquin, Susan, and Chün-fang Yü. "Introduction." In *Pilgrims and Sacred Sites in China*, edited by Susan Naquin and Chün-fang Yü, 1–38. Berkeley and Los Angeles: University of California Press, 1992.

Narusawa Akira 成沢光. *Seiji no kotoba: Imi no rekishi wo megutte* 政治のことば: 意味の歴史をめぐって. Tokyo: Heibonsha, 1984.

Neelis, Jason E. *Early Buddhist Transmission and Trade Networks: Mobility and Exchange Within and Beyond the Northwestern Borderlands of South Asia*. Leiden: Brill, 2011.

———. "Networks for Long-distance Transmission of Buddhism in South Asian Transit Zones." In *Buddhism Across Asia: Networks of Material, Intellectual and Cultural Exchange*, edited by Tansen Sen, 3–18. Singapore: Institute of Southeast Asian Studies, 2014.

Nikaidō, Yoshihiro. *Asian Folk Religion and Cultural Interaction*. Göttingen: V&R unipress, 2015.

Nishida Nagao 西田長男. *Nihon Shintō shi kenkyū* 日本神道史研究. 10 vols. Tokyo: Kōdansha, 1978–1979.

Niunoya Tetsuichi 丹生谷哲一. "Chūsei ni okeru jiin no dō ni tsuite" 中世における寺院の童について. In *Nihon shakai no shi teki kōzō: Kodai·chūsei* 日本社会の史的構造: 古代・中世, edited by Ōyama kyōhei kyōju taikan kinen kai 大山喬平教授退官記念会, 463–485. Kyoto: Shibunkaku Shuppan, 1997.

Ogino Minahiko 荻野三七彦. "Sekizan no kami to Shinra Myōjin" 赤山の神と新羅明神. In *Jikaku Daishi kenkyū* 慈覺大師研究, edited by Fukui Kojun 福井康順, 141–155. Tokyo: Waseda Daigaku Shuppanbu, 1964.

Ōhashi Nobuya 大橋信弥. "Ōmi ni okeru torai shizoku no kenkyū" 近江における渡来氏族の研究. *Seikyū gakujutsu ronshū* 青丘学術論集 6 (1995): 7–74.

Ōhashi Nobuya and Ogasawara Yoshihiko 小笠原好彦. *Shin・shiseki de tsuzuru kodai no Ōmi* 新・史跡でつづる古代の近江. Kyoto: Mineruva Shobō, 2005.

Oka Naomi 岡直已. *Shinzō chō koku no kenkyū* 神像彫刻の研究. Tokyo: Kadokawa Shoten, 1966.

Okada Masayuki 岡田正之. "Jikaku daishi no nittō kikō nit suite" 慈覚大師の入唐紀行に就いて (4). *Tōyō gakuhō* 東洋学報 13, no. 1 (1923): 110–150.

Okada Shōji 岡田荘司. "Toraigami to jinushi gami" 渡来神と地主神. *Shintō gaku* 神道学 79 (1966): 19–32.

Okubo Ryōshun 大久保良峻. "Taimitsu shoryū no keisei" 台密諸流の形成. In *Asia bunka no shisō to girei* アジャ文化の思想と儀礼, edited by Fukui Fumimasa hakase koki taishoku kinen ronbunshū kankō kai 福井文雅博士古稀退職記念論集刊行会, 783–798. Tokyo: Shunjūsha, 2005.

Ōmori Keiko 大森恵子. "Miidera no Benzaiten shinkō no kakudai to mōjin geinōsha no kakawari" 三井寺の弁財天信仰の拡大と盲人芸能者の関わり. *Sangaku shugen* 山岳修験 45 (2010): 62–82.

Ōmori Tarō 大林太良. *Higashi to nishiumi to yama: Nihon no bunka ryōiki* 東と西海と山: 日本の文化領域. Tokyo: Shōgakkan, 1990.

Ooms, Herman. *Imperial Politics and Symbolics in Ancient Japan: The Tenmu Dynasty, 650–800*. Honolulu: University of Hawaiʻi Press, 2009.

Origuchi Shinobu 折口信夫. *Okina no hassei* 翁の発生. Tokyo: Aozora Bunko, 2004.

Orzech, Charles D., Richard K. Payne, and Henrik H. Sørensen. "Introduction: Esoteric Buddhism and the Tantras in East Asia: Some Methodological Considerations." In *Esoteric Buddhism and the Tantras in East Asia*, edited by Charles D. Orzech, Richard K. Payne, and Henrik H. Sørensen, 3–18. Leiden; Boston: Brill, 2011.

Ōwa Iwao 大和岩雄. *Hata-shi no kenkyū: Nihon no bunka to shinkō ni fukaku kan'yoshita torai shūdan no kenkyū* 秦氏の研究: 日本の文化と信仰に深く関与した渡来集団の研究. Tokyo: Yamato Shobō, 1993.

Oyamada Kazuo 小山田和夫. "Ennin to Enchin to no kankei" 円仁と円珍との関係. In *Ronshū Nihon Bukkyo shi: Heian jidai* 論集日本仏教史: 平安時代, edited by Hiraoka Jōkai 平岡定海, 3:133–162. Tokyo: Yūzankaku, 1986.

———. "'Sōgō Bunin Shōshutsu' no shōshutsu ishiki ni tsuite" 『僧綱補任抄出』の抄出意識について. *Risshō daigaku jinbun kagaku kenkyū nenpō* 立正大学人文科学研究所年報 25 (1987): 13–20.

———. *Chishō daishi Enchin no kenkyū* 智証大師円珍の研究. Tokyo: Yoshikawa Kōbunkan, 1990.

Palmer, Dalton. "Searching for the Law: Ennin's Journal as a Key to the Heian Appropriation of Tang Culture." PhD diss., University of California, Irvine, 2009.

Park Namsu 朴南守. *Han'guk kodae ŭi tong Asia kyoyŏk sa*. 한국 고대의 동아시아 교역사 (Ancient Korean kingdoms and East Asian trade history). Seoul: Churyusŏng, 2011.

Paul, Paramita. *Wandering Saints: Chan Eccentrics in the Art and Culture of Song and Yuan China*. Zutphen, the Netherlands: Wöhrmann Print Service, 2009.

Payne, Richard, ed. *Tantric Buddhism in East Asia*. Boston: Wisdom Publications, 2006.

Pinnington, Noel. "Invented Origins: Muromachi Interpretations of Okina Sarugaku." *Bulletin of the School of Oriental and African Studies* 61, no. 3 (1998): 492–518.

Poth, Or. "Nasty Boys or Obedient Children? Childhood and Relative Autonomy in Medieval Japanese Pedagogical Texts." In *Child's Play: Multi-Sensory Histories of Children and Childhood in Japan*, edited by Sabine Frühstück and Anne Walthall, 10–40. Oakland: University of California Press, 2017.

Proffitt, Aaron P. "Mysteries of Speech and Breath: Dōhan's 道範 (1179–1252) *Nenbutsu shō* 祕密念佛抄 and Esoteric Pure Land Buddhism." PhD diss., University of Michigan, 2015.

Pu, Muzhou. *In Search of Personal Welfare: A View of Ancient Chinese Religion*. Albany: State University of New York Press, 1998.

Pye, Michael. "The Structure of Religious Systems in Contemporary Japan: Shintō Variations on Buddhist Pilgrimage." *Occasional Papers*, Center for Japanese Studies, University of Malburg 30 (2004): 3–46.

Quinn, Shelley Fenno. *Developing Zeami: The Noh Actor's Attunement in Practice*. Honolulu: University of Hawai'i Press, 2005.

Quinter, David. "Creating Bodhisattvas: Eison, Hinin, and the 'Living Manjusri.'" *Monumenta Nipponica* 62, no. 4 (2007): 437–458.

———. *From Outcasts to Emperors: Shingon Ritsu and the Mañjuśrī Cult in Medieval Japan*. Leiden; Boston: Brill, 2015.

Rambelli, Fabio. "Religion, Ideology of Domination, and Nationalism. Kuroda Toshio on the Discourse of Shinkoku." In *The Legacy of Kuroda Toshio*, edited by James C. Dobbins, special issue of the *Japanese Journal of Religious Studies* 23, nos. 3–4 (1996): 387–426.

———. "The Emperor's New Robes: Processes of Resignification in Shingon Imperial Rituals." *Cahiers d'Extrême-Asie* 13 (2002a): 427–453.

———. "Secret Buddhas (*Hibutsu*): The Limits of Buddhist Representation." *Monumenta Nipponica* 57, no. 3 (2002b): 271–307.

———. "Secrecy in Japanese Esoteric Buddhism." In *The Culture of Secrecy in Japanese Religion*, edited by Scheid Bernhard and Mark Teeuwen, 107–129. London: Routledge, 2006.

Reader, Ian. *Pilgrimage in the Marketplace*. New York: Routledge, Taylor & Francis Group, 2014.

Reischauer, Edwin O. *Ennin's Diary: The Records of a Pilgrimage to China in Search of the Law*. New York: Ronald Press Co., 1955a.

———. *Ennin's Travels in Tang China*. New York: Ronald Press Co., 1955b.

Ricoeur, Paul. "Imagination in Discourses and in Action." In *Rethinking Imagination Culture and Creativity*, edited by Gillian Robinson and John F. Rundell, 118–135. London and New York: Routledge, 1994.

———. *La mémoire, l'histoire, l'oubli*. Paris: Seuil, 2000. English translation: *Memory, History, Forgetting*. Chicago: University of Chicago Press, 2004.

Robson, James. *Power of Place: The Religious Landscape of the Southern Sacred Peak (Nanyue) in Medieval China*. Cambridge, MA: Harvard University Press, 2009.

Ruppert, Brian D. *Jewel in the Ashes: Buddha Relics and Power in Early Medieval Japan*. Cambridge, MA: Harvard University Asia Center, 2000.

———. "Pearl in the Shrine: A Genealogy of the Buddhist Jewel of the Japanese Sovereign." *Japanese Journal of Religious Studies* 29, nos. 1–2 (2002): 1–33.

———. "Dharma Prince Shukaku and the Esoteric Buddhist Culture of Sacred Works (*Shōgyō*) in Medieval Japan." In *Esoteric Buddhism and the Tantras in East Asia*, edited by Charles D. Orzech, Henrik H. Sørensen, and Richard K. Payne, 794–802. Leiden: Brill, 2011.

Saeki Arikiyo 佐伯有清. *Shinsen shōji roku no kenkyū (kenkyū hen)* 新撰姓氏録の研究 (研究篇). Tokyo: Yoshikawa Kōbunkan, 1965.

———. *Chishō daishi den no kenkyū* 智証大師伝の研究. Tokyo: Yoshikawa Kōbunkan, 1989.

———. *Enchin* 円珍. Tokyo: Yoshikawa Kōbunkan, 1990.

Said, Edward W. *Orientalism*. New York: Vintage Books, 1979.

Saitō Hideki 斎藤英喜. *Amaterasu no fukami e: Kodai shinwa o yominaosu* アマテラスの深みへ: 古代神話を読み直す. Tokyo: Shin'yōsha, 1996.

———. *Yomikaerareta Nihon shinwa* 読み替えられた日本神話. Tokyo: Kōdansha, 2006.

———. *Onmyōdō no kamigami* 陰陽道の神々. Kyoto: Bukkyō Daigaku Tsūshin Kyōikubu: Seisaku Hatsubai Shibunkaku Shuppan, 2007.

———. "Chūsei Nihongi to shinwa kenkyū no genzai" 中世日本紀と神話研究の現在. *Kokubungaku: kaishaku to kanshō* 国文学: 解釈と鑑賞 76 (2011): 134–142.

———. *Araburu Susanoo, shichi henge: 'Chūsei shinwa' no sekai* 荒ぶるスサノヲ, 七変化: '中世神話' の世界. Tokyo: Yoshikawa Kōbunkan, 2012.

Sakaguchi Kōtaro 阪口光太郎. "Shinra Myōjin no katasumi kara 'Kakugisōzuki' yoin" 新羅明神の片隅から『覚基僧都記』余韻. *Bungaku ronsō* 文学論藻 72 (1998): 54–72.

Sanford, James. "Amida's Secret Life: Kakuban's Amida hishaku." In *Approaching the Land of Bliss: Religious Praxis in the Cult of Amitabha*, edited by Richard K. Payne and Kenneth K. Tanaka, 120–138. Honolulu: University of Hawai'i Press, 2003.

Sasaki Reishin 佐々木令信. "Sangoku Bukkyō shikan to zokusan hendo" 三国仏教史観と粟散辺土. In *Kokka to tennō* 国家と天皇 (仏教と日本人 bukkyō to nihonjin 2), edited by Kuroda Toshio, 275–315. Tokyo: Shunjūsha, 1987.

Satō Hiroo 佐藤弘夫. "Shinkoku shisō kō" 神国思想考. *Nihonshi kenkyū* 日本史研究 390 (1995): 1–30.

———. *Amaterasu no henbō: Chūsei shinbutsu kōshōshi no shiza* アマテラスの変貌: 中世神仏交渉史の視座. Kyoto: Hōzōkan, 2000.

Sawada, Shikyo. "Aki no yo no naga monogatari: A Lengthy Story for a Long Autumn Night." Master's thesis, University of British Columbia, 1976.

Sax, William S. *God of Justice: Ritual Healing and Social Justice in the Central Himalayas*. Oxford; New York: Oxford University Press, 2009.

Schafer, Edward H. *Pacing the Void: T'ang Approaches to the Stars*. Berkeley: University of California Press, 1977.

Schipper, Kristofer M. *The Taoist Body*. Berkeley: University of California Press, 1993.

Schottenhammer, Angela. "The 'East Asian Mediterranean.'" In *Trade and Transfer across the East Asian "Mediterranean,"* edited by Angela Schottenhammer, 1–10. Wiesbaden: Harrassowitz, 2005.

———. "The Sea as Barrier and Contact Zone: Maritime Space and Sea Routes in Traditional Chinese Books and Maps." In *The Perception of Maritime Space in Traditional Chinese Sources*, edited by Angela Schottenhammer and Roderich Ptak, 2–13. Wiesbaden: Harrassowitz, 2006.

———. *The East Asian Mediterranean: Maritime Crossroads of Culture, Commerce and Human Migration*. Wiesbaden: Harrassowitz Verlag, 2008.

Sekimori, Gaynor. "Star Rituals and Nikko Shugendo." *Culture and Cosmos* 10, nos. 1–2 (2006): 217–250.

Sen, Tansen. *Buddhism, Diplomacy, and Trade: The Realignment of Sino-Indian Relations, 600–1400*. Honolulu: University of Hawai'i Press, 2003.

Setodani Akira 瀬戸谷晧. "'Harima fudoki' no naka no Ame no hiboko" 播磨風土記の中の天之日矛. *Fudoki no kōkogaku* 風土記考古学, Vol. 2: *Harima no Fudoki* 播磨風土記, 1994.

Shiga-ken Bunkazai Hogo Kyōkai 滋賀県文化財保護協会, ed. *Shōmu Tennō to so no jidai* 聖武天皇とその時代. Otsu: Shiga-ken Bunkazai Hogo Kyōkai, 2005.

Shih, Shan. *The Sixteen Arhats and the Eighteen Arhats*. Peking: Buddhist Association of China, 1961.

Shimozaka Mamoru 下坂守. "Onjōji denrai no 'Hōhiki' ni tsuite" 園城寺伝来の『宝秘記』について. In *Onjōji monjo* 園城寺文書, 7:444–451. Tokyo: Kōdansha, 2004.

Shinbutsu Imasu Ōmi 神仏います近江. Otsu: Shinbutsu Imasu Ōmi Jikkō Iinkai, 2011.

Shindō Tōru 新藤透. "'Shira no kiroku' to Shinra Myōjin shiryō" 『新羅之記録』と新羅明神史料. *Toshokan jōho media kenkyū* 図書館情報メディア研究 3, no. 1 (2005): 19–28.

———. *Matsumae Kagehiro* 'Shinra no kiroku' *no shiryōteki kenkyū* 松前景広『新羅之記録』の史料的研究. Kyoto: Shibunkaku Shuppan, 2009.

Shiozawa Hirohito 塩沢裕仁. "Sekizanjin ni tsuite" 赤山神について. In *Kodai Nihon no ibunka kōryū* 古代日本の異文化交流, edited by Suzuki Yasutami 鈴木靖民, 28–47. Tokyo: Bensei Shuppansha, 2008.

Shirai Yūko 白井優子. "Inseiki ni okeru Miroku shinkō no hensen" 院政期における弥勒信仰の変遷. *Shichō* 史潮 58 (2005): 74–89.

Smith, Anthony D. *National Identity*. London: Penguin, 1991.

Smyth, Gerry. *Space and the Irish Cultural Imagination*. Houndmills, Basingstoke, Hampshire: Palgrave, 2001.

Souyri, Pierre-François. *The World Turned Upside Down: Medieval Japanese Society*. New York: Columbia University Press, 2001.

Sponberg, Alan, and Helen Hardacre, eds. *Maitreya, the Future Buddha*. Cambridge and New York: Cambridge University Press, 1988.

Stein, Rolf A. "Buddhist Mythology." In *Asian Mythologies*, edited by Yves Bonnefoy and translated by Wendy Doniger, 119–121. Chicago: University of Chicago Press, 1991a.

———. "The Guardian of the Gate: An Example of Buddhist Mythology, from India to Japan." In *Asian Mythologies*, edited by Yves Bonnefoy and translated by Wendy Doniger, 122–136. Chicago: University of Chicago Press, 1991b.

Stone, Jacqueline I. *Original Enlightenment and the Transformation of Medieval Japanese Buddhism*. Honolulu: University of Hawai'i Press, 1999.

Strickmann, Michel. *Chinese Magical Medicine*. Edited by Bernard Faure. Stanford, CA: Stanford University Press, 2002.

Strong, John S. "The Legend of the Lion-Roarer: A Study of the Buddhist Arhat Piṇḍola Bhāradvāja." *Numen* 26, no. 1 (1979): 50–88.

Sueki Fumihiko 末木文美士. "Bukkyōteki sekaikan to esunosentorizumu" 仏教的世界観とエスノセントリズム. In *Nihon Bukkyōshi ronkō* 日本仏教思想史論考, 94–124. Tokyo: Daizō Shuppan, 1993.

———. "Annen: The Philosopher Who Japanized Buddhism." *Acta Asiatica* 66 (1994): 69–86.

———. *Chūsei no kami to hotoke* 中世の神と仏. Tokyo: Yamakawa Shuppansha, 2003.

Sugawara Shinkai 菅原信海. *Sannō Shintō no kenkyū* 山王神道の研究. Tokyo: Shunjū Sha, 1992.

Sumino Beňichi 住野勉一. *Keitai ōchō seiritsuron josetsu* 継体王朝成立論序説. Osaka: Izumi Shoin, 2007.

Suzuki, Masanobu. *Clans and Genealogy in Ancient Japan: Legends of Ancestor Worship*. Abingdon, Oxon, and New York, NY: Routledge, 2017.

Suzuki Masataka 鈴木正崇. *Kami to hotoke no minzoku* 神と仏の民俗. Tokyo: Yoshikawa Kōbunkan, 2001.

Suzuki Tōzō 鈴木棠三. *Tsushima no Shintō* 対馬の神道. Tokyo: San'ichi Shobō, 1972.

Swanson, Paul L, and Clark Chilson. *Nanzan Guide to Japanese Religions*. Honolulu: University of Hawai'i Press, 2006.

Tabata Chiaki 田畑千秋 and Hiramoto Ruri 平本留理. "'Kokon chōmonjū' kan ni, dai yonjū wa kara dai yonjū wa yakuchū" 『古今著聞集』巻二, 第四〇話から第四九話訳注. *Ōita Daigaku Kyōiku Gakubu kenkyū kiyō* 大分大学教育学部研究紀要 22, no. 1 (2000): 164–174.

Tachi Ryūshi 舘隆志. *Onjōji Kōin no kenkyū* 園城寺公胤の研究. Tokyo: Shunjūsha, 2010.

Takada Teruo 高田照世. "Yama no kami no kanjō to Shushōe" 山の神の勧請と修正会. *Ch'asedae inmun sahoe yon'gu* 차세대 인문사회 연구 3 (2007): 379–398.

Takahashi Yusuke 高橋悠介. *Zenchiku nogakuron no sekai* 禅竹能楽論の世界. Tokyo: Keiō Gijuku Daigaku Shuppankai, 2014.

Takatori Masao 高取正男. "Ushirodo no gohōjin" 後戸の護法神. In *Ronshū: Nihon no seikatsu to shinkō* 論集: 日本人の生活と信仰, edited by Ōtani Daigaku Kokushi Gakkai 大谷大学国史学会, 385–407. Kyoto: Dōhōshashuppan, 1979.

Take Katachō 武覚超. *Hieizan jodōshi no kenkyū* 比叡山諸堂史の研究. Kyoto: Hozōkan, 2008.

Takeda Kazuo 竹田和夫. *Kodai · chūsei no kyōkai ishiki to bunka kōryū* 古代・中世の境界意識と文化交流. Tokyo: Bensei Shuppan, 2011.

Takeda, Sachiko 武田佐知子. "Roads in the *Tennō*-centered Polity." In *Capital and Countryside in Japan, 300–1180: Japanese Historians Interpreted in English*, translated by Joan Piggott, 148–165. Ithaca, NY: Cornell University East Asia Program, 2006.

Tamura Enchō 田村円澄. "Nihon Bukkyō shi kenkyū no michi" 日本仏教史研究の道. *Nihon no Bukkyō* 日本の仏教 1 (1994): 156–158.

Tanaka Fumio 田中史生. "Chō Hōkō jidai no Dazaifu kōeki to Kōrokan" 張宝高時代の太宰府交易と鴻臚館. In *Kōrokan to so no jidai* 鴻臚館とその時代, edited by Fukuoka-shi hakubutsukan, 140–143. Fukuoka: Fukuoka-shi hakubutsukan, 2007.

Tanaka Takako 田中貴子. "Torai suru kami to dochaku suru kami" 渡来する神と土着する神. In *Nihon no kami: Kami no shigen* 日本の神: 神の始原, vol. 1, edited by Yamaori Tetsuo 山折哲雄, 173–208. Tokyo: Heibonsha, 1995.

Tanaka Yasuhiko 田中泰彦. *Kyō no fukujin meguri* 京の福神めぐり. Kyoto: Kyōto Shinbunsha, 1990.

Teeuwen, Mark. "Knowing vs. Owning a Secret: Secrecy in Medieval Japan, as Seen through the Sokui Kanjō Enthronement Unction." In *The Culture of Secrecy in Japanese Religion*, edited by Bernhard Scheid and Mark Teeuwen, 172–203. London: Routledge, 2006.

Teeuwen, Mark, and Fabio Rambelli, eds. *Buddhas and Kami in Japan: Honji suijaku as a Combinatory Paradigm*. New York: Routledge Curzon, 2003.

Teeuwen, Mark, and Hendrik van der Veere. *Nakatomi Harae Kunge: Purification and Enlightenment in Late-Heian Japan*. Munich: Iudicium, 1998.

Teiser, Stephen F. *The Ghost Festival in Medieval China*. Princeton, NJ: Princeton University Press, 1988.

Teraoka Shigeki 寺岡茂樹. "Rōba no sugata no hōsōgami ni tsuite no ichi kosatsu" 老婆の姿の疱瘡神についての一考察. *Kyoto minzoku* 京都民俗 25 (2008): 45–62.

Tokunaga Seiko 徳永誓子. "Kumano sanzan kengyō to Shugendō" 熊野三山検校と修験道. *Chūsei shi kenkyū* 中世史研究 27 (2002): 75–100.

———. "Shugendō no Seiritsu" 修験道の成立. In *Shugendō shi nyūmon* 修験道史入門, edited by Tokieda Tsutomu 時枝務, Hasegawa Kenji 長谷川賢二, and Hayashi Makoto 林淳, 77–92. Kyoto: Iwata Shoin, 2015.

Tōno Haruyuki 東野治之. *Kentōshi to Shōsōin* 遣唐使と正倉院. Tokyo: Iwanami Shoten, 1992.

Totman, Conrad D. *A History of Japan*. Malden, MA: Blackwell Publishers, 2000.

Tsuda Tetsuei 津田徹英. "Rokuji myōō no shutsugen" 六字明王の出現. *Museum* 553 (1998a): 27–54.

———. "Uho・henbai to Sonjōō・Rokuji Myōō no zuzō" 禹保・反閇と尊星王・六字明王の図像. *Nihon shūkyō bunkashi kenkyū* 日本宗教文化史研究 2 (1998b): 75–83.

———. "Jimon no Sonjōō o megutte" 寺門の尊星王をめぐって. *Museum* 581 (2002): 17–37.

———. "The Images of Star and Their Significance in Japanese Esoteric Art." *Culture and Cosmos* 10, nos. 1–2. (2006): 145–194.

Tsugita Masaki 次田真幸. *Kojiki* 古事記. Vols. 1–3. Tokyo: Kōdansha, 1977–1984.

Tsuji Zennosuke 辻善之助. "Shinra Myōjin kō" 新羅明神考. In *Nihon Bukkyōshi no kenkyū* 日本仏教史之研究, 1: 211–220. Tokyo: Kinkōdō Shoseki, 1931.

Turnbull, Stephen. *Japanese Warrior Monks AD 949–1603*. Oxford: Osprey Publishing, 2003.

Tyler, Royall. *The Miracles of the Kasuga Deity*. New York: Columbia University Press, 1990.

Ueda Masaaki 上田正昭 and Kim Talsu 金達寿, eds. *Chōsen to kodai Nihon bunka: Zadan kai* 朝鮮と古代日本文化: 座談会. Tokyo: Chūō Kōronsha, 1982.

Ueno Kayoko 植野加代子. *Hata-shi to Myōken shinkō* 秦氏と妙見信仰. Tokyo: Iwata Shoin, 2010.

Ukeda Masayuki 請田正幸. "Toraijin ron・joshō" 渡来人論・序章. *Rekishigaku kenkyū* 歴史学研究 582 (1988): 13–22.

Uno Shigeki 宇野茂樹. *Shiseki to bijutsu* 史迹と美術 384 (1968): 133–143.

Unschuld, Paul U. *Huang Di Nei Jing Su Wen: Nature, Knowledge, Imagery in an Ancient Chinese Medical Text, with an Appendix, the Doctrine of the Five Periods and Six Qi in the Huang Di Nei Jing Su Wen*. Berkeley: University of California Press, 2003.

Uozumi Sogoro 魚澄惣五郎. "Onjōji to Ashikaga Takauji" 園城寺と足利尊氏. In *Onjōji no kenkyū* 園城寺之研究, edited by Tendaishū Jimonha go'onki jimukyoku 天台宗寺門派御遠忌事務局, 417–428. Otsu: Onjōji, 1931.

Urban, Hugh B. *The Economics of Ecstasy: Tantra, Secrecy and Power in Colonial Bengal*. New York: Oxford University Press, 2001.

Valentine, James. "On the Borderlines: The Significance of Marginality in Japanese Society." In *Unwrapping Japan*, edited by E. Ben-Ari, B. Moeran, and J. Valentine, 36–57. Manchester: Manchester University Press, 1990.

Vásquez, Manuel. "Studying Religion in Motion: A Networks Approach." *Method and Theory in the Study of Religion* 20, no. 2 (2008): 151–184.

Verschuer, Charlotte von. *Across the Perilous Sea: Japanese Trade with China and Korea from the Seventh to the Sixteenth Centuries*. Ithaca, NY: Cornell University Press, 2006.

Visser, Marinus W. *The Arhats in China and Japan*. Berlin: Oesterheld & Co, 1923.

Von, Glahn R. *The Sinister Way: The Divine and the Demonic in Chinese Religious Culture*. Berkeley: University of California Press, 2004.

Wakabayashi, Haruko N. "From Conqueror of Evil to Devil King: Ryōgen and Notions of Ma in Medieval Japanese Buddhism." *Monumenta Nipponica* 54, no. 4 (1999): 481–507.

———. *The Seven Tengu Scrolls: Evil and the Rhetoric of Legitimacy in Medieval Japanese Buddhism*. Honolulu: University of Hawai'i Press, 2012.

Wang Yong 王勇 and Kuboki Hideo 久保木秀夫. *Nara: Heianki no nitchū bunka kōryū: Bukku rōdo no shiten kara* 奈良・平安期の日中文化交流: ブックロードの視点から. Tokyo: Nōsangyoson Bunka Kyōkai, 2001.

Watanabe Nobukazu 渡邉信和. "'Shinra Myōjin hassin wa etsu no koto' kō" 「新羅明神発心者悦事」考. In *Mabuchi Kazuo hakushi taikan kinen setsuwa bungaku ronshū* 馬淵和夫博士退官記念話説文学論集, 267–280. Tokyo: Taishūkan Shoden, 1981.

Watase Masatada 渡瀬昌忠. "Ōmi kōtoka to Sūfukuji" 近江荒都歌と崇福寺. *Kokubungaku kaishaku to kyōzai no kenkyū* 国文学: 解釈と教材の研究 23, no. 5 (1978): 65–72.

Watson, Burton, trans. *Record of Miraculous Events in Japan: The Nihon Ryōiki*. New York: Columbia University Press, 2013.

Wedemeyer, Christian K. *Making Sense of Tantric Buddhism: History, Semiology, and Transgression in the Indian Traditions*. New York: Columbia University Press, 2012.

Weiss, David. "Constructing Identity through Myth: Susanowo as a Liminal Figure in Discourses on Japanese and Korean Identity." PhD diss., University of Tübingen, 2016.

Williams, Duncan R. *The Other Side of Zen: A Social History of Sōtō Zen: Buddhism in Tokugawa Japan*. Princeton, NJ: Princeton University Press, 2005.

Wu, Pei-jung. "The Manjuśrī Statues and Buddhist Practice of Saidaiji: Iconography, Interior Features of Statues, and Rituals Associated with Buddhist Icons." PhD diss., University of California, Los Angeles, 2002.

Yamada Yūji 山田雄司. "Gōryōkai seiritus no zentei jōken: Ekibyōkan no henyō" 御霊会成立の前提条件: 疫病観の変容. In *Nihon shakai no shiteki kōzō*: Kodai·chūsei 日本社会の史的構造: 古代・中世, edited by Ōyama Kyōhei kyōju taikan kinen kai 大山喬平教授退官記念会, 103–124. Kyoto: Shibunkaku Shuppan, 1997.

Yamagiwa Teppei 山極哲平. "Chintaku reifujin shinkō kenkyūshi no seiri" 鎮宅霊符神信仰研究史の整理. *Kokubungaku* 国文学 91 (2007): 143–153.

Yamamoto Hiroko 山本ひろこ. *Ishin: Chūsei Nihon no hikyōteki sekai* 異神: 中世日本の秘教的世界. Tokyo: Heibonsha, 1998a.

———. *Chūsei shinwa* 中世神話. Tokyo: Iwanami Shoten, 1998b.

Yamao Yukihisa 山尾幸久. "Ōmi Ōtsu no miya to Shiga kanjin" 近江大津宮と志賀漢人. *Higashi Ajia no Kodai Bunka* 東アジアの古代文化 76 (1993): 17–50.

Yamaori Tetsuo 山折哲雄. *Kami to Okina no minzokugaku* 神と翁の民族学. Tokyo: Kodansha, 1991.

———, ed. *Inari shinkō jiten* 稲荷信仰事典 (Shinbutsu shinkō jiten shirīzu 3). Tokyo: Ebisu Kōshō Shuppan, 1999.

Yamasaki Masatoshi 山崎雅稔. "Jōkan 8 nen Ōtenmon shikka jiken to Shinra zokuhei" 貞観8年応天門失火事件と新羅賊兵. *Jimin no rekishi gaku* 人民の歴史学 146 (2000): 1–13.

Yanagita, Kunio 柳田國男. *About Our Ancestors: The Japanese Family System*. Translated by Fanny Hagin Mayer and Ishihara Yasuyo. Tokyo: Japan Society for the Promotion of Science, 1970.

———. "Oshiragami kō" 大白神考. In *Yanagita Kunio zenshū* 柳田國男全集, 15: 201–417. Tokyo: Chikuma Shobō, 1990a.

———. *Ishigami (Shakujin) mondō* 石神問答. In *Yanagita Kunio zenshū* 15: 7–200. Tokyo: Chikuma Shobō, 1990b [1910].

Yi Hyŏnsuk 이현숙. "Silla toilgi chonyombyong ui yuhaeng gwa daeungchaek" 신라 통일기 전염병의 유행과 대응책 (Epidemics during the Unified Silla period). *Han'guk kodaesa yŏn'gu* 한국고대사연구 31 (2003): 209–256.

Yi Pyŏngdo 李丙燾, trans. *Samguk sagi* 三國史記. Seoul: ŭryu Munhwasa, 1977.

Yi Songsi 李成市. *Higashi Ajia no ōken to kōeki: Shōsōin no hōmotsu ga kita mō hitotsu no michi* 東アジアの王権と交易: 正倉院の宝物が来たもうひとつの道. Tokyo: Aoki Shoten, 1997.

———. *Mandŭrŏjin kodae: Kŭndae kungmin kukka ŭi Tong Asia iyagi* 만들어진 고대: 근대 국민국가의 동아시아 이야기 (Invented history of the ancient: The story of modern nation-states in East Asia). Translated by Pak Kyŏng-hŭi. Seoul: Samin, 2002.

Yi Yujin 이유진. "Ennin ŭi yŏhaeng gwa Tong Asia segye insik" 엔닌 (円仁)의 여행과 동아시아 세계 인식 (Ennin's travel and his understanding of East Asian world). *Tongyang sa hakhoe donggye haksul t'oronhoe* 東洋史學會冬季學術討論會 28 (2009): 1–20.

Yiengpruksawan, Mimi. *Hiraizumi: Buddhist Art and Regional Politics in Twelfth-Century Japan*. Cambridge, MA: Harvard University Press, 1998.

Yokouchi Hiroto 横内裕人. "Shirō shōkai: Tōdaiji toshokan zō Kakuken sen 'Sangokudentōki': kaidai・eiin・honkoku" 資料紹介―東大寺図書館蔵覚憲撰『三国伝灯記』: 解題・影印・翻刻. *Nanto bukkyō* 84 (2004): 98–152.

Zitterbart, Susan. "Kumano Mandara: Portraits, Power, and Lineage in Medieval Japan." PhD diss., University of Pittsburgh, 2008.

Index

Page numbers in boldface refer to figures and tables.

About the Author

Sujung Kim is assistant professor of religious studies at DePauw University. She received her PhD in East Asian languages and cultures from Columbia University in 2014, with a focus on esoteric Buddhism in medieval Japan. While her research centers on the premodern transcultural interactions between Japan and Korea, her interdisciplinary research interests include modern/contemporary Korean Buddhism, Buddhist visual and material culture, as well as performative aspects of Buddhist narratives.